W9-CZM-394

HOW TO MANAGE
BY
RESULTS
THIRD EDITION

HOW TO MANAGE
BY
RESULTS
THIRD EDITION

DALE D. McCONKEY

A DIVISION OF AMERICAN MANAGEMENT ASSOCIATIONS

Library of Congress Cataloging in Publication Data

McConkey, Dale D
  How to manage by results. (Third edition)

  Includes index.
  1. Management by objectives. I. Title.
HD31.M152 1976   658.4   76-41332
ISBN 0-8144-5393-7

© 1976 AMACOM
A division of American Management Associations, New York.
All rights reserved. Printed in the United States of America.

Third Printing

This book is dedicated to
two members of my family who have successfully
progressed through the halls of academia—
my son, Dale D. Jr.
(A.B. in psychology, Ohio University, 1973)
and my daughter, Lori L.
(B.S. in education, University of Wisconsin, 1976)

PREFACE

THE TWIN GOALS of managerial and organizational effectiveness often are elusive. As is often the case with elusive solutions to complex problems, managers from biblical times to the present have tried many approaches. The effectiveness of many of these attempts has been highly suspect.

Some have bordered upon treating a sick patient with a chocolate-covered pill. Others have been tantamount to the layman's undertaking complex brain surgery armed with little more than the peripheral knowledge gained by reading a medical article in a popular magazine. Still others have resulted in treating only a portion of the problem. Finally, other approaches have addressed symptoms rather than causes.

Management by objectives is not, per se, immune from falling into the witch doctor category. It is a deceptively simple system—so deceptively simple, in fact, that many managers, quasi-consultants, teachers, and writers have been deceived and in turn have deceived others. There continues to be an alarmingly high number of people with a readymade solution running around looking for the problem. Thus MBO has become a popular buzzword often bordering on the occult. Such is unfortunate! Such need not be the case!

In the hands of an enlightened, competent management group MBO has impressive and well-earned credentials, credentials that have been awarded only after the system passed intensive, exhausting examination under varying circumstances. More than 20 potential benefits have been identified as being the realistic expectations of the manager who practices MBO successfully. When this number of benefits is multiplied by the number of managers in an organization, the cumulative benefit of MBO to the organization becomes obvious. Evidence, which is continuing to accumulate, indicates that if two companies out of a competitive group of eight companies are practicing MBO, these two companies are usually more successful than the six who are not using the system. The reason for this success is not difficult to understand.

MBO is, after all, a logical approach for lining up the efforts of all managers to help achieve the most desirable ends of the organization. Every manager has a common sense of direction and wasted, diluted effort is minimized.

This book was written for practical operating managers who must make their mark in the real, often frustrating world of management, a world in which problems are always difficult and the answers are never easy. To those managers who are contemplating the adoption of MBO or are just embarking on such an endeavor, I hope the book will help them avoid or at least minimize the three major traps experienced by other novices; namely: (1) adopting MBO in ignorance, (2) implementing MBO in haste, and (3) directing MBO in blindness. To those managers who have already embraced MBO, I hope this book will provide additional guidance and thoughts for improving their management effectiveness through MBO.

Although an author must accept full responsibility for all thoughts expressed in a book (and I accept this responsibility), no work is ever the exclusive domain of the author. Invariably much of his thinking is the product of those who have influenced him. Thus this book leans heavily on the knowledge I have gained from working with the senior executives of more than 500 profit and nonprofit organizations in the United States, Canada, the United Kingdom, Europe, Latin America, Japan, and India.

DALE D. MCCONKEY

CONTENTS

1

MBO
Today and Yesterday

AN OVERVIEW

MORE THAN TEN YEARS have passed since I wrote my first book on MBO, *How to Manage by Results.* Over twenty years have passed since Peter F. Drucker, the father of management by objectives, first issued his prophetic proclamation that all organizations should be managed by objectives.[1]

These years were most dynamic in the continuing development and refinement of the MBO system. What I wrote in the 1965 version and in the subsequent 1967 revised version constituted only a small portion of the MBO experience as we know it today. Because of the dynamic nature of MBO, any book on the subject risks becoming considerably out of date if it isn't revised about every five years.

It will be helpful to the reader in establishing a perspective to review the major developments that have taken place during the past twenty years of MBO practice. These have been both numerous and varied.

MILESTONES IN MBO

Although it is difficult to apply the word "milestone" to only some elements in a series of events, certain events can be singled out as the most

[1] Peter F. Drucker, *The Practice of Management* (New York: Harper & Row, 1954).

significant in the evolution of MBO. The first concerns the translation of the MBO concept into reality. "Objectives" of one variety or another have been known and used by managers since biblical times. It remained for Peter Drucker, writing in 1954, to use them as the basis for a management system. Drucker, always the able catalyst to management thinking, set the stage by proposing that objectives serve as the vehicle for administering and directing a systems approach to managing an organization. Others would develop the system and render it operative. Approximately 22 years after Drucker's lucid pronouncement, MBO has become a practical reality embodied, successfully and unsuccessfully, in thousands of diverse organizations throughout the world. Concept has been translated into practice.

The second milestone concerns the three-stage evolution of MBO from its fledgling stage to the present. Initially, almost complete emphasis was devoted to improving the performance of the individual manager by providing him with goals toward which to strive and by according him recognition for his achievements.

Next, emphasis switched to the organization as a total entity, and the goal was overall organizational effectiveness on a short-range basis. Finally, the long-run future of the organization was emphasized by balancing and directing the results of individual managers to achieve organizational priorities.[2]

The third milestone was realized when MBO advanced from a special-purpose management tool or technique into a full-fledged management system.

The early efforts of the pioneers in MBO arose primarily from a complete disenchantment with the techniques then popular for evaluating or appraising managerial performance. The evaluation techniques of the late 1950s measured the degree to which managers were thought to possess, or to fail to possess, highly subjective traits or factors. Factors commonly evaluated were cost-awareness, grasp of function, initiative, innovation, punctuality, loyalty, cooperation, potential for advancement, and other qualities. The traits were not keyed to actual results, and two evaluations of the same manager could differ by 180 degrees because of the orientation and prejudices of the examiners.

Gradually, measurable objectives and results replaced evaluations of traits. This required the development of effective objectives for managers, and here we see the beginnings of the new system. The development of objectives appropriate for use in evaluating performance paved the way

---

[2] See Robert A. Howell, "Managing by Objectives—A Three-Stage System," *Business Horizons*, February 1970, pp. 41–45.

for allowing objectives to serve as the focal point for all other major parts of the management process.

EXTENT OF ADOPTION

The precise extent to which MBO has been adopted is impossible to gauge. To date there are no valid findings or data. Any attempt to arrive at the number of organizations that have adopted MBO is complicated by the need for a clear understanding of the extent to which an organization must practice MBO to be included in the data. Moreover, the collection of data would be further confused because of the uncertainty concerning what MBO is.

Some managers classify themselves as MBO practitioners simply because they operate with budgets. Others do so because they work with general goals and objectives, and others because they believe they are following a few MBO principles—as they understand them. And still others profess to be full-fledged MBO managers because they give their subordinates some voice in decision making.

The above variations notwithstanding, there is no question that MBO has been adopted extensively. Applications are found in abundance in large and small companies and in all areas of the business sector, in both capital goods and consumer goods companies and in companies with product lines as divergent as turbines and facial tissues and with goals as different as producing a product and providing a service.

The nonprofit sector, having witnessed the attention devoted to MBO in the private sector, has begun to adopt MBO at a rather startling pace. This trend is discernible among government units, in hospitals and the health-care field, among religious organizations, and in educational systems.

Service organizations—whose growth is outpacing manufacturing entities—constitute another vital area of growth. Many insurance companies, banks, and retail establishments are exploring and adopting the MBO system.

A pattern of adoption within geographical locations is also evident. From the United States, MBO has spread to England, Europe, Japan, Canada, and other parts of the globe. Thus MBO has been widely adopted and is being extensively practiced.

It can be demonstrated, without attempting to quantify the results, that practicing MBO in depth does result in improved communication, coordination, control, and motivation of managers. These desirable ends are considered the minimum an organization should expect from its MBO efforts, and there is little if any disagreement that these benefits do accrue when MBO is employed for at least two to three years.

Before proceeding to a discussion of the specific changes MBO has helped bring about, the absence of "pure" MBO systems must be indicated. If pure MBO is defined as a system in which all the commonly accepted principles of MBO are practiced in A-to-Z fashion, few if any organizations actually practice MBO.

Major differences exist in the applications of MBO, in the procedures for accomplishing the applications, and in the degree of conviction with which MBO is pursued. For example, some organizations embrace the method primarily as a means of evaluating their managers, while others use it primarily for planning. Still others employ MBO as the overall management system. Even within different divisions of the same company, there are considerable differences in the approach and applications. For example, in one multi-billion-dollar, multidivision company, some divisions are practicing MBO as a way of life while other divisions have barely heard of it.

IMPACT ON MANAGING

The impact of MBO on the management process and on the manager has been profound and dramatic. Nowhere is this impact more demonstrable than in the change in the very definition of "management." Formerly, if a person were asked to define management, he might reply, "It's getting things done through people." If pressed to amplify this definition, he might add, "by planning, organizing, directing, and controlling." This rather common and traditional definition of management was rendered obsolete by a study completed by a committee of the Association of Consulting Management Engineers and reported by the Business Management Council.[3] The study concluded that management consists of three steps: establishing objectives, directing the attainment of objectives, and measuring results.

Figure 1 shows the management wheel, which resulted from the study. The 3 major steps in managing are divided into their 12 elements. Thus, in lieu of defining management by general terms or by citing a list of functions that the manager carries out, management now is defined as comprising three major steps, all highly oriented toward objectives. Now the former main functions are subfunctions of the three larger steps. This change in emphasis and the rationale leading to the change have brought about far-reaching changes in many of the traditional approaches to the

[3] *BMC Report Number 1* (New York: Business Management Council, 1968).

Figure 1. Elements of managing.

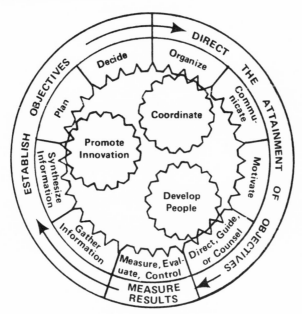

Source: Business Management Council, New York.

manager's job. Several of these key changes are described in subsequent sections of this chapter.

Not the least of these changes has been the major distinction established between "running" a business and "managing" a business. Those who run a business are usually frantically busy doing many different things—often working excessively long hours—and hoping that something will happen. Those who manage a business make things happen by deciding what they should be doing and then lining up all their resources and actions to make it happen. The latter are usually in control of their operations; operations of the former are frequently out of control.

Management Styles

Twenty years of MBO experience have demonstrated that MBO enjoys a better chance for success if its practitioners follow a particular management style. The more successful companies have been those whose management can be characterized by a balanced, participative style that encourages maximum participation while discouraging permissiveness. For obvious reasons, MBO will be least successful with an autocratic management. While MBO can achieve some measure of success in a bureaucratic atmosphere, its effectiveness will be greatly decreased by the excess of red tape, controls, and procedures.

The balanced, participative style is usually defined as one in which the maximum number of the following attributes is actually practiced to a maximum degree:

In-depth delegation.

Maximum participation in the objective-setting and planning processes.

Managers permitted to make some mistakes.

Change encouraged and planned for.

Policies and procedures minimal and subject to change when necessary.

Controls tight but only the minimum imposed to keep the unit in control.

A meaningful reward system.

A high degree of self-management, self-discipline, and self-control on the part of managers.

Increased Use of Behavioral Sciences

More and more, MBO is raising the status of behavioral scientists from mere voices crying in the wilderness to valuable, recognized members of the management process. According to my concept, management thinking passed through three stages of development (see Figure 2) on its way to the fourth stage, the MBO system.

Stage 1. Stage 1 was exemplified by the birth and adoption of the so-called scientific management approach. This stage relied heavily on a more impersonal approach to managing people, and was characterized by emphasis on standards, work measurement, and methods improvement. Its leading advocates were Taylor and the Gilbreths.

Stage 2. This stage, which emphasized the human, or personal, factor in managing people, was a natural outgrowth of the impersonal approach of Stage 1. Much of the thinking of Stage 2 can be attributed to Elton Mayo and those who follow his work.

Stage 3. Stage 3 can be described as an era of discontinuity, an era in which a sizable chasm developed between the purists and the behavioral scientists. The purists (frequently the hard-nosed production managers who frowned on behavioral scientists and regarded them as socialist theorizers) advocated the scientific management approach. The behavioral scientists, on the other hand, often regarded the scientific managers as hard-nosed profit-seekers with inadequate regard for the human factor

Figure 2. History of approaches to managerial appraisal.

STAGE 1 *Measuring by Traits* *Pre-MBO*	STAGE 2 *Measuring by Objectives* *1955–1972*	STAGE 3 *Measuring by Objectives* *and Efficiency 1972–*
Emphasis was on measuring managers based on trait factors, such as health, initiative, loyalty, punctuality, and grasp of function.	Emphasis was on measuring managers based on degree to which they achieved, or failed to achieve, their objectives.	Emphasis was on objectives and how efficiently managers achieved their objectives.
This was an extremely weak approach because it was not related to results which the manager achieved.	This was a much better approach as it was results-oriented. However, it emphasized effectiveness: were the objectives achieved or not? It failed to consider efficiency: was the achievement based on good management practices?	This has the added advantage of coupling effectiveness (were the objectives achieved?) with efficiency (did the manager accomplish the results by luck or by sound management?).

and with little appreciation of the how and why of motivating people.[4]

Stage 4. The end of Stage 3 came in the late 1950s. The move to participative management within the MBO system started a narrowing of the gap between impersonal and personal management approaches. MBO, while continuing to emphasize the importance of achieving the necessary objectives of the organization, also placed a premium on marshaling and directing all the human assets toward those objectives. Applications of the behavioral sciences were evident. This trend continues to grow as MBO serves increasingly as a marrying agent.

Increasing Use of Staff Managers

Prior to MBO, the staff manager was frequently regarded as a necessary evil, as one who dealt with intangibles that could not be measured. Often he received neither the opportunity to make a profit-oriented contribution nor acceptance and recognition for his accomplishments when they were achieved.

The advanced applications of MBO now permit staff managers to

[4] For an in-depth discussion of the third stage, see Harold Koontz, *Appraising Managers as Managers*, AMACOM, 1972.

write measurable objectives, to measure rather finitely their contributions against their objectives, to receive deserved recognition in the process, and to take their proper place as members of the profit-making team. With staff managers currently averaging 20 to 40 percent of an organization's total personnel budget, their increased utilization must be credited as being one of MBO's greater contributions. While some organizations have been slow to bring staff managers into the MBO system, the number that now consider staff managers as an integral part of MBO is steadily increasing.[5]

Managerial Appraisal

One of the most dramatic changes brought about by MBO has been its impact on measuring managerial performance. MBO has been instrumental in the three-stage progression concerning managerial appraisals highlighted in Figure 2.

Job Description

MBO has all but eliminated the traditional job description, which cataloged what the company required of the job, not of the manager in the job. The emphasis in MBO descriptions is on the manager because the system recognizes that it is the person who makes the job in the managerial ranks (see Figure 3 for a comparison of the differences between the

Figure 3. Comparison of traditional and MBO job descriptions.

	Traditional	*MBO*
Major thrust	Heavily oriented to long statements of activities.	Oriented to objectives.
Change factor	Seldom changes unless major function is added or subtracted from the job.	Objectives portion changes at least once each year.
Priorities	Lack of change precludes recognizing changing priorities.	Changing priorities are recognized through changing objectives.
Improvement	Lack of recognition of change precludes inclusion of improvement as a factor.	Continual improvement can be programmed into the changing objectives.
Orientation	Heavily job-tailored; frequently ignores the man and differences in men.	Man-tailored; individual strengths can be capitalized on.

[5] See Dale D. McConkey, *Management by Objectives for Staff Managers* (New York: Vantage Press, 1972).

traditional and the MBO job description and Figure 4 for an illustration of what an MBO job description should be).

The importance of the document that describes the manager's accountability cannot be overemphasized. This document serves as the basis for evaluating the manager's performance, for rewarding it, and for gauging the countless other actions related to individual performance. The sum of all these activities determines the future of the total entity.

Compensation Practices

MBO has had a pronounced impact on compensation practices, both in the basis on which payments are made and in the form the payments take.

Basis for compensating. Prior to the widespread adoption of MBO, it was quite common for compensation to be based on so-called merit principles. However, "merit" was a highly elusive term, and few organizations succeeded in realizing it in actual practice. Too often, for example, merit became synonymous with longevity. Invariably, there was a tenuous con-

Figure 4. Example of MBO job description.

JOB TITLE: Vice-President and General Manager, Operating Division B.

PURPOSE
Management of Division B to achieve growth and profits according to approved plans.

RESPONSIBILITIES (relatively stable from year to year)
1. Planning to achieve long- and short-term objectives.
2. Monitoring the efficient execution of approved plans.
3. Development and administration of division policy and procedures and of standards of performance; implementation of corporate policies and procedures.
4. Marketing for Division B services.
5. Operations
   Maintenance.   Efficiency.
   Job quality.   Equipment design and
   Safety.   construction supervision.
6. Personnel and financial services not provided by corporate office.

ACCOUNTABILITY
1. Achieve pretax return of 11 percent on capital employed.
2. Achieve minimum sales of $27 million.
3. Achieve pretax profit of $3 million.
4. Increase profit contribution at division level by 4 percent over 197x.
5. Develop at least one new product with potential sales volume of $100,000 annually.

---

nection between a manager's compensation and the results achieved or the contribution made.

As often as not, compensation plans did everything possible to destroy the prime objectives of compensation: promoting equity and motivation. Rewards that were not tied to specific results, and were not given to the manager in proportion to the results achieved, could hardly be considered equitable or a motivating force to encourage better performance. MBO has precipitated fundamental changes by insisting that compensation be tied closely to achievement of objectives and paid in proportion to the degree to which the objectives are achieved or exceeded.

Form of payments. Incentive compensation, in one form or another, has been around for many years, but it remained for MBO to give real meaning and purpose to its use. Formerly, incentive payments were often limited to a small percentage of an organization's top managers and were usually handed out on a profit-sharing basis in which payments were related more to total organizational performance than to the individual performance of the manager. This too has changed. The percentage of managers covered by incentive plans is on the increase.

Incentive payments are viewed more and more from the standpoint of the contribution of the individual manager. Even though the company as a whole may have enjoyed record profits, there is no guarantee that the individual manager will share in the bonanza. Emphasis is placed on his or her individual record (results).

Recognizing the limitations imposed by salary payments (fixed versus variable compensation costs, inability to recognize wide swings in individual performance, and the failure of salaries to emphasize a direct tie-in with profitability), many companies are stressing variable incentive payments over straight salaries. The group of managers whose total compensation contains a significant amount of incentive compensation is definitely enlarging. Arch Patton, a leading researcher on executive compensation, has stated that a successful MBO system in the United States seems to require an incentive plan for sound ongoing administration.[6]

Thus MBO has reoriented the basis of compensation from nebulous merit to results, changed the emphasis of payments from salary to incentives, and increased the number of managers participating in incentive plans. Of at least equal importance in the rewards process, MBO has provided the possibility for recognizing contributions when promotion time arrives.

[6] Arch Patton, "Does Performance Appraisal Work?" *Business Horizons,* February 1973, p. 89.

Planning

Probably no other aspect of the management process has received such a substantial jolt from MBO as planning has. Formerly, planning was an exercise in writing tolerated to satisfy the company's requirements; now, its value and help to the individual manager are increasingly appreciated. More important, the manager recognizes the real need for planning and can appreciate why it is necessary.

Edward Green, one of the authorities in the area of corporate planning, has compared what he terms the traditional approach to planning with the more modern approach, which is markedly oriented toward MBO. Figure 5 outlines Green's comparison.

Delegation

MBO has at last brought real meaning to the definition of "delegation." Formerly, delegation was defined as "getting things done through other people." This wholly inadequate definition failed to recognize that "things" can be good, bad, or indifferent. Unfortunately, the much-touted delegation was approached in the same inadequate fashion.

Now delegation is approached in a manner that is conducive to more positive results. Under MBO, a subordinate is not told to go out and do something or to get things done. Instead, the person is delegated specific objectives or end results for which he or she is accountable. Both the subordinate and the boss know the specific end results that must be achieved.

One of the cardinal mandates of MBO is that the manager must have sufficient authority to accomplish objectives. For the first time, in many instances, managers are receiving clear definitions of the authority they may exercise. Statements such as "he or she shall enjoy authority commensurate to carry out his or her job" are rapidly giving way to rather finite statements of authority.

The impact of MBO on the overall management process and especially its effect on delegation have provided a viable foundation for practicing participative management. Delegating by specific objectives permits a manager to determine much of his own destiny, to help set his objectives, to do much of his own planning to achieve the objectives, to operate with the authority he knows he has, and to take the initiative when corrective action is required. The emphasis on delegating end results permits participation and helps considerably in preventing permissive management.

In an era in which one of the popular buzzwords of the day is "job enrichment," with attention so far directed almost exclusively to the em-

Figure 5. Comparison of old and new planning approaches.

	Static Planning (Old Way)	vs.	Dynamic Planning (New Approach)
Purpose	Get a "plan."		Achieve optimum results.
Basic premise	Forecasts are accurate.		Future is unpredictable.
Technique	Static, periodic.		Dynamic, continuous.
Process	Rigid, formal, pre-scribed.		Flexible, selective adaptation.
Management style	Traditional, authoritative.		Decentralized, participative.
Responsibility	Top management. VP, planning. Centralized planning staff.		Every manager. Director, planning services. Decentralized planning coordinators.
Types of planning Strategic Operational Logistic	Separate plans.		Integrated planning.
Functional planning Marketing Financial Personnel, and so on	Separate plans.		Integrated planning.
Time spans Short Medium Long-range	Separate plans.		Integrated planning.
Support	Resistance and resentment.		Enthusiastic participation.
Durability	Tapers off to discouragement.		Growing value and enthusiasm.
Cost/benefits	Too much time-effort-paper. Higher cost. Limited benefits.		Better decisions and programs. Less time and effort. Better results.

SOURCE: Edward J. Green, "The Communication Crisis," Marshall Allan Robinson lecture, University of Pittsburgh, 1972.

ployee instead of the manager, MBO has made considerable strides in enriching the manager's job. The practice of MBO in depth culminates in each manager's becoming "president" of his own little "company" within the total organization. When this end is reached, the manager experiences substantial job enrichment because his destiny depends largely upon his own efforts.

Decision Making

The decision-making process also has come in for its share of change as a result of MBO. Two aspects of MBO have been causative forces in this change. The first is the feedback and data, tailored and directed to the individual manager; the second is the structuring of strict accountability for each manager.

Feedback

Advocates of decentralization have long maintained that decisions should be made at the lowest possible level of management at which all information necessary to the decision comes together. However, the principle has been honored more in the breach than in practice.

Some of the reasons why the principle has not been widely practiced concern the characteristics of the data many managers receive: an overabundance of raw data but little of the selected intelligence required for decision making, data prepared for the needs of the manager's superior instead of for the manager, and data collected for costing and revenue purposes rather than for use by the manager.

MBO places a premium on data prepared under the best principles of enlightened responsibility accounting—the right data, at the right time, at the right place, for the right manager. Now, with in-depth delegation and the proper data, decisions can be made at the lowest possible level, nearest the point of action, and at the time the action is taking place.

Accountability

Prior to MBO's requirement for strict accountability by individuals, decisions often were delayed because of what one writer has referred to as decision drift; that is, the tendency to avoid decision making when it is not clear who should make the decision. Often, the timid manager will purposely delay or ignore making a decision unless forced to make it. The undesirable expedient of decision making by committee often results.

MBO, by clearly defining who is accountable for what, pinpoints the manager who should make a particular decision. This has definitely lessened procrastination and avoidance of decision making.

MBO FAILURES

As discussed later, MBO has not been a 100 percent success. Many attempts have been failures, absolute failures. Others, while not failing completely, have not delivered the full benefits of which they are capable (failures by degree). Both types of failures have resulted from succumbing to the numerous pitfalls that can develop in the system.

The experience of various and diverse organizations over roughly 20 years has singled out a number of reasons for the failure of some organizations to make their mark with MBO.

MBO TIME SHOCK

The progressive use of MBO within an organization has an attendant time shock to managers. F. D. Barrett, president of Management Concepts, Ltd., describes this shock feature as threefold, coming about when the manager realizes that:

> Writing meaningful objectives requires several days, not just a few hours
>
> The time required to realize the full impact of MBO is not a matter of months but a few years
>
> A pronounced change takes place in the amount of time the manager spends actually "managing" rather than "doing." Increasingly, doing gives way to managing.[7]

Unfortunately, the impact of time shock has been too little appreciated by some organizations, and the effectiveness of their MBO approaches has suffered. The impact of this shock (actually it is a necessary period of transition) can neither be ignored nor brought to a forced conclusion. It is as necessary and natural as the progression of a child from adolescence to adulthood. Any attempt to move too rapidly or to fail to gain from the experience arising from the requisite steps will result in an inferior development process.

FUTURE OF MBO

As the application and impact of MBO are yet unfolding, any evaluation must be a dynamic one. However, evidence to date indicates that the effect of MBO has been most dramatic, both on the overall approach to managing and on the many parts of the management process.

[7] F. D. Barrett, "The MBO Time Trip," *The Business Quarterly*, Autumn 1972, pp. 44–47.

Probably its signal benefit has been its insistence on improving organizational effectiveness through improving the effectiveness of the individual manager. This transition has been well summarized by Barrett in his comparison between "Model A" management (pre-MBO) and "Model B" management (post-MBO). See Figure 6. The average organization—I dislike the term but am hard pressed to come up with a better description—should expect that this transition will start to take place three to five years after beginning its MBO system.

Figure 6. Transition in management styles under MBO.

Pre-MBO	Post-MBO
Day-to-day managing	Future-focused
Amateur, seat-of-pants	Full-fledged professional
Inward-looking	Outward-looking
Product-oriented	People-oriented
Organization-oriented	Consumer-oriented
Activities-oriented	Results-oriented
Administration of routine	Creation of innovations
Emphasis on "how to"	Emphasis on "what to"
Emphasis on money, machines, materials	Emphasis on people, minds, time
Centralized, technocratic, functional control	Decentralized initiative from subordinates
Authoritarian style	Participative style
Directives and supervision	Delegation and reporting
Individualism	Teamwork

Source: Reprinted by permission of the author, F. D. Barrett, "The MBO Time Trip," *The Business Quarterly* (Autumn 1972), pp. 44–45.

MBO and its benefits are too well established, having survived the test of about 20 years of practice, to be considered a passing fancy or a fad. The system has earned its place as part of the permanent management scene. The future will bring the continued use and increased applications of MBO. Real progress remains to be made in several major areas. Managers must become more adept at setting top priorities. As all of an organization's efforts are geared through MBO to meeting top priorities, management's efforts must be directed to ensuring that the most desirable priorities are selected. Otherwise, MBO causes an organization to become increasingly efficient at something it should not be doing in the first place.

Having set the optimum priorities, management must increase its competence in planning to achieve the priority objectives. Failure to develop better planning expertise will render it impossible to exploit the full potential of priority objectives.

Other areas of the MBO system necessitate continual refinement. For example, even though much excellent work has been done in relating managerial appraisal to actual contribution, more work remains to be done on this subject. Similarly, additional progress must be made to establish a more direct correlation between a manager's contribution and his rewards. The tie-in presently is not direct enough.

Last, the effectiveness of MBO in general will continue to suffer unless an organization's management recognizes that the key word in management by objectives is "management" and not "objectives." MBO is a whole new way of life for many organizations. It is a way of managing. Those organizations that embrace the system without recognizing this and without first examining their management philosophy and practice will continue to adopt MBO on a "planned failure" basis. Even worse, they will become easy prey for the increasing number of MBO advocates with a solution who are running around looking for a problem.

The utilization of the continually growing number of workers in the knowledge industry represents another area of high potential payback from MBO. The system has much to commend it for application to these workers. The failure to align their efforts to priorities and full utilization of their talents will constitute a costly oversight for their organizations.

Experience has proved that MBO, by itself, will accomplish nothing but chaos. In the hands of a capable management that is ready for it and knows how to use it, it has much to offer. For the right management, it holds promise of a bright future.

Thus this book must be viewed in its proper context. It's much like a photograph taken at a specific point in time, which freezes the action as of that time. MBO is continuing to evolve and change. This book covers the practical, proven experience as of 1976. What is written here undoubtedly will require major revision within a few years.

2

What Is Management by Objectives?

ONE OF THE SALUTARY BENEFITS that any current book on management by objectives should attempt to deliver to the reader is the elimination of the mystique with which many writers and speakers have attempted to surround MBO. There is nothing magical about MBO. It won't accomplish magical things, nor does one have to be adept at magic to practice MBO effectively.

Nor is there anything terribly new about many aspects of MBO. Many pieces of the MBO system have been around for many years. Many managers—in fact most managers—are already practicing parts of MBO regardless of whether or not these parts are so labeled.

Probably the most significant or new aspect of MBO is the underlying intent or rationale behind it. Primarily, MBO resulted from the pulling together of all the more effective management techniques and applications and combining them into one systematic, integrated, total way of managing an organization. Viewed in this light, MBO is little more than a common-sense approach to achieving greater positive results at all levels of management.

The words "all levels of management" are used advisedly. MBO contemplates that an organization, as a total entity, will determine the overall results it must achieve and then line up the actions of each and every manager to achieve these predetermined overall results. Thus one of MBO's greatest virtues is its potential ability to promote a rifle approach to achieving desired results rather than a scattergun approach in which many managers dissipate their time and effort keeping busy on unnecessary and routine activities.

MBO DEFINED

Now let's take a look at what will hopefully serve as a clearer definition of MBO. Before doing so, a word of caution is in order. An effective MBO system should never have in it even one definition or technical distinction that isn't absolutely required. MBO should promote results such as profitability, not semantic jungles that turn managers into professors of English.

There are almost as many definitions of management by objectives as there are writers, practitioners, and theoreticians who have concerned themselves with the subject. Thus the definitions run the gamut from two or three lines of oversimplification to many paragraphs of oversophistication. Hopefully, the following definition, which will be used throughout this book, represents a balance between the two extremes. I do not intend this as the ultimate definition but rather as one that will provide the reader with the necessary guidance for understanding the MBO system of managing. This is my definition:

> MBO is a systems approach to managing an organization—*any* organization. It is not a technique, or just another program, or a narrow area of the process of managing. Above all, it goes far beyond mere budgeting even though it does encompass budgets in one form or another.
>
> First, those accountable for directing the organization determine where they want to take the organization or what they want it to achieve during a particular period (establishing the overall objectives and priorities).
>
> Second, all key managerial, professional, and administrative personnel are required, permitted, and encouraged to contribute their maximum efforts to achieving the overall objectives.
>
> Third, the planned achievement (results) of all key personnel is blended and balanced to promote and realize the greater total results for the organization as a whole.
>
> Fourth, a control mechanism is established to monitor progress compared to objectives and feed the results back to those accountable at all levels.

Other Definitions

Excellent definitions of MBO are provided by executives who are actually practicing MBO. Several of these follow. Note the common practice of using the terms "management by objectives" and "management by results" interchangeably.

James O. Wright, president of Federal-Mogul Corporation, has briefly spelled out the management by results approach as follows:

> First, decide what the broad objectives of the company should be. These are the strategic goals. They involve such basic questions of policy as: What profit return should be aimed for? How big do we want to become? What products should we sell? In what markets?
>
> Next, develop operating plans in each functional area as the means of reaching the broad objectives. This involves determining what plants to build, and where, and how; where the money is to come from, and of what kind; how the markets will be reached; and what R&D effort will be required—all this, of course, being spelled out in detail. Full consideration, too, should be given to planning the development of people who will have the needed managerial and technical skills.
>
> Then all members of management down through first-line supervision should be acquainted with what's expected of them in carrying out the plans. . . .
>
> Finally, use the coach-and-counsel method in helping subordinates play their part as the plans go into action.[1]

Emphasis here is on the specific *what* and *when*. General statements are of little if any value in management by results. Charles E. St. Thomas, president of St. Thomas Associates, Inc., expresses this point well:

> "To increase our business" is a meaningless four-word statement typical of the "goals" that many companies put on paper. What company doesn't want to increase its business? Writing such an objective is wasted effort unless the goal includes some details. "To increase our business in 11 western states by 22 percent over the next 24 months by direct selling," for example, tells what the department or company wants to do, and where, when, and how it proposes to do it. It is an objective, a directive, and a yardstick.[2]

Still another definition is provided by Arch Patton of McKinsey & Company:

> Companies that have explored ways and means of providing specific goals for their executives have tended to adopt an approach designed to integrate the short-term goals of individual executives with company objectives. In its simplest form, this goal-setting effort involves three key steps:

[1] As paraphrased in *Management News*, AMACOM, May 1965.
[2] *The Manager's Letter*, AMACOM, February 20, 1965.

1. Developing long- and short-term company or division goals, both tangible and intangible.
2. Assigning specific responsibility to functional executives by agreement between superior and subordinate.
3. Reviewing results at the year's end, giving adequate weight to the difficulty of accomplishment and preserving a reasonable balance between tangible and intangible goals.[3]

Probably one of the best definitions of management by results was given by Harlow H. Curtice, then president of General Motors:

> It is really an attitude of mind. It might be defined as bringing the research point of view to bear on all phases of the business. This involves, first, assembling all the facts; second, analysis of where the facts appear to point; and third, courage to follow the trail indicated even if it leads into unfamiliar and unexplored territory. This point of view is never satisfied with things as they are.[4]

THE KEY WORD

As I said earlier, the key word in the term "management by objectives" is not the word "objectives" but the word "management." Again, this is a necessary and important distinction. The failure to appreciate this distinction has been at the root of many of management's failures in attempting to practice MBO.

The following sequence of events usually occurs when "objectives" is considered the key word. First, and generally, objectives are overemphasized in relation to the system. Second, the setting of objectives becomes a fetish. Third, managers are required to write a list of objectives for their jobs. Those objectives are commonly written in a vacuum, without completion of the necessary preliminary action that must precede the objectives. The result to the manager is a list of uncoordinated and unbalanced objectives whose meaning, importance, and function seem incomprehensible. Often, the manager is puzzled as to how the objectives can help him manage his job better. Actually, objectives written in this manner can impede rather than aid job performance.

The successful MBO manager views objectives as only one part—admittedly a vitally important part—of a total system. He ensures that the management system is in place so that he can position objectives into the

[3] "Developing Executives to Beat the Profit Squeeze," *Business Horizons*, Winter 1962, p. 49.
[4] Statements before the Subcommittee on Antitrust and Monopoly of the U.S. Senate Committee on the Judiciary, December 2, 1955.

system rather than have them stand on their own and see them as the system. The manager must first master the system: determine what it is, what it isn't, its rationale, the prerequisites to be met, the pitfalls to be wary of, the mechanics of the system, the components. Then, and only then, does he address himself to objectives proper. The system and its components are examined in detail later in this chapter.

THE DEFINITION IN PRACTICE

The MBO system begins with the establishment of overall objectives for the total organization for the target period. Once the top management of the organization has established these overall objectives, they constitute the sum total of the results that must be accomplished by all the managers of that organization; that is, at the end of the target period, the total of the results accomplished by all the managers must add up, as a minimum, to the overall objectives that were set earlier.

MBO is adaptable to any type of organization as long as that organization has a mission to perform. The only difference is that the type and content of the objectives will differ. In a police department, the objective may be to lower the crime rate to a stipulated level. In a school system, the objective might be to provide specific educational benefits at various cost levels. In a corporation, the overall objective might be to achieve a certain profit level or certain return on investment.

Once the top objectives have been approved, the next step is to translate them into the action each manager must take. The objective-setting process is complete when every manager, both line and staff and at all levels from top management down to and including the lowest-level manager, has objectives that, when added up, will at least equal the overall objectives of the enterprise. Another way to describe MBO is that it is the full, in-depth delegation of pieces of the overall organizational objectives down the line so that each manager is accountable for accomplishing part of the higher-level objectives.

THE SYSTEMS APPROACH

MBO can be referred to as a systems approach to managing an organization. The "systems" nature of the approach as it is presently practiced becomes clear when we delve into the definition of a system, which I'll describe as being a combination of actions (or components) that, when acting as a whole, cause something to happen. The components of an electric doorbell provide a good example of a system and its operation. The components in this case are a power source (electricity), a conducting medium (electrical wire), a triggering mechanism (the button), and an action vehicle (the bell mechanism). All four components must be present and must play their proper role if the desired action—the ringing of the bell—is to take place. In the case of MBO the system comprises objectives, plans, managerial direction and action, control (monitoring), and feedback. The absence of any one of these key components of the MBO system will render it inoperative. In the early days of MBO there was often a lack of one, two, or even more of the key components. For example, it has long been fashionable to uphold the virtue and use of objectives and an even cursory review of the literature reveals the extensive adoption of objectives on a wide scale. As we shall see later, the quality and value of the early objectives were subject to considerable criticism. But until recently, there was a glaring lack of one of the other key components that must always accompany objectives if they are to be accomplished: the plans for making them work. The inherent defects in the type of objectives formerly used and the lack of plans for accomplishing them resulted in major weaknesses in the other components of the system: managerial direction and action, control and feedback.

THE EMERGENCE OF MBO AS A SYSTEM

Before MBO could emerge as a system it was necessary to correct these weaknesses by strengthening each component and meshing each improved component into a smoothly working, effective whole.

Objectives

Typically, objectives were formerly little more than general statements of management's wishes. It was not uncommon to find objectives such as:

Achieve the greatest possible cost/benefit ratio for all expenditures.

Manage our organization in the most efficient manner possible.

Provide the highest-quality products to our customers.

Provide the necessary motivation to our people.

All these wishes are laudable and because they are, they became known as "Motherhood" objectives. However, they did little if anything to fulfill the basic requirements of meeting objectives. They did not provide concrete directions to managers in that they did not tell them what must be accomplished, how much must be accomplished, who was to accomplish it, or when it must be accomplished.

MBO required that objectives be removed from the nebulous, blue-sky thinking category into a new category in which they would be specific and measurable and thus would provide proper direction for all the managers in an organization. This was accomplished by applying the "3Ws": What will be done? When will it be done? Who will do it?

With the advent of specific, time-limited, and clearly delineated objectives we began to witness the beginnings of the systems approach. The word "beginnings" is used advisedly because it remained to formulate concrete plans for accomplishing the specific objectives.

Plans

Prior to MBO as it is presently practiced, it was an all-too-frequent practice for organizations to structure their objectives, even highly specific ones, and then fail to develop the concrete plans and actions that, when completed, would result in the accomplishment of the objectives. It seemed almost as if they were relying on the Almighty to see to it that the objectives did in fact get accomplished. MBO stopped this praying and wishing and substituted "backbone management" for "wishbone management."

The role of plans in MBO may be illustrated by a common objective for a production manager whose objective is to increase output per employee by x percent.

To justify that this is a realistic and obtainable objective and to provide the means by which he will achieve it, this manager must develop concrete plans. These plans should include a statement of the step-by-step action he will pursue to achieve the objective.

Once his plans have been formulated, he must test them for reasonableness. Are the plans as realistic as he can make them? Has sufficient justification been included with respect to his assumptions and alternatives? Have all possible alternatives been considered? Do the plans contain any unjustified or blue-sky thinking? Will the plans hold up under a penetrating analysis? If the plans come true as written, is it reasonable to expect that the objective will be achieved?

Managerial Direction and Action

The next component of the MBO system requires the manager to give proper direction and take action to accomplish what the company wishes to achieve—in other words, to carry out his objectives and plans. This component includes major functions such as organizing, communicating, motivating, coordinating, and developing subordinates. It brings to life the objectives and plans the manager established; it's the action vehicle of MBO.

Control (Monitoring)

Returning again to the conditions existing prior to MBO, we find that management's control function was largely inadequate and going through its infancy. Controls were either too general or, when they were specific, they were attempting to monitor nonspecific matters. Consequently the controls did not serve their intended purpose. Control was largely an after-the-fact reporting of what actually happened as opposed to what someone thought *should* happen.

Under MBO a specific objective is decided upon first. Second, a specific control is tailored to measure the specific objective. In other words, we first determine where we want to go and then decide upon the one best method for determining whether or not we are getting there.

Another problem with controls as they were formerly used was that they were not designed to serve the differing needs of the various levels of management. Too frequently, control was considered as being necessary only at the upper levels of management but not really necessary at intermediate and lower levels. Under MBO each manager has controls for each of the objectives for which he is responsible, and these controls are tailored to his particular needs at his level.

As a very minimum, each control must include the objective (or subject matter) being measured, the method of measuring, the frequency of measuring, and to whom the control information will be sent.

Feedback

Control is useless unless the information is placed in the hands of those who must make the decisions and subsequently use the information to check the validity of their decisions and take appropriate corrective action when necessary. Thus we come to feedback and its part in the MBO system. Feedback requires that each manager receive the type of information, in the right form and at the right frequency, that he requires to carry out the accountabilities of his job. The manager need not be deluged with information but should receive only that which he requires.

3

Prerequisites for Successful MBO

THE EXPERIENCE of organizations in which MBO has been judged to be the most successful has demonstrated that several conditions or prerequisites must be met. These prerequisites include: (1) the most effective management style, (2) organizational clarity, and (3) feedback on performance.

A general comment is in order before proceeding to a discussion of each of these prerequisites. No organization will meet each of these one hundred percent. This would be an impractical ideal. However, the greater the degree to which these prerequisites are met, the greater the degree of success that will usually result from MBO efforts. In fact, one of the more common causes of failure in MBO is a misguided attempt to proceed without meeting these prerequisites.

MANAGEMENT STYLE

The prevalent management style found in most successful MBO systems is now referred to as the participative style. The late Douglas McGregor gave impetus to this style when he wrote:

> The essential task of management is to arrange organizational conditions and methods of operation so that people can achieve their own goals best by directing their own efforts towards organizational objectives.

This is a process primarily of creating opportunities, releasing potential, removing obstacles, encouraging growth, providing guidance. It is what Peter Drucker has called "Management by Objectives" in contrast to "Management by Control." *

Essentially, participative management is a decentralized, team approach to managing in which each manager is given the greatest possible latitude to determine or influence his job and his future, but always within the requirements of what the organization as a whole must accomplish during the target period. The highlights of participative management can be summerized as follows:

Responsibility: Major voice in determining his job.
Accountability: Major voice in determining results (objectives) he must achieve.
Planning: Does his own planning for his unit.
Authority: Major voice in determining clear-cut authority for himself.
Decision making: Freedom to make decisions for his unit.
Supervision: Emphasis is on self-supervision with minimal control from above.
Management: Wide latitude to manage his own resources.
Communications and feedback: Tailored to his individual needs on a need-to-know basis.

Participative management requires that the manager and his superior first agree on the specific results the subordinate will achieve and when, the authority the subordinate enjoys, and the resources the subordinate may use. Then the subordinate is left alone, within minimal but effective control from the superior, to manage his own unit.

Common Misconceptions

It is unfortunate that some critics of participative management—often those who don't understand it or have never seen it actually practiced—have succeeded in perpetuating several misconceptions. The major of these misconceptions are:

Participative management is "permissive" management.

Once adopted, participative management must be practiced 100 percent of the time regardless of the circumstances.

All managers must be granted the same amount of participation.

Participative versus Permissive

Permissive management may be defined as a misguided and naive approach in which each manager is allowed to do as he pleases, until the

* *The Human Side of Enterprise* (New York: McGraw-Hill, 1960).

company goes bankrupt. Why? Because it fails to consider the requirements of the corporation. Participative management begins with the company's requirements, its objectives and priorities, and then gives each manager a major voice in determining how he or she will help carry out the requirements.

Participative management is a highly rewarding style. It is also a very demanding one, imposing on each manager the following demands:

To accept *accountability* for the results of his unit.

To *plan* for his unit.

To accept and carry out *authority*.

To make *recommendations* relative to the operation of his unit.

To make *decisions* as called for by his authority.

To seize the initiative in *problem solving* for his unit.

In short, participative management requires the manager to stand up and be counted at all times.

100 Percent of the Time

The goal of this style of management should be to practice it as *consistently* as possible, not 100 percent of the time. Attempting to do the latter would often constitute abdication on the part of the superior manager.

Often the higher-level manager must make decisions and take action that may impact on a subordinate even though he may not always be able to discuss the subject with the subordinate in advance. Emergencies and other pressing circumstances would make it foolish for the superior to delay action until the subordinate can be consulted.

Equal Participation by All?

Those who argue that all subordinates should be given the same amount of participation appear to overlook two important facts. One, every manager differs as to the degree to which he is achievement-oriented. Second, each manager differs in competence.

Both of these major variables must be considered when determining how much leeway and freedom each manager can be given. Otherwise, managerial effectiveness will suffer.

ORGANIZATIONAL CLARITY

A prerequisite to management effectiveness is the absolute requirement that all managers be held responsible for results. Inherent in this premise is the necessity for pinpointing just which manager is responsible for which results. Also, the results for which each manager is held accountable must be consistent with the authority that has been delegated to him. To put it another way, the manager cannot be held responsible for results if he hasn't been delegated sufficient authority to accomplish the expected results. Any gap between responsibility and authority will usually result in failure to achieve objectives and in a high degree of frustration on the manager's part. Establishing objectives for each manager will help spot organizational weaknesses and duplication or inconsistent assignment of authority, but it will not correct them. This must be handled by top management. The folly of endeavoring to set objectives in the midst of organizational confusion is evidenced by a couple of examples.

Some Common Confusion

The president of a medium-size food company was understandably concerned by the high rate of rejected products being turned out by the production department. In his zeal to correct the situation, he tried to hold the director of quality control responsible for an objective that required the director to lower the reject rate by a certain percentage. While the objective itself was certainly in order under the circumstances, it was doomed to failure from the start because the director lacked the authority to accomplish it.

Despite what his title implies, a quality control director is *not* responsible for controlling quality; this is a responsibility for which only the production people can be held accountable. A quality control manager can analyze the quality of production, isolate causes of problems, suggest remedial action, and recommend quality control specifications, but only production management is responsible for the quality of production once the specifications are approved. To be able to hold the director of quality control responsible for the product rejection rate would require that he be given the unquestioned right to direct the production department—to shut down lines, to boss the workers, to dictate work methods, and to control every other operation that could have a bearing on quality levels. Doing this would strip production management of *its* responsibility.

Clearly the food company president should have ensured that the profit objective in this instance was structured so as to make the director of quality control responsible for recommending accurate quality control specifications and procedures; once these were adopted, the production manager should have been held responsible for a prescribed reduction in the rejection rate in accordance with the approved specifications. In this way, the objectives for which each manager was held accountable would have been consistent with his authority and performance and the effectiveness of the objectives would have been enhanced instead of weakened.

In similar fashion, the chief executive of a plastics fabricating company instructed his vice-president of personnel to recommend an objective calling for the vice-president to reduce the plant absentee rate by 2 percent. In addition to the cost of absenteeism itself, the company was losing business because of its inability to deliver products on time.

As in the case of the quality control director, this objective was impossible to meet because the executive didn't have the authority to accomplish it. The personnel vice-president can maintain records of absences, analyze and investigate to determine the reasons for the absences, identify the repeat offenders, and, on the basis of all this, make appropriate recommendations to the managers concerned. However, he cannot control the absentee rate because he has no authority to issue warnings to offending employees or to correct the departmental conditions that may be contributing to the absences. He must leave the corrective action to the respective managers to whom the absent employees actually report. In this instance, the personnel vice-president should have had his objective structured so that it reflected his authority to analyze and recommend, and the other managers should have been held accountable for actually taking the necessary corrective action within the approved absentee control policy.

Conflicting Responsibility

Other types of organizational cloudiness will cause a lessening of profit potential. Take, for example, the credit and collections manager who reports to the sales executive. The typical credit manager is responsible for facilitating sales by extending the maximum line of credit he believes justified by the customer's credit rating. Concurrently, the credit manager must take all possible action to minimize bad debts. Balancing greater sales and low bad debts is generally fraught with contradictions. As long as the credit manager must report to and take orders from the sales executive—whose main interest in life is generating increased sales volume—there is an ever present likelihood that the credit manager's ability to achieve his objectives will be clouded by the sales executive's contradictory objective.

Three other instances of organizational fuzziness that weaken the individual manager's effectiveness are, first, there has been no clarification of responsibility for chain store sales in a given territory, and both a headquarters sales manager and a local area sales manager are permitted to make sales to chain stores in the same area. Second, the purchasing manager is responsible for purchasing all materials centrally, but the line manager is responsible for the cost of all purchases made for his department, including the materials that go into his production. Third, the sales manager, who is responsible for net sales revenues, constantly books short-term, low-volume orders that pyramid production costs without regard for the production manager's stated responsibility to hold down production costs.

The majority of potentially troublesome organizational conflicts can usually be resolved by clear statements of accountability, the goal being to pin down as specifically as possible the responsibilities of each manager. In other instances, a desired objective may require that several managers be jointly responsible for the completion of an objective. This frequently occurs in highly integrated operations such as the large fruit-importing and sales company that grows the fruit in foreign countries, transports it to this country in its own ships, and sells it through its own marketing organization in the United States. The officers in charge of fruit growing, shipping, and marketing each play a key role as part of a fully integrated profit center, and all three are responsible for maximizing profits of the three departments as a whole.

The officer in charge of fruit growing runs a cost center, as does the shipping officer. The marketing officer's prime responsibility is to secure maximum revenue. The factor that makes especially close coordination mandatory is the relatively short pricing period; depending upon short-term changes in the amount of fruit entering a particular U.S. port at a given time, the price received for fruit can fluctuate all over the map. Under these circumstances, it is sometimes possible to maximize total profits by shipping less than the maximum amount to avoid glutting a particular market area and driving the price down.

When this happens a natural contradiction develops between the executives in charge of growing and shipping. As both operate cost centers, both are normally interested in growing and shipping the maximum number of units, thereby favorably offsetting the high fixed costs that characterize their departments. However, if they were always to grow and ship the maximum number of units, the overall profitability of the company would frequently suffer because their shortsighted gains would later be lost by deteriorating prices on the selling end. In this particular instance, it is necessary that the profit-planning objectives for each of the three integrated departments be set in such a way that this situation is clearly recognized.

Additional discussion will demonstrate how this is accomplished in the instance of the shipping executive, whose effectiveness is usually based on the load factor of his ships. In essence, the load factor is the measure of the percentage of actual load being transported as compared to the total load possible, considering the ship's capacity. Normally, a shipping officer makes his greatest contribution as he approaches the 100 percent load factor. In the case of the fruit company, however, he may be making his optimum contribution to the profits of the three departments as a whole if his ships are traveling at, say, 90 percent of capacity. If so, the 90 percent load factor would become his objective even though at first glance it would appear that he is inefficient to the tune of 10 percent. Thus it becomes important not only to delineate just who is responsible for what, but also just what each is responsible for.

Finally, organizational clarity is required if a company is to measure individual managerial performance against objectives and to provide each manager with the information he requires for control and decision-making purposes.

The next section in this chapter discusses the need for management information or feedback, which must be closely tailored to the organization structure and individual responsibilities. Responsibility accounting can be effective only if the right information is provided to the right person—the one who must take action or make the decision. Therefore, if the right type of data is to be provided to a manufacturing superintendent, the responsibilities and functions of this superintendent must be clearly understood, not only by him, but also by the personnel who must supply the data. If his responsibility encompasses accountability for the cost of raw materials purchased, this must be clear and the management information he receives must reflect it. If, on the other hand, the purchasing manager is responsible for the cost of goods, he, not the superintendent, must receive the data.

The principle of organizational clarity can be summarized as follows:

> The organization structure and individual responsibilities must be sufficiently clear so that they permit the formulation of individual objectives that are consistent with authority and responsibility and, in turn, so that it is possible to develop a management information system that is also consistent and responsive to individual responsibility and authority.

Chapter 9 discusses the clarification of the manager's responsibility before he begins to write objectives.

FEEDBACK

Feedback on performance is an absolute requirement for two vitally important reasons. The first has to do with the requirements of an achievement-oriented manager. The second purpose of feedback is to permit the manager to stay on target by making interim decisions and revisions during the target period.

Achievement orientation. A large body of experience and knowledge has proved the soundness of two premises: First, the more achievement-oriented a manager is, the more he demands feedback on his performance. He wants to know how well he's doing at all times. He doesn't want to take action and then be left in the dark as to the results of his action. Second, the more achievement-oriented a manager is, the less tolerant he is of paperwork, unnecessary routines, and raw data. He wants a minimum amount of data—quality, action-oriented data organized so as to constitute "intelligence" on which he can make decisions and take action.

Decisions and revisions. Once objectives and plans have been approved, they can't just be filed away and forgotten. They must be used as a guide to required action during the target period. Thus the manager must always know how well or poorly he's performing. He must know at the earliest possible time when his objectives aren't working out; otherwise, he can't take corrective action and make the revisions that are sometimes necessary to keep objectives and plans realistic at all times. In the absence of timely, meaningful feedback, he runs a strong chance of having his operation get out of control and his objectives and plans becoming obsolete.

Types of Feedback

The two major types of feedback are:

1. The continuous, day-to-day feedback the manager needs to track progress on his objectives and plans. This may be called operational feedback. This feedback is tailored for, and used primarily by, the manager himself.

2. Periodic feedback, generally in the form of performance appraisal or evaluation from the manager's boss. Both the manager and his boss are very much involved in this form of feedback.

This section will concern itself with day-to-day, operational feedback. Chapter 18 covers feedback in the form of performance appraisal or evaluation.

Traditional Weaknesses

Control often became a dirty word in many traditional approaches to feedback. Often, it was prepared by accountants with a looking-backward orientation. Mistakes were overemphasized instead of providing managers with future-oriented information on which positive action could be taken. As a natural result, feedback often became associated with "gigging" or "auditing" managers. The following are other common weaknesses in traditional feedback:

□ The information was collected primarily for revenue or costing purposes without regard to the needs of the individual managers who might be involved in the actions that generated the revenue or created the costs.

□ The information was prepared for the wrong person—often not for the manager on the firing line but for his supervisor.

□ Attempts were made to provide specific feedback on general matters. This is a contradictory situation because control implies specificity. For example, in the absence of specific objectives and plans, the manager's responsibility was very general and nebulous in nature. Applying specific controls became very difficult at best. Overcontrol was frequently the result.

□ Traditional feedback also has been plagued by an overabundance of the wrong type of information, which the hapless manager must plow through attempting to locate the one or two nuggets of information he really needs. This problem was compounded with the advent of the computer. Many organizations continue to operate with fourth-generation hardware and first-generation computer personnel when it comes to feedback information.

Emphasizing the Positive

The exacting requirements for feedback will be met only if those responsible will emphasize the positive, if they'll stop looking backward on a gigging, auditing basis and switch their focus to the future. A future orientation provides feedback that emphasizes keeping the manager out of trouble in the first place and spotting trouble for him or her as quickly as possible when it does occur. Also, it requires treating feedback as a decision-making tool rather than as a hanging device for mistakes. It must emphasize helping the manager improve and not be based on making him "prove it."

Emphasizing the Individual

Much of the success of MBO lies in the increased motivation and commitment that results from putting each manager in business for himself. The terms "self-supervision," "self-management," and "self-control" are key to establishing this much-sought entrepreneurial relationship. And all of them act in concert.

Self-supervision means that once the manager and his boss have agreed upon the objectives the subordinate must achieve, he should be fairly free to supervise himself with only minimal (but effective) supervision from above. Self-management means that once the two parties agree to the resources that have been allocated (budget), the manager should be free to manage these resources.

Naturally, if the emphasis is on self-supervision, then commensurate emphasis must be placed on self-control. The manager must be in a position to properly control those matters he is supervising and managing. He can't supervise and manage unless he can also control at his level. Thus controls must be designed and tailored primarily for the manager who is accountable for achieving the objectives, not for his boss.

Qualities of Effective Feedback

The more important attributes of well-functioning operational feedback are these:

□ It should specifically and accurately measure what it is intended to measure.

□ It should incorporate the best features of responsibility accounting, in which the right type of data is provided to the right manager responsible for decision making.

□ It should be in the simplest form possible and should be presented in such a fashion that trouble spots are quickly identifiable.

□ It should be prepared and submitted as rapidly as required to permit corrective action before additional loss is experienced and while there is still time to pursue alternative courses of action.

□ It should be closely tailored to the specific company so that critical cost and revenue factors peculiar to that particular business are being measured accurately.

□ It should serve a dual role for decision making—as a guide to the manager at the time the decision is made and, later, as a control after the decision is made and the action is being pursued.

□ It should be formulated with the complete participation of managers at all levels so that full consideration may be given to what each manager requires in order to direct and measure his own operations properly. (Managers at different levels require different types of information.)

MANAGERIAL PARTICIPATION

A management information system cannot be the sole creation of the finance department. While finance may coordinate the collection and reporting of data, every manager who will be using the data must be permitted full participation when determining its type and form. No financial person, regardless of competence, can presume to know what the critical factors are for a particular operation or what type of information is important to and required by a particular manager.

Many presidents would be shocked to discover how many of their managers are spending countless hours keeping their own books and compiling their own data just because the reports they receive from the finance department don't meet managerial needs. "Junior accounting" by operating managers is costly. For one thing, operating managers are wasting time on accounting matters when they could be making more profit for the company by doing their regular jobs. For another, they lack adequate training and experience in accounting, so they run the risk of making a wrong decision on the basis of their own inadequate and possibly erroneous figures. In addition, the finance department is wasting money turning out reports that the operating managers aren't using. This alone seems sufficient justification for insisting that financial people spend as much time as possible out in the field with operating personnel, getting to know their operations, problems, and needs, so that finance can fulfill the vital role it should be playing.

4

THE STARTING POINT
Overall Corporate Objectives

IT IS FROM THE OVERALL objectives of the company that the objectives established for individual managers are derived. These constitute the starting point for the management by results approach.

At the crux of the concept is the translation of these objectives into required action at all levels of management. (The means by which multiple-level objectives are established are covered in Chapter 5.) The objectives provide leadership, a sense of direction. They set the tone of the united efforts, and the extent to which they are well thought out and well formulated determines in large part the success of the entire management group. Unless their intention is clear and they are based upon the best possible estimate of the company's total capability, the full benefit of management by results will not be realized.

The setting of overall objectives is the real test of top management's abilities. Should this group be indecisive, flounder confusedly, or set inadequate or erroneous objectives, its errors will be compounded as the whole organization focuses on activities aimed at goals that were wrong in the first place.

For illustration, consider the top management that becomes so deeply enmeshed in the day-to-day operations of the business or vacillates to such a degree that it fails to set corporate objectives at all or, even worse, changes them so frequently that they are almost meaningless. No lower-level manager, forced as he is to take his direction from those above him, can possibly work at anything approaching his full capabilities when he receives either no guidance or conflicting guidance.

SPECIFIC VERSUS GENERAL OBJECTIVES

In setting overall objectives, care must be exercised to distinguish between those that are specific in purpose and those that are more in the nature of credos—general statements of interest or policy intended to create what some writers on management term an "atmosphere." Included in the first category are specific targets such as sales volumes and rates of return required during a stated period. The second includes such nebulous statements as: "When a better mouse trap is built, XYZ Company will build it" or: "Our aim is to please our customers." Needless to say, it is only the specific objectives that have any significance for management by results.

This is not to imply that a company should not have certain broad, overall guides that continue relatively unchanged from year to year. These are frequently helpful in singling out the general direction in which management wishes to move. For example, State Mutual Life Assurance Company of America has as one of these general guides a statement to the effect that its purpose is "to fulfill the insurance needs of the greatest possible number of people."

To show the importance of such a statement, its former president, H. Ladd Plumley, cites a hypothetical bright young executive who proposes that the company stop writing policies of less than $10,000. The proposal has merit in view of the increasing demand for larger policies and the lower unit costs of writing such policies. "But we're not interested in serving a limited market consisting of a bon ton clientele," says Plumley. The guiding statement makes this unmistakably clear. And so the young executive's proposal is turned down immediately.

A TASK FOR TOP MANAGEMENT

The overall objectives are the responsibility of top management—typically the chief executive officer and staff with the assistance and concurrence of the board of directors. In short, they represent the thinking and inclinations of the very highest echelons—who, however, cannot act without having a great deal of information and intelligence passed up the line from the levels below. That is, the directors must be in possession of such necessary materials as economic studies on current and projected trends in their particular industry and the country as a whole, market research reports and forecasts, operating reports and costs, evaluations of the management team, historical data on the performance of the company, variances in the current budget picture, and many other indices that enable top management to gauge the company's ability to achieve certain goals in the future.

Armed with such information, management sets about determining what objectives it *wants* to achieve. It must concern itself with both long-range objectives (say, for a five-year period) and short-range objectives (usually for one year ahead)—those that the company must pursue in order to implement its plans. In many instances, as each twelve-month period is completed, the five-year plan is simply extended accordingly; thus it always remains a five-year plan.

This procedure can best be illustrated by the case of the relatively young consumer products company that has been marketing its products on a regional basis. As it continues to grow, it lays out an expansion program that, at the conclusion of ten years, should find the company marketing its products on a national scale. However, it approaches this program on an initial five-year basis. In other words, the company sets sales (as well as raw materials and production) targets for each of five successive years and continues extending the program by one-year increments until the planned expansion has been realized.

MENTAL WRESTLING

Generally, from its exhaustive review of all pertinent factors, management will probably conclude that the overall objectives for a particular year should include a policy stating objectives of the following kinds:

A stated return on capital employed.

A stated amount of appreciation in earnings per share.

A certain sales volume or share of the market.

In addition, management may set other specific targets for itself: growth through acquisition, for example, or companywide cost reduction.

Another objective that top managers should consider is the personnel required to carry out all other objectives. (This one is particularly important in setting long-term objectives.) More and more, corporations are also establishing objectives concerning the environment and ecology. Public responsibility is becoming increasingly prevalent as another subject for top corporate objectives.

Considerable mental wrestling must be undergone when setting overall objectives. In one firm, which was basically a one-product company, an exhaustive analysis left management with two long-range objectives: (1) to return the present business to a satisfactory earnings level and (2) to broaden the earnings base through vertical or horizontal diversification. While both were highly important to the future growth of the company, management finally decided, owing to the magnitude of its current problems and the experience and background of its management group, to devote the next five years to rebuilding the present business. Only when this had been accomplished would it undertake the second major objective—diversification. By proceeding in this order, management believed it would enhance the possibilities of long-term growth and at the same time produce a more immediate return for its shareholders.

This order of procedure, which required that management give priority to shareholder earnings, also forced it to cope with the matter of priorities for major projects. Should the company postpone expenditures on which it could not hope to realize a return for some years but which might offer a handsome payback subsequently? Or should it, where at all possible, put the future welfare of the business above current needs? These questions, and many more, had to be resolved.

WHOSE RESPONSIBILITY?

It may be meaningful to repeat that overall corporate objectives are applicable, as the term implies, primarily to the company as an entity. They are not the individual responsibility of any particular member of management, with the possible exception of the chief executive, who *is* responsible for the total entity. Rather, they are the responsibility of all management combined.

It is the results approach by which overall objectives are applied to individual executives and by which they become individual and departmental objectives. The broad corporate objectives set the framework— provide the kickoff point, as we have said. It is with them that all subordinate objectives, all functional activities, and all individual and group effort must be in harmony. To the extent that any of these are not compatible with the overall objectives, the greater the likelihood of the unnecessary effort and the excessive costs, which we have seen are inimical to true management effectiveness.

The broad objectives, then, provide the strategy. Once they have been set, management can turn its attention to the tactical objectives by which the strategic objectives are accomplished.

The next chapter provides the details as to how the overall corporate objectives are translated into other objectives at each successive lower level of management.

5

Establishing Multiple-Level Objectives

As EXPLAINED in the preceding chapter, the objective-setting process for a company begins with establishing the overall objectives and priorities of the corporation for the target period under consideration. It then proceeds through each succeeding level of management down the line until objectives have been established at the lowest level that will be covered by the system. Usually the lowest level covered is first-line supervision; for example, a section supervisor in the office and a foreman in the plant who have supervisory employees reporting to them.

DIFFERING APPROACHES

Not all companies carry out the objective-setting process in the same manner. Many variations are evident as one studies different organizations. The three following approaches have been tried or recommended to one degree or another.

1. Company A begins its annual objective-setting process by first enunciating the overall corporate objectives and then passing them down the line to be used by the lower levels as they set their objectives (top down).

2. Company B follows the opposite practice by having the process start at the lower levels and then building them up to reach the overall corporate objectives (bottom up).

3. Company C follows a third approach by endeavoring to establish all objectives at practically the same time through numerous meetings attended by several levels of management and through extensive dialog (all at once).

Each of these approaches has serious weaknesses if an attempt is made to follow it as a pure approach.

The Company A, or top down, approach will frequently culminate in a situation in which lower-level managers believe the results have been predetermined, and they will tend to feed back up the line whatever they believe the higher levels want to hear. This approach can stifle the participation and dialog that are so important to MBO effectiveness.

The weaknesses inherent in the bottom up, or Company B, approach center around the differences in emphasis by various organizational levels. The lower the manager is on the ladder, the more oriented he is to the present. Future orientation increases as we move up the management ladder. Thus if objectives begin at the bottom, they will be heavily bent to the present and very often will involve perpetuating the status quo. Another disadvantage is that the lower-level managers will lack any guidance whatsoever as to what is expected of them.

Company C's approach of trying to establish all objectives at once is probably the least effective of all three. Even though it does generate maximum participation, the participation would result in wholesale confusion and chaos except in the extremely small organization having only a handful of managers.

A BETTER APPROACH

The subsequent paragraphs illustrate an approach commonly followed. It will provide sufficient guidance to the reader so that he or she may adapt it to the particular circumstances that may exist in his or her own organization.

Two provisions of the definition of MBO that was cited in an earlier chapter serve as the basis for a better approach—one that minimizes the disadvantages of the above three approaches and capitalizes on the advantages. The two provisions are that those responsible for directing the company first establish the overall objectives and priorities and that all managers are required, permitted, and encouraged to contribute their maximum.

Top-Level Objectives

According to this combination approach, a team is selected to recommend objectives at each level in the company. For example, Figure 7 shows a simplified organization for a company. The president heads the top team of the persons reporting to him; the team is indicated by the triangle. It is the job of this team to formulate and recommend the broad, all-encompassing objectives of the company, which were discussed in the preceding chapter. During the three- to five-day meeting, which is usually required each year to formulate these objectives, each team member is responsible for helping set the objectives of the company as a total entity. He isn't concentrating on objectives for his own department; this will come later.

At the conclusion of this meeting, the president has a list of possibly six to eight recommended top objectives for the company. The types of broad, but specific objectives that result from this meeting were discussed in the last chapter.

Next, the president (usually with the concurrence of the board of directors) approves the objectives. This permits objectives to be set at the next level, the departments reporting to the president; that is, the vice-presidents of the major functions.

Lower-Level Objectives

Now that the overall corporate objectives have been set, each vice-president composes his team to recommend the departmental objectives.

Figure 7. Team for developing overall corporate objectives.

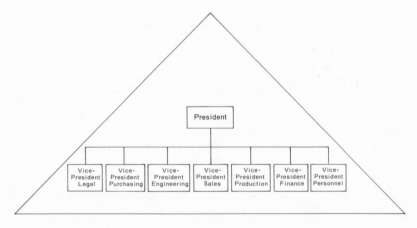

Figure 8. Team for developing multi-level objectives.

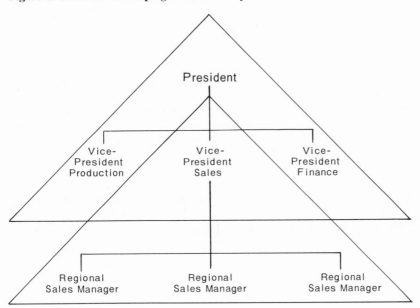

Figure 8, which is an extension of the previous organization chart, reflects the team of the sales vice-president. Each of the other vice-presidents has a comparable team. The overlapping triangles indicate that the vice-president of sales belongs to two teams—as a member of the president's team and as the leader of his own team.

The job of the team led by the vice-president of sales is to arrive at a list of recommended objectives for the entire sales department. The overall corporate objectives provide guidance and direction. In effect, the top sales team determines what it must accomplish during the target period to ensure that its department is helping carry out the overall corporate objectives. For example, what objectives must the combined sales department achieve to support the accomplishment of the top corporate objectives?

That question, when answered properly, will constitute the objectives the sales team will recommend for the department as a whole. Once these objectives have been approved, they, plus the overall corporate objectives, serve as the basis for moving the objective-setting process down the line to the next level. The team approach will be repeated at that level and at all other lower levels.

Link-Pin Concept

Setting objectives by levels is commonly known as the link-pin concept and owes its name to the series of overlapping triangles by which it can be portrayed. Figure 9 illustrates the link-pin concept as it might appear for the four levels of management below the president in a typical company.

Although this chart shows only the team emanating from the sales vice-president, it should be noted that each member of Team A has a team, as does each member of Team B. The same is true for each member of Team C.

Objectives at the Lowest Level

As noted in Figure 9, the three area sales managers (Team D) do not have a team because they are the lowest level of management and do not have other managers reporting to them. Normally, the link-pin approach does not contemplate that teams will comprise nonmanagerial employees.

Although the area sales manager probably wouldn't appoint a formal team to help him establish his objectives, he has much to gain by attempting to secure as many recommendations and as much commitment from his people as is practical and possible. They can give him appreciable help in carrying out his objectives, provided that they have the interest.

Making Recommendations Up the Line

Continuous care must be exercised to prevent the preceding process from ending up in a top-down approach, as was illustrated earlier by Company A.

Obviously, one of the ways to prevent this is to ensure that each team member is given the greatest possible voice in recommending and debating the objectives set at the higher level. For example, the seven vice-presidents reporting to the president should have a major voice in determining the overall corporate objectives. This also requires a willingness on the part of each team member to stand up and be counted, to play an active role rather than a passive one.

There's a second way to encourage the much-needed participation up the line by lower-level managers. Assume, for example, a vice-president who is a member of the president's team. The vice-president knows that on a certain date in the future he must participate with all other vice-presidents in helping establish the overall objectives for the organization. Well in advance of the meeting, if he's smart, he'll take advantage of every possible opportunity to secure the recommendations and comments

Figure 9. Link-pin approach to setting multiple-level objectives.

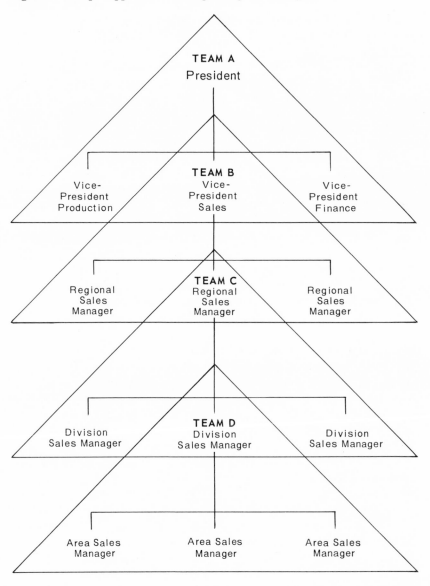

of each of the managers below him. This can be accomplished by a combination of meetings, telephone calls, face-to-face contact with individuals, and written communications. Thus he enters the top team meeting armed not only with his own thinking and recommendations but also with those of his subordinate managers.

Once the manager has prepared his objectives, a critical task awaits his superior, who must then evaluate the subordinate's proposed objectives and measure them against the objectives for which he will be held accountable. Multiple-level objective setting requires constant decision making at all levels. Each higher-level manager must approve the objectives for his unit as a whole and the objectives for each manager reporting to him. Obviously, rubber stamping the subordinate's objectives will result in an ineffective, permissive approach. This the superior avoids by asking himself the following questions about each recommended objective:

Does it represent a sufficient task for the manager during the measuring period?

Is it a practical, attainable objective?

Is it clearly stated in terms of the task, the measuring period, the method of measuring to be used?

Is it compatible with the company's overall objectives for the period?

Only after the superior has answered these questions is he in a position to pass upon an objective. If he approves one that is too easy—one that is an insufficient task for the measuring period—the company will suffer in two ways. First, it will not have received value due for the period. Second, the development of the manager will have been impeded, since he has not been provided with a proper incentive to spur his performance. Rather, his objective has contributed to substandard performance.

As contrasted with the relative ease of setting work standards in routine, highly repetitive production operations, the job of establishing managerial objectives is complex. The superior who must review a subordinate's objectives has no handy indexes to use, and herein lies one of the most difficult aspects of management by results. The minute the superior has put his stamp of approval on those objectives, the subordinate has every reason to accept them as being his mandate and his operating objectives for the next two, three, or five years—depending upon the target period. Thus if at the end of the period the manager has in fact satisfactorily met his objectives, he has a right to believe he has done a good job.

But let's look more closely at this line of thinking. Let's consider, for example, an objective that is to be achieved in two years, but for which a period of twelve or eighteen months would be entirely realistic. Does this mean that a manager who takes the full two years is goofing off? Not altogether.

In the first place, the manager knows he has two years to meet the objective, and so he schedules each phase of the task for completion at a certain date during the two-year period. In the second place, if he completes one phase ahead of schedule, he is very likely to use the time he and his staff have gained to work on other matters he considers to be important. True, by working on these other matters he may be making poor use of priority time that could be better spent on his primary objective. However, neither his boss nor anyone else has told him that the company might be glad to see the job completed, if possible, in less than the full two years. In such a situation, the fault probably rests more with the superior than with the manager, if either is culpable, since it is the superior who is mainly responsible for fitting the manager's objectives into the overall matrix of the company's planning.

An effective system should provide for interim measuring of performance within the total allowed time for achieving an objective. One approved for a two-year period might be reviewed, say, every six months. This has two distinct advantages: (1) It serves as a further check on the validity of the original objectives and its timing and (2) it permits corrective action to be taken before an improperly conceived objective or a poor manager has gone beyond the point of no return.

For illustrative purposes, let us assume that a production manager's objective is to produce for inventory (that is, for next year's sales season) 10,000 dresses at a unit cost of $11. At the time of the interim review, it is readily apparent that the dresses cannot be produced for less than $12.50 per unit. Not only does having this important information available prior to the end of the target period enable the production manager's superior to evaluate the reasons for the variance, but it also puts the sales department on notice that a higher selling price may be necessary to maintain profit margins and warns the financial department that new cost and income projections may be necessary.

CONCLUSION

The link-pin approach discussed previously illustrated only the sales function. The entire process of beginning with the overall corporate objectives

Figure 10. An objectives triangle.

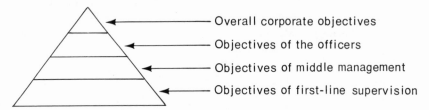

Overall corporate objectives

Objectives of the officers

Objectives of middle management

Objectives of first-line supervision

and working toward multiple-level objectives in all major functions and departments can be viewed in terms of an objectives triangle (see Figure 10). At the apex of the triangle are the broad objectives of the company as a whole. Below these, the triangle begins to widen out as each succeeding level of management establishes its objectives. As the triangle shows, the objectives of each manager at the top level are made up of the objectives of all the managers below him. The objectives of all the managers in a particular unit add up to the objectives of the manager responsible for that unit. And the objectives of all the managers at all levels throughout the company equal the overall corporate objectives for the period under consideration.

6

Components of the Objective-Setting Process

No MANAGER can jump, unprepared, into the writing of objectives.

Feeble attempts to write objectives are often the result of the senior manager's asking his subordinates to write a list of objectives for their jobs. Even if the subordinates do succeed in writing the list of objectives, the objectives are seldom worth the paper they are written on. The reason the objectives are faulty is that the managers were required to write their objectives at what is really Step 7 of the objective-setting process. The necessary first six steps—the steps designed to prepare the manager to write meaningful objectives—were all but completely overlooked.

An excellent example of the consequences of trying to begin at Step 7 is provided by the approach of the president of a plastic products company. Let's call him Mr. Jones. Jones had little experience or knowledge of MBO but had heard the many allegedly wonderful things MBO will accomplish. Like many others have done, Jones got carried away with enthusiasm. In rapid-fire succession he called a meeting of his managers, gave them a brief overview of his understanding of MBO, informed them that the company had adopted MBO, and directed each manager to prepare a list of objectives for his job. Each manager did prepare—in an atmosphere of considerable frustration and fear—a list of objectives. As might be expected, the objectives included these failings:

They did not address the real needs and priorities of the company.

Lower-level objectives didn't support higher-level objectives.

Even though each of three managers was managing one unit of an integrated operation, their objectives were not supporting each other.

Several of the managers were pulling at cross-purposes with respect to optimizing results for the company as a whole.

Objectives addressed themselves to subjects ranging from the highest of priorities to the unnecessary routine.

Figure 11 illustrates all the required steps in the objective-setting process. Note that the actual writing of objectives should take place at Step 7, not at Step 1.

THE PREPARATORY STEPS

Steps 1 through 6 are designed to make objectives meaningful when the manager arrives at Step 7 and is ready to write his objectives. In summary, these first six steps provide the manager with the following necessary guides to lead him gradually and naturally into writing pertinent, high-payback objectives:

Step 1: An intelligence base. Guidance as to higher-level requirements and priorities. This is the prime basis for assuring *vertical* compatibility of objectives.

Step 2: A coordination network. Identification of the other managers and types of information on which coordination must be effected. This is the prime basis for assuring *horizontal* compatibility of objectives.

Step 3: Clarification of job responsibility. Securing agreement as to what the manager is truly responsible for.

Step 4: Selection of high-payback areas. The priority areas of the manager's responsibility that will be prime candidates for objectives in Step 7 (key results areas).

Step 5: Capability analysis. Determining the manager's ability to achieve a high level of results in the key results areas and, second, determining priorities.

Step 6: Formulation of assumptions. Establishing a foundation for continuing the objective-setting process by making a value judgment as to what will happen with respect to each of the major variables that may impact on the manager's operations during the target period.

Only by completing each of these preliminary steps will the manager be in a position to write his objectives when he arrives at Step 7. If he attempts to omit or slight any of these steps, he will have deprived himself of the guidance and intelligence these steps are designed and able to provide. Also, he has weakened his foundation for writing his objectives.

Figure 11. The objective-setting process for the individual manager.

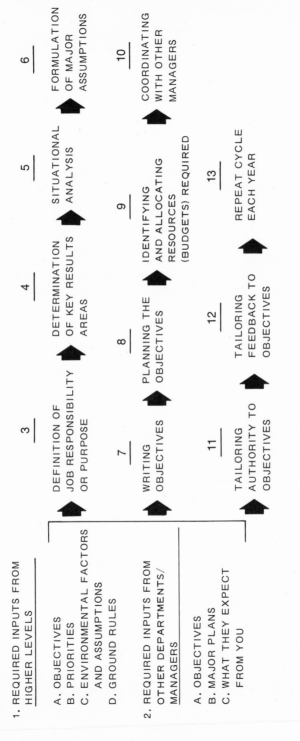

Chapters 7 through 12 explain and illustrate, with actual examples, each of the six preliminary steps.

Step 7: Writing objectives. As noted previously, the actual objectives are written in this step, only after the manager has adequately completed the necessary first six steps. Chapter 13 covers the actual writing of objectives.

THE ACTION STEPS

Obviously, there is absolutely no reason for the manager to have undertaken the laborious but necessary effort in arriving at meaningful objectives in Step 7 unless he succeeds in getting his objectives into action. In other words, his objectives must get translated into action and provide the manager with a living, dynamic means of achieving a higher level of results. They must provide him with a day-to-day way of managing and coping with change during the target period.

The purpose of Steps 8 through 13 is to permit the manager to translate his objectives into action. These action steps include:

Step 8: Programming objectives. Planning the major action steps and a timetable or schedule stating how the objective will be achieved.

Step 9: Allocating. Identifying and allocating the resources (budget) that will be required to achieve the objectives and plans. How much in resources will be required or how much revenue will be generated?

Step 10: Coordinating with other managers. Ensuring that the manager has effected the necessary coordination with the other managers who are involved in his objectives.

Step 11: Tailoring authority. Making certain that each manager has sufficient authority (power) to carry out his objectives and plans.

Step 12: Tailoring feedback. Designing the monitoring and control information so that the manager can stay in control of his operation and take corrective action as necessary.

Step 13: Recycling each year. The repeating of the steps in the objective-setting process as each target period is completed and planning is undertaken to cover the next target period.

Unless the action steps are pursued, the manager will usually end up having an approved list of objectives that don't cause anything to happen. Frequently, his objectives are filed away and all but forgotten about until the time again rolls around to write another list of objectives. Thus the objectives are never given the opportunity to help the manager achieve better results; they don't serve as a guide to action; they don't permit him to stay in control of his operation, to take corrective action when necessary;

and, in summary, they don't become a way of managing. The objectives have become static statements rather than living guides.

A few additional words are in order before proceeding into the subsequent chapters, which provide the detailed explanation of the 13 steps. Each of the 13 steps is but one step of an integrated approach. None of the 13 steps stands by itself. For example, Step 7 (writing the objectives), Step 8 (planning to achieve the objectives), and Step 9 (resource allocation) together constitute a balance. When one is changed, usually one or both of the other steps must also be changed to maintain the balance. For this reason, it is suggested that you read completely through all the steps before trying to place each step, and all of them, in perspective.

7

PREPARATORY STEP 1

Required Inputs from Higher Levels

ONE OF THE GUIDING PRINCIPLES of MBO is that each manager is responsible for helping achieve the objectives of the management levels above him. For example, the senior officers of a corporation are responsible for structuring objectives that will help achieve the overall corporate objectives. An advertising manager reporting to a marketing vice-president is responsible for helping carry out the objectives of the total marketing function. A research manager is responsible for achieving a portion of the objectives of the research department as a whole. In other words, each manager has a piece of the action of those objectives above him.

Therefore, if a manager is to help carry out the higher-level objectives, he must have certain information with respect to these objectives. Otherwise, he will end up writing objectives from his own narrower vantage point, often in a vacuum. Also, it is impossible to achieve vertical compatibility of the objectives of all levels of management.

As a very minimum, every higher-level manager owes the following information to lower-level managers before the latter can begin thinking about their objectives:

1. The higher-level objectives.
2. A statement of the major priorities for the target period.

3. Environmental factors and assumptions that serve as the basis on which objectives and plans are to be written.
4. Ground rules for writing and submitting objectives and plans.

HIGHER-LEVEL OBJECTIVES

Normally, for example, the lower-level financial manager is provided with the objectives that have been established for all levels above him. As an illustration, the following managers would receive these objectives:

Level	Objectives Received
President	
Financial vice-president	Top corporate objectives
Controller	Top corporate objectives
	Financial V.P.'s objectives
Manager of accounting	Top corporate objectives
	Financial V.P.'s objectives
	Controller's objectives

Major disagreements exist as to how far down the line the top corporate objectives should be distributed. I recommend wide as opposed to restricted distribution of higher-level objectives. However, there can be no disagreement that, as a very minimum, each manager must receive the objectives of the level immediately above him.

PRIORITIES

The extent and import of the higher-level priorities for the target period are not always readily apparent from the objectives themselves. Therefore, it is preferable to have the objectives accompanied by a list of the specific priorities for the target period. Following is a list of priorities, by subject matter only, that one corporation issued to its managers for their guidance:

Asset management
Percent of division profit contribution
No-loss divisions
Improve market penetration
No loss in market position
Elimination of marginal products
Overhead cost control
Improved purchasing
Expanded value analysis

Improved safety rates
Management development
Installation of MBO through second level in division
Inventory reduction (raw materials and in process)
Improved capacity
Order balancing
Reduction of debt/equity ratio
Meeting inflation
Performance appraisal of managers

ENVIRONMENTAL FACTORS/ASSUMPTIONS

In its simplest form, an environmental analysis results from a study of factors and circumstances outside the company that may exert an impact on its operations. Primarily, the study will be concerned with what is expected to occur in the industry and the economy in general and covers matters such as industry growth, customer demands, and the state of the economy.

Assumptions are current estimates of major external factors over which the company has little if any control but which may exert a major impact on its operations during the target period. Note that "assumptions" appears in two steps of the flow chart—Step 1 and again in Step 6. The basic difference is this: The assumptions in Step 1 are the broad, overall ones that provide guidance to all managers on matters of common concerns, such as inflation. In contrast, the assumptions in Step 6 are more specific and apply primarily to the manager who is writing his own objectives, such as an assumption on manpower availability for the personnel manager. Assumptions are used by the managers as the basis for writing their objectives. Examples of overall corporate assumptions include: (1) inflation will continue at the rate of x percent, (2) the cost of borrowing will be x percent, and (3) no tax laws adverse to profitability will be enacted.

Usually the environmental analysis and the statements of major assumptions are prepared centrally—often by an economist or director of planning—and distributed to lower-level managers for their use.

GROUND RULES

These are the major guides under which managers are to prepare their objectives and plans. Examples include:

Capital will be available for all projects meeting the following tests.

There will be no net growth in people.

All plans will include a contingency factor of x percent.

Charge-out costs will be agreed to as of 1/1/77, and reviewed for revision as of 7/1.

No action will be taken in 1977 to enhance 1977 performance if such action will adversely affect performance in subsequent years.

In 1977 emphasis will be on showing up present operations versus developing new ones.

How do ground rules provide guidance to the manager? Take, for example, the second ground rule listed above: "There will be no net growth in people." This, in effect, tells the manager not to waste valuable time developing objectives that will require additional people. Thus he concentrates on other subjects.

CONCLUSION

Step 1 involves, essentially, the preparation of an intelligence or information base on which the manager will subsequently write his objectives. This step helps the manager ensure that his objectives are vertically compatible.

8

PREPARATORY STEP 2

Required Inputs from Other Managers

IN STEP 1, the manager received the information necessary for lining up his objectives on a vertical basis. Step 2 permits him to line up his objectives on a horizontal basis. This is important because, as we shall see later, all objectives must be compatible with all other objectives on both a vertical and horizontal basis.

In addition to helping achieve the higher-level objectives, each manager must interact with other functions and managers in the organization. He must do something for these other managers or they must do something for him. Thus he must know what these other departments will require of him, and what he requires of them, during the target period for which he writes his objectives. He receives his major guidance in this regard by receiving from the other departments their tentative objectives, tentative major plans, and specific briefings as to what is required from his department.

The manager may secure this information by receiving draft copies of the objectives and plans, by meetings with the other managers, or by personal visits and consultations. Often, a combination of all three methods is used.

Note that the information the manager receives from the other managers is tentative in nature because all managers in the organization are working through the objective-setting process at the same time. As each manager progressively firms up his final objectives and plans, he must continue to coordinate the changes made from the tentative drafts that were originally coordinated. This continuing coordination must take place on a need-to-know basis. In other words, if the operations of Manager A and Manager B are closely connected, both managers must continually coordinate with each other as they prepare their objectives and plans.

THE COORDINATION NETWORK

It is often helpful to a manager if he will periodically identify and spell out the nature of his coordination network. A coordination network identifies the other managers in an organization with which the manager must effect coordination. Figure 12 illustrates one approach to charting the coordination network.

The network is completed by identifying the managers with whom coordination must be effected and the primary subject matter on which the coordination must be effected. Staff managers in particular may have to exert special effort to ensure that they receive the necessary information in Step 2; this is covered in detail in Chapters 21 and 22.

EXAMPLES OF INPUTS

Examples of the types of input a manager must receive in Step 2 are:

Production manager: information from the sales manager as to the volume and schedule of sales.

Treasurer: information from all managers concerning the amount of capital that will be required.

Quality assurance manager: information from the production manager, especially about planned changes in production methods or processes that may affect quality.

General counsel: information from the research department that may involve patent protection and information from the sales manager with regard to antitrust or fair trade laws.

Engineering manager: information from all managers whose plans contemplate major construction projects.

CONCLUSION

Step 2 helps the manager ensure that his objectives will be horizontally compatible with the objectives of his associates in the organization.

These inputs, combined with those higher-level ones secured in Step 1, constitute the data or intelligence base the manager will use to proceed to the next steps in the objective-setting process.

Figure 12. Charting a coordination network (internal only).

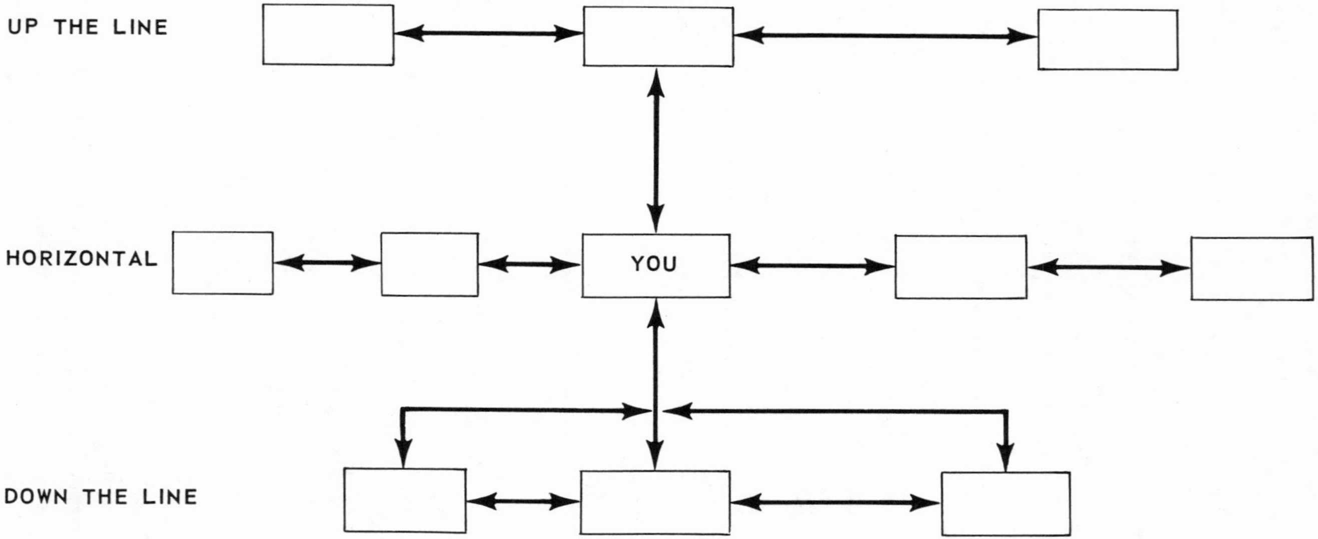

UP THE LINE

HORIZONTAL

DOWN THE LINE

YOU

9

PREPARATORY STEP 3

Clarifying Responsibility

To PERFORM WELL, every manager needs to know what is expected of him. In this step the manager should sit down with his superior and get the clearest possible definition of what will be expected of him during the target period. Any confusion that exists after this meeting will undoubtedly be reflected in the wrong areas being covered by wrong objectives or in areas that were not covered at all.

Thus there are two primary reasons why this step should be completed before proceeding further. First, the objectives that will ultimately be written will flow from and be a part of this responsibility. The manager must have the clearest possible understanding of what his real responsibility is. Second, a considerable body of research has indicated that there is an average of 25 percent difference of understanding between a subordinate and his boss as to what is expected of the subordinate. Frequently, for example, a manager may spend considerable time working on a project his superior doesn't even know the subordinate has under way. Also, the superior may assume that a subordinate is performing a certain function while the latter isn't aware that he should be working in that area.

THE JOB DESCRIPTION

Undoubtedly, much of this confusion between superior and subordinate has resulted from the overreliance upon the traditional job description for managers. While the traditional job description may have some use and value for nonmanagerial personnel (production and clerical workers), it has proved woefully inadequate for managers. The more serious inadequacies are, first, that emphasis is placed on activities to be pursued rather than results to be achieved. Second, sufficient emphasis is not devoted to revising the description to reflect the changing priorities of the organization. Typically, the same description remains on the books year after year. Further, there is no provision for continual improvement from one period to the next because the descriptions seldom change. Finally, job descriptions, by their very name and nature, emphasize the job rather than the person even though, in the case of managers, the person makes the job, not vice versa. And the higher the manager is in the organization, the more the person makes the job.

It is, of course, entirely possible to compensate for several of these weaknesses by supplementing the traditional job description with other documents and forms. For example, the weakness of an activity orientation can be mitigated by a supplemental list of specific objectives the incumbent must achieve over a short-run period. However, supplementing the basic document involves considerable unnecessary time, effort, and cost. Instead, why not include in one dynamic document all the necessary ingredients? It is possible, as shown in the ensuing paragraphs.

DYNAMIC VERSUS STATIC RESPONSIBILITY

Because MBO is a dynamic system, it does not countenance a static job description of the traditional type used by business as a means of describing responsibility.

Construction of an effective job description ("statement of accountability" is probably more descriptive) for use in delegation necessitates continuous zeroing in on the specific accountability of the incumbent. First, it should outline the broad responsibility of the incumbent (the scope of the job). Next, it should list the key results areas in which he must perform within the scope. Third, it should specify the objectives he must accomplish with the key results areas (his accountability). This continual zeroing in will be apparent as you proceed through the objective-setting flow chart. In this step—Step 3—the manager clarifies his overall responsibility. In Step 4, he selects those specific subjects or areas of his total responsibility in which he must turn in a high level of performance to be successful. Finally, in Step 7 he defines his specific accountability in terms of the objectives he must achieve.

DEFINING RESPONSIBILITY

Responsibility describes the manager's global assignment: he's in charge of the financial function or he's the manager of finance; he's in charge of personnel or he's the personnel manager. Responsibility establishes the fences around the area the manager directs. It can be viewed as an arena in which he conducts his managerial actions. It is more general than accountability in that it does not spell out the specific results to be achieved. For example, the responsibility of a typical financial officer might include directing the following functions: capital management, accounting, data processing, office services, and reporting systems. These constitute his operating area. They do not include the results he must achieve in these five major functions.

Responsibility is usually defined in a combination of two ways: (1) the major functions and/or personnel assigned to the manager and (2) the parameters of the manager's responsibility (a) by organizational unit—for example, corporatewide, subsidiary, plant, division, department—and (b) by geographical area—for example, United States, Eastern Division, worldwide.

A major purpose of defining responsibility should be to ensure that the jurisdiction of each manager in the organization is described in a way that minimizes the confusion that would result if two or more managers were responsible for the same function and avoids gaps—intances in which *no* manager is responsible for a function.

10

PREPARATORY STEP 4

Identifying
Key Results Areas

ONE OF THE MOST important steps, which is too frequently overlooked or neglected when managers prematurely write objectives, is the identification of key results areas (KRAs). This is unfortunate because KRAs are a prime tool for helping the manager direct his efforts to those areas of his job where he can make his optimum contribution.

WHAT ARE KEY RESULTS AREAS?

Simply stated, KRAs are those highly selective areas (by subject matter) of a manager's job in which he must achieve a high level of performance to be successful during the target period. Other definitions of KRAs are:

> Those major areas of a job in which high performance is required to optimize results.
>
> The major keys to success in a job.
>
> Critical subjects for the target period.
>
> The areas in which a manager must achieve results to be most successful.
>
> The critical, make-or-break areas of a job.
>
> The highest-priority matters for success during the target period.

Figure 13. Failure to select key results areas.

Function	View of Job	Objectives
Controller	1. Maintain accounting records	1. Reduce cost of accounting division by 10%
	2. Prepare reports	2. Submit monthly operations report by fifth day of month
	3. Administer budget	3. Investigate and report on all variances exceeding plus or minus 5%
Purchasing Director	1. Process purchase orders and requisitions	1. All requisitions will be processed within three days of receipt
	2. Place orders	2. Place all orders within five days
	3. Assure deliveries	3. 98% on time delivery schedule
Public Relations Manager	1. Secure news releases	1. Place three articles per month
	2. Write speeches for administrators	2. All speeches to be written one month in advance
	3. Promote community relations	3. Arrange annual "open house"

WHAT PURPOSE DO THEY SERVE?

Probably the most valuable purpose KRAs serve is to help the manager direct his limited resources (time, money, people, and plant and equipment) to the most important matters where the return on his effort will be the greatest. In doing so they help prevent him from falling into the "activity" or "busyness" trap: getting busy and staying busy without first determining at *what* he should get busy.

Figure 13 illustrates what usually will happen to a manager when he tries to write objectives without first having identified his KRAs. Note that the three managers in the figure view their jobs in rather routine fashion. After listing some of the routine activities of their jobs, they immediately reduced these activities to objectives. They failed to consider what was important before writing their objectives, and therefore they can't optimize their effectiveness. This is a rather common trap if KRAs are not selected first.

GUIDES TO SELECTING KRAs

When selecting KRAs it is usually helpful to think in positive, not negative, terms. Consider these contrasts:

Results, not activities   *Results*, not a process
Output, not input   *Results*, not procedures
Ends, not means   *What*, not how
Results, not tools

Let's look at the rather simple job of a carpenter who builds houses or other units. What are his KRAs? In the first draft of his KRAs he lists:

First Draft
Driving nails
Swinging hammer
Ordering materials
Sawing boards
Measuring materials

Note that the subjects listed by the carpenter would best be described by the words in the negative mode. He has listed the tools of his trade, inputs rather than outputs, and activities instead of results. He has listed the effort he expends and not the results he achieves.

Now we ask the carpenter how he measures whether or not he is successful when the year is over. We ask him how he knows whether or not he did a good job. We ask him to identify his primary end results. The carpenter prepares a second draft, which now includes:

Second Draft
Number of units completed
Quality of completions
Schedule of completions
Materials costs
Labor costs

The carpenter has now recorded several of his actual key results areas. Note that in his second draft he has switched his emphasis away from the inputs and activities of his first draft to those important end results in which he must turn in a high level of performance to be successful.

This example demonstrates the distinction between inputs and outputs and activities and results. Obviously, the swinging of a hammer is an activity, or an input. There is really no reason for the carpenter to swing a hammer or pound nails unless some end result, or output, is achieved. The output, or result, is the number of units completed. Key results (and the subsequent objectives that may flow from them) must address themselves to the ultimate accomplishment being sought.

A TWO-STAGE APPROACH

Many managers find it easier to select KRAs by approaching them in two stages. In the first stage the manager makes a list of major job responsibilities or job functions. In the second stage, he examines each job responsibility to determine if KRAs should be assigned to it. The following illustrates this two-stage approach for a financial manager:

Major Job Responsibilities	Key Results Areas
Accounting	Accurate, timely measurement of organizational performance
Treasury	Cost of capital Availability of capital Return on investable funds
Credit and collections	Aging of accounts Bad-debt level
Data processing	Machine utilization Personnel utilization Cost/benefit level

MAJOR CATEGORIES OF KRAs

KRAs often fall into one or more of four major categories or classifications. Managers should analyze their jobs in light of these categories to determine if their KRAs are appropriate. The broad categories are:

Quantity. Examples: revenue and production levels.

Quality. Examples: customer satisfaction, product quality.

Timeliness. Examples: scheduling and customer demands.

Cost. Examples: cost of services and manufacturing cost levels.

PITFALLS IN SELECTING KRAs

Experience has proven that a few cautions are in order when selecting KRAs.

Avoid considering measurability. How performance might be measured is a consideration in Step 7 (writing objectives). Considering it sooner may lead to the premature rejection of a KRA. For example, a common KRA for a training manager is behavioral change. If the training manager permits his thinking to jump ahead, he may list some of the problems of measuring behavioral change and decide there is no point in listing it as a KRA. The same might be true of other KRAs, such as customer satisfaction and public responsibility.

Every result can be measured to some degree and by one means or another. This should be left for Step 7. We measure actual performance on objectives, not on KRAs.

Avoid goals and objectives. KRAs should identify subject matter, not goals or objectives—the latter will come later. Take costs, for example. Usually this KRA should be listed as "cost levels," which identifies subject matter. Sometimes managers list this as "decrease costs." Again, the latter wording is a goal and is premature. Until the manager completes Steps 5 and 6, he has no firm idea as to what he may be capable of doing in the areas of costs. In actuality, costs may remain static, decrease, or increase.

TYPICAL KRAs

Listed below are typical key results areas for several different managerial jobs. These are intended as examples only. They are not intended to be all-inclusive or representative of all jobs bearing these titles. The actual KRAs for two jobs with the same title but in different organizations may vary significantly depending upon actual job responsibility and the priorities that are set at higher levels.

Manufacturing Manager

Production volume
Production costs
Production schedule
Production quality
Production capacity
Production efficiency

Financial Manager

Availability of capital
Cost of capital
Return on investable funds
Aging of receivables
Bad-debt levels

Director–
Volunteer Blood Center

Financial sustenance
Donor participation
Product utilization
Research competence
Community acceptance
Public reputation

Director of Dietetics–
Hospital

Nourishment adequacy
Quality of service
Quality of food
Patient satisfaction
Regulatory compliance
Cost levels

Purchasing Manager

Price optimization
Inventory optimization
Materials quality
Level and quality of vendor services
Vendor relations effectiveness
Value analysis effectiveness

Personnel Manager

Wage and salary equity
Behavioral change
Manpower availability
Recruitment quality
Timeliness of labor settlements

Sales Manager	*Data Processing Manager*
Sales profit margin	Applications effectiveness
Sales levels	Machine utilization rate
Sales mix	Personnel utilization rate
Customer satisfaction	Operating cost level
Sales force effectiveness	Cost/benefit ratio
	Customer satisfaction
	Output quality

Certain KRAs are common to all managerial positions; for example, subordinate effectiveness and cost levels.

CONCLUSION

The purpose of Step 4 is to select or identify those more important areas of the job in which the manager *should* achieve a high level of performance if he is to be successful. Once having identified these areas, he must next devote his attention to the question: *Can* he achieve a high level of performance in these KRAs? Step 5, covered in the next chapter, addresses itself to this question.

11

PREPARATORY STEP 5

Situational Analysis

THE PURPOSE of Step 5 is to help the manager analyze his capability to achieve a high level of performance in his KRAs. In other words, Step 5 is the capability-determination step.

In this step the manager must identify the advantages that he will enjoy during the target period and thus the factors that may enhance his ability to perform at a high level. Advantages usually fall into two groups: strengths and opportunities. Also, he must identify the disadvantages he will face, those factors that may impede his ability to perform at a high level. Disadvantages include weaknesses and threats.

Figure 14 shows a form for recording these major advantages and disadvantages. This analysis is frequently referred to as a SWOT analysis (Strengths, Weaknesses, Opportunities, and Threats).

PROCEDURE

A SWOT analysis is completed on each key result area. Thus a manager having seven KRAs would complete a total of seven SWOT analyses.

The left side of the form, which deals with Strengths and Weaknesses, is primarily oriented toward the present, while the right side, which deals with Opportunities and Threats, has a future orientation—primarily the target period under consideration.

Strengths are those major advantages that are operating to favor the manager and on which he should try to capitalize.

Figure 14. SWOT analysis.

The Present		The Future	
Strengths	Weaknesses	Opportunities	Threats

Weaknesses are those major disadvantages that will impede performance and that he should try to overcome.

Opportunities are those major future advantages that the manager should do everything possible to exploit to his favor. The more opportunities that can be identified, the more flexibility the manager will have to allocate his resources to the areas of greatest return and thus optimize his contribution or performance during the target period.

Threats are those major future happenings or changes that may exert a significant impact on the manager's performance. The manager should attempt to minimize these threats or, failing this, plan to cope with them.

SWOT ILLUSTRATED

As noted earlier, a common KRA for a manufacturing manager is manufacturing cost levels. Figure 15 shows the results of a SWOT analysis prepared by one manufacturing manager as he analyzed manufacturing costs. Figure 16 illustrates a SWOT analysis for the assets utilization KRA of a general manager of a corporate subsidiary. Figure 17 provides a SWOT analysis for the manpower availability KRA of a personnel manager.

Figure 15. SWOT analysis—manufacturing costs.

S	W	O	T
High volume	Rate of labor turnover	Better sales forecasting	No money
Sufficient labor market	Materials shortages	Production standardization	Unstable economy
Adequate manufacturing space	Poor plant layout	New equipment	Strikes
Good standards	Limited tooling	Better training	Changing labor market
Strong first-line supervisor	No capital budget	New plant layout	Design obsolescence
Good design	Frequent engineering changes	Corporate purchasing contracts	OSHA metrics

BENEFITS OF SWOT ANALYSIS

Well-thought-through and carefully prepared SWOT analyses should provide the manager with two valuable guides. First, they help lead him into the subject matter for his objectives when he reaches Step 7. Second, they should provide general guides as to what level of achievement the objective can be set at; for example, a long list of strengths and opportunities and only a few weaknesses and threats usually indicate that the manager may be able to perform at a high level of achievement. An excess of weaknesses and threats over strengths and opportunities generally indicates a probable low level of performance. Obviously, these are general guides only.

Figure 16. SWOT analysis—assets utilization.

S	W	O	T
New credit capability	Receivables problem	Value analysis product redesign	Resin shortage
Tight inventory control	Excess inventory	Develop new earnings per share product	Increased competition
Subcontract basis for parts	Poor utilization of plant and equipment	Export more product	High interest rates
High-quality products	Limited production line	Push collection by legal action	Inflation
Efficient labor force	Change in engineering management	Install MBO	

Figure 17. SWOT analysis—manpower availability.

S	W	O	T
Ample recruiting budget	Isolated location	New management trainee program	National shortage of technical personnel
Favorable salary rates	Lack of local continuing education opportunities	Promotional opportunities from retirements	Labor competitors entering local area
Excellent fringe benefits	Provincial management reputation	Better utilization of present manpower	Impact of inflation on salary rates
Trained recruiters	Above-average turnover		Changes in management's position on management development
Excellent product reputation			Increasing costs of recruiting and hiring

USING THE SWOT ANALYSIS FOR PRIORITIZING

Now we come to the prime purpose of the SWOT analysis: to begin leading the manager into the probable subject matter of his objectives, which he will write in Step 7. The manufacturing manager referred to previously will be used to illustrate this one.

The manufacturing manager now has in front of him a completed SWOT analysis on each of his KRAs, including the one on manufacturing cost levels, which was discussed previously. Now he must complete the exhaustive decision-making process of prioritizing all the information in front of him. Which are the more important subjects? Which should be done first? In what order should the subjects be approached?

When answering these questions and ordering his priorities, the manager must consider several criteria, including:

Higher-level priorities (which he received in Step 1).
Cost considerations.
Payback and return.
Income requirements.
Time required.
Personnel required.
Sequencing with other managers involved.
Customer demands.
Resources available.
Legal requirements.

Now let's return to Figure 15, the SWOT analysis of manufacturing costs. After prioritizing, the manager decides the two major weaknesses of rate of labor turnover and materials shortages are so serious that they must be corrected during the target period. Thus he identifies them as the probable subject for objectives. Also, he believes that the opportunity of product standardization has high potential and thus identifies this as the subject for a probable objective.

Three possible objectives have flowed from the SWOT analysis of one KRA. The manufacturing manager will analyze each of his other SWOT analyses to select probable objectives; when he has finished he may have anywhere from 8 to 12 subjects for possible objectives. For reasons that will be enumerated later, all 8 to 12 subjects may not culminate in objectives.

12

PREPARATORY STEP 6

Formulation of
Major Assumptions

THIS IS THE SECOND TIME that "assumptions" have appeared in the flow chart, the first time being back in Step 1 as a part of the guidance provided from higher-level management.

The basic difference between the two sets of assumptions is that the assumptions in Step 1 are the broad, overall ones covering the company as a whole. They provide common reference points to all managers in the organization to whom the assumptions are pertinent. For example, an assumption as to what the prime rate of interest will be during the target period would be a broad, major assumption covering all managers in a bank. Other examples in Step 1 are assumptions dealing with matters such as the level of the economy, the rate by which inflation will increase, and possible legislation that may have an impact on the company's operations.

Assumptions formulated in Step 6 are those that apply in particular to the individual manager. They are more specific in subject matter and coverage. For example, a personnel manager in charge of recruiting may formulate an assumption concerning availability of manpower; a financial manager, one dealing with the availability of capital; a marketing manager, one concerning product obsolescence; and a plant manager, one covering collective-bargaining settlements in a plant.

WHAT IS AN ASSUMPTION?

Generally, assumptions are defined as:

> Best estimates of the impact of major external factors over which the manager has little if any control but which may exert a significant impact on his performance or ability to achieve desired results.

A manager is faced with many variables and imponderables that he can neither control nor predict with 100 percent accuracy. Because they may influence his results, he must formulate an assumption as to what the factors are and the degree to which they will impact on him.

USES OF ASSUMPTIONS

Assumptions make planning possible. Without the use of assumptions it would be all but impossible to undertake any planning for the future.

One of the criticisms most frequently made by the unskilled about profit planning—or any type of planning, for that matter—is that no one can accurately anticipate the things that will happen in the future; therefore, planning must necessarily be a lot of long-hair gobbledygook. They reason that not even the most highly qualified weather experts can really know what the weather will be like a year in the future, that no one can predict with accuracy when a particular product or material will become obsolete because of advances in technology, that only employees and their union leaders can determine when a strike will disrupt operations, and that only a fortune teller would be willing to go on record as to when customers will switch from plain cigarettes to filter tips. To these persons any serious planning belongs in the category of crystal-balling.

Without the proper use of assumptions, these critics would have valid arguments on their side. Planning does deal with events in the future, and it is not possible to predict with unfailing accuracy when or how these events will come to pass. In fact, most skilled profit planners, as one of their assumptions, make the cold assertion that *no* assumptions used in their profit plans will take place exactly as assumed. One very successful company actually incorporates in the introduction to its annual profit plan the statement: "Implicit in the planning process is the fact that events in 1977 will certainly be different from what is predicted. Inevitably, circumstances will require changes in the plans, and these changes must be orderly and planned. Plans are less important than planning."

Essentially, assumptions serve three useful purposes to good profit planning. These may be summarized as follows.

First, assumptions permit the planning process to begin and progress. Without assumptions there would be so many uncertainties that one would not know where to begin. By isolating those future occurrences that would have the most significant impact on profits and by making assumptions about them, management then has a base on which to begin its planning. For example, an employee strike is always a possibility in any business. Unless management makes a definite assumption about the chances that there will be a strike, the situation would be so nebulous that planning would be impossible.

If, after evaluating all aspects of its labor relations picture to the best of its ability, management is able to conclude that there will be no strike, it is possible to begin the planning process. Conversely, even if management concludes that there will be a strike, the planning process can begin because there is a definite assumption on which to build plans. It is the wishy-washy type of thinking—that is, when management doesn't take a stand one way or another—that hampers effective planning. In this particular example, if the probability of a strike occurring is approximately the same as the probability of one not taking place, management might be well advised to structure two alternative plans to cope with both possibilities.

Next, assumptions serve as one of several checks on the validity of plans. Selecting applicable assumptions and undertaking a critical analysis of the probability that each assumption is as accurate as possible takes considerable guesswork out of the planning process.

Example: Most companies today are faced with increasing labor and materials costs that, unless offset in some way, will decrease profitability. When making its plan, a company draws certain assumptions with respect to its ability to offset these costs; a frequently used assumption is that increases in the cost of materials and labor will be compensated for by price increases. Before a company can make this assumption, it must thoroughly evaluate key factors such as its present selling price versus that of its competitors, the impact on sales volume of a price increase, the possibility of consumers switching to a lower-cost product (for example, the classic switch from coal to oil) and all other ramifications a price increase might occasion.

When management has completed its evaluation of this assumption, it has added another check on the validity of the profits it has planned for.

Finally, once the objective-setting process has been completed and the target year has begun, assumptions serve as continuing checkpoints with respect to possible required revisions to the plans. By having these assumptions clearly spelled out, management has always before it the basis on which the plans were constructed. If during the year actual events differ from the assumptions, management is alerted immediately that it must take action to keep objectives, plans, and resource allocations realistic and current.

APPLICABLE ASSUMPTIONS

If management were required to make assumptions about everything that might or might not happen in the future, it would face an insurmountable task. Fortunately, such detail is unnecessary. Assumptions must be made only about those major factors that will exert an impact on the operation during the period covered by the plan. Thus the first task facing management is to determine the specific future factors that might influence its particular business.

Managers are faced with a tremendous task when they go about isolating the factors affecting their operations so that applicable assumptions may be made. The end result of this soul searching must be a definitive statement of the significant factors on which the success of the operation is based or will be based in the future.

It will be evident from the preceding discussion that the formulation of assumptions proceeds in orderly steps:

1. Isolate those future events that are most likely to have a significant effect on the company's business.
2. Evaluate as accurately as possible the probable impact of these events.
3. Determine whether an assumption is necessary, and, if so, formulate the assumption.
4. Record all assumptions.
5. Continuously track the validity of all assumptions.

PROBABILITY ESTIMATES

An increasingly used and useful technique adopted by the management of many companies is that of probability estimates in conjunction with assumptions.

Reduced to the barest essentials, probability estimates are management's best judgment, expressed in either quantitative or relative terms, of the degree to which an assumption is likely to come true. They aid in the decision-making process by providing management with a more definite evaluation of events that may occur so that the pros and cons of one event may be weighed against the advantages and disadvantages of another event or action. Probability estimates can be expressed in two ways. In the highly quantified version, the probability is expressed in terms of percentages; for example, there is a 10 percent or a 90 percent probability of a strike. Relative terms are used in the second version; for example, there is a high or a low probability of a strike.

The value of probability estimates may be shown by an example. Assume that a merchandise manager can save $1 million next year by signing a contract now to buy a large quantity of high-fashion dresses. As these dresses are seasonal items, any work stoppage in the purchaser's company could cause considerable loss. In view of the possibility of a strike next year in the purchaser's company, the purchaser is faced with a decision that hinges to a large extent on the degree of probability that a strike will take place. If the probability of the strike is rated at 10 percent, the chances of the purchaser's signing the contract are better than average; if the strike probability is rated at 90 percent, the decision will be quite different.

Contrast the situation in which probability estimates were used with the one with which the decision maker would be faced if they were not used. Under the latter conditions he would have two pieces of information to guide his decision: (1) A large amount of money could be saved, and (2) there could be a strike, which would turn the saving into a loss. Given only this information, the decision maker is at a loss as to whether to take the risk and sign the contract. Reliable probability estimates can help minimize the risk.

SOURCES OF ASSUMPTIONS

Two areas in particular should be examined to determine what types of assumptions may be necessary. The first is the manager's key results areas; the second is the SWOT analysis, particularly the "Threats" column. For example, consider the manpower availability KRA of the personnel manager. He may have to formulate assumptions covering both the supply and the price of personnel recruited. The manufacturing manager's KRA of manufacturing costs may require assumptions as to labor contract settlements and the possibility of being able to revise work standards.

Typical threats facing a manager today are energy-related cost increases and ecology-oriented legislation. These may require managers to formulate assumptions in order to cope with them.

CONCLUSION

Once the manager has completed Step 6 and the five steps that preceded it, he has done the homework absolutely required to arrive at writing meaningful objectives. He has now reached Step 7.

13

Writing
Effective Objectives

ASSUMING that the manager has satisfactorily completed the first six preparatory steps, he should now be in a position to write meaningful objectives that will help him manage better. The value of his objectives will vary in direct proportion to the quality of his preparatory work.

WHAT IS AN OBJECTIVE?

An objective is a specific description of an end result to be achieved. It states *what*—the specific end result to be achieved—and *when*—a target date or period by which the objective will be achieved.

An objective *does not* describe *how* the objective will be achieved. Step 8 in the objective-setting process tells how the objective will be achieved. The next chapter will explain why a manager should not prematurely determine how the objective will be achieved.

CRITERIA FOR EFFECTIVE OBJECTIVES

The more effective objectives will meet several commonly accepted criteria. These criteria are examined in the following paragraphs.

Specific and Realistic

First, and most important, objectives must be specific. They must be stated in terms of *what* must be accomplished and *when* it must be completed. To the maximum extent possible, they should be quantified; that is, dollar volume, sales volume, return on investment, units of production, and the like should be stated explicitly. For example:

Poor: Increase sales during 1977.

Better: Increase institutional sales by 8 percent in the Eastern division during 1977.

Where it is not possible to quantify, qualitative indexes should be used and care should be exercised to avoid vague, general statements of desired results. Thus:

Poor: Upgrade the quality of clerical employees hired during 1977.

Better: Hire during 1977 only those typist applicants who demonstrate their ability through previous experience and by passing the typing proficiency test, the clerical proficiency test, and Test B of numerical ability.

Objectives should never be stated as activities but always as end results. Thus:

Activity: Conduct five one-day training sessions for surgeons.

Result: By September 1, have three surgeons competent to practice surgical procedure XYZ.

Objectives should also be realistic—that is, attainable. Those that are too easily attainable are harmful, as we have pointed out, to both the manager and the company. Conversely, those that are too difficult result in an overstatement of the company's projected goals and, in terms of long-run effectiveness, cause managers to lose confidence in the results approach.

In the absence of highly extenuating circumstances, for example, it would be questionable to set as an objective for the year an increase of 10 percent in return on investment when the historical trend for the past ten years has shown an annual increase ranging from 1 to 4 percent. An increase of 3 to 7 percent would be more realistic, and the objective for the year probably should be set somewhere in this area.

Consistent with Authority

A manager's objectives must be consistent with the authority that has been delegated to him. To approve for him an objective that he does not have the authority to carry out is self-defeating and can well lead to inter-managerial disputes if he tries to accomplish it.

Take the job of reducing the number of rejects by, say, 5 percent. This will normally be beyond the realm of quality control; it is more likely to lie within the jurisdiction of the production manager. Therefore, it will be more realistic to delegate this objective to the production manager, aided by the quality control manager.

Objectives for each manager down the line must likewise be consistent with those of all other managers and with the overall objectives of the company. Any that are not consistent or that are set merely to keep a manager fully occupied are not in harmony with results management.

If the major objective for the director of sales is to increase sales by 10 percent, the major objectives for the divisional sales managers reporting to him should reflect the percentage of increase each must realize if the overall 10 percent increase is to be met. As another case in point, a company with a major public relations problem in the financial area would be ill-advised to permit its public relations director to concentrate his or her energies on a program designed to dramatize the benefits of the free enterprise system.

Provision for Flexibility

To maintain proper priorities and consistency with changing company goals and objectives, the objectives for most managers should probably be changed from one target period to another. As a general guide, the same *what* and *when* should seldom be repeated. The point here is that when a manager (especially one in a staff department) comes up with the same objective for succeeding periods, it is important to make sure that it has been well thought out and does not represent mainly a perpetuation of existing practices.

To the greatest degree possible, objectives should permit interim checking and evaluation during the target period. Those that allow for quarterly or semiannual review are much preferable to those that can be accurately evaluated only after the lapse of a year of more. For example:

Poor: Build and equip a new plant by January 1.
Better: Complete specifications for approval on March 1; complete construction by September 1; install all equipment and have in operation by January 1.

In other words, the objective should be broken down into its component parts so that it is possible to progress.

Unmistakable Meaning

Objectives should be expressed in terms that both the subordinate and the superior clearly understand—and that have the same meaning for both. Much of the effectiveness of management by results is sacrificed if the subordinate interprets objectives in one way and his superior sees them in another.

The first draft of objectives for a data processing manager included the following:

Achieve the highest possible machine-utilization rate consistent with the best interest of service to the company.

This vague, general statement of intent is incapable of being measured. Furthermore, it is so vague that it provides little guidance to the manager or his subordinates. Obviously, the relative words "highest possible" must be defined. The objective is made more specific and measurable by rewording it to read:

Achieve a machine-utilization rate of 85 percent by September 1, 1977, and maintain it at that rate for the remainder of 1977.

For this reason, objectives should be put in writing. If they are only stated orally, they are subject to being misinterpreted, forgotten, confused, unintentionally or intentionally changed or modified. Most of us undoubtedly know the vital role of effective communication in business; the results approach is no less dependent on mutual understanding than any other management device.

Should Contain "Stretch"

MBO contemplates continual improvement on the part of managers. Therefore, objectives should be set at a level of difficulty and achievement that requires managers to exert more than normal effort or a "business as usual" approach. There is no easy formula for determining how much stretch an objective should require. Essentially, the determination of stretch must be based on the superior's evaluation of the subordinate's objectives in light of the probable circumstances that will exist during the target period. To the extent it can be secured, the following will serve as useful guides—but only guides—when evaluating stretch:

Superior's observation and knowledge of subordinate's capability, drive, motivation, and so on.

The subordinate's past record.

The subordinate's recommendation and comments.

Performance levels of other managers on the same or similar jobs in the organization.

Performance on similar jobs in other organizations.

External requirements; for example, legal requirements may establish the minimum level at which the manager must perform.

Demands of the situation; for example, customer demands of other departments may establish minimum performance levels.

Should Match Experience and Capability

One of the major virtues of MBO is its effectiveness as a means of management development. However, the full realization of this benefit requires matching the complexity and difficulty of objectives to the manager's experience and capability. Set too high, the objectives can lead to frustration and thwarting of development. Set too low, they can demotivate the manager. Particular care in this regard must be exercised when working with the newer, less experienced manager.

HOW MANY OBJECTIVES?

Obviously, there is no set number of objectives for all managers. However, if the commonly accepted principle is followed that objectives should cover only the highest-priority matters for the target period, then somewhere around five to seven objectives is probably a good rule of thumb for most managers. This number usually increases in the case of specialists and staff managers who deal primarily in programs and specific projects.

Also, the number usually increases at the lower levels of management. Special considerations for staff and lower-level managers are covered in subsequent chapters.

VERTICAL AND HORIZONTAL COMPATIBILITY

Financial objectives are not an end in themselves nor are they written exclusively for the financial department. Thus all objectives written in any unit of the department must be compatible with, and help carry out the higher-level objectives (vertical compatibility). They must also be supportive of the objectives of other departments and units (horizontal compatibility). Double-checking all financial objectives for dual compatibility helps ensure that the department is carrying out the role expected and required of it.

THE WORDING OF OBJECTIVES

Contrary to the advice of some writers, there is no set wording or format that will cover the multiplicity of objectives emanating from the financial department and its many units. Rather than trying to follow a set format, primary emphasis should be devoted to having the objective—regardless of the wording used—meet the criteria discussed here.

IS IT REALLY IMPORTANT?

Care must be taken to avoid setting objectives that include matters that are easily measurable but are of less importance than others that are not so readily measurable. This can become a problem if too much emphasis is placed on quantitative objectives. For example, if we insist that an industrial relations director quantify all his objectives, he may set one that requires him to reduce the cost of recruitment advertising by 15 percent. This quantified objective may replace a qualitative one that would have required him to upgrade completely the effectiveness of the organizational planning program. The latter goal is more difficult to measure, certainly, but it is infinitely more pertinent to the company's needs.

All objectives should be reviewed critically in light of two questions: (1) Is the work necessary? and (2) Is it compatible with all other plans for the period? In addition, they should concentrate on those activities that yield the largest payback—in other words, the real bread-and-butter matters. If possible, less important objectives should be included in the major ones and handled concurrently, or they can be postponed until the major ones have been accomplished.

Finally, all objectives should be stated in terms that will ensure that a serious attempt will be made to carry them out and to check progress against them regularly. It is undoubtedly better never to have set a goal in the first place than to have set it and forgotten it.

SAMPLE OBJECTIVES

Following are examples of objectives for top-level managers in various companies. Since these objectives are for illustration only, no completion dates have been included.

Plant Manager Complete construction and equipping of approved addition to new plant within cost of $20,000.
Produce x number of units of y product at z costs.
Install, and have operational, approved XYZ packaging line.

Industrial Relations Director Reduce cost of recruiting each research Ph.D. from $1,000 to $750 without sacrificing quality.
Formulate a full-strength, one-for-one incentive system for Packaging Department designed to lower per-unit labor costs by 3 percent.
Maintain cafeteria costs at 1976 levels without loss in food quality.

Research Director Reduce costs of fertilizer application by 5 percent.
Complete development of ABC product and make it available for production.
Apportion research costs on basis of 25 percent basic and 75 percent applied.

Quality Control Director Recommend measures for reducing by 5 percent the quantity of ABC product rejects.
Reduce quality control labor costs by 15 percent by centralized rather than decentralized inspection.
Reduce inspection time on *x* items by 35 percent by installation of electronic measuring devices.

Controller Reduce clerical accounting labor by $100,000.
Reduce by seven days the time lag in preparation of standard cost follow-up reports.
Reduce by 25 percent the working cash required in bank deposits.

Sales Director Increase sales of ABC product by 3 percent.
Hold private-label sales to 7 percent of total sales.
Maintain advertising promotion expenses at last year's level without adversely affecting sales.

General Counsel Reduce by 10 percent the cost of outside legal services.
Recommend approach for complying with antitrust divestiture decree that will result in not more than a 3 percent reduction in total sales.
Hire and train two antitrust specialists at a cost of $35,000.

Public Relations Director Reduce costs of holding regional public relations seminars by 10 percent.
Hold direct-mail program costs to $.05 per unit.
At a cost of $20,000, conduct survey of company's public relations position and needs.

Corporate Secretary Reduce cost of shareholder mailings by 5 percent by decreasing their frequency and making them more comprehensive.
Ensure that company is properly registered to do business in all 28 states in which it markets.
Hold cost of printing the annual report to $25,000.

Engineering Director Complete construction on Boiler No. 2 and place it on line.
Reengineer packaging line No. 10 to provide one-hour surge facility.
Complete rewiring of Plant No. 6.

CONCLUSION

Now that the manager has determined *what* he is going to achieve and has expressed this in the form of objectives, he must turn his attention to *how* he will achieve his objectives.

14

ACTION STEP 8

Planning to
Achieve the Objectives

THIS CHAPTER is concerned with the highly critical, but often neglected
area of formulating plans to make the objectives come true. In this step,
commonly referred to as programming the objectives, the manager spells
out *how* his objectives will be achieved. Also, this is the first of the action
steps designed to bring life to the objectives that were written in Step 7.

As noted, this is a critical part of the objective-setting process. Too
often, considerable attention is accorded to writing objectives, but little is
spent in programming them for achievement. Objectives without plans to
achieve them are largely a delusion. An objective won't be accomplished
just because it has been written or approved. Step-by-step plans must be
developed for achieving it. The plans are the primary means of giving life
to the objective and transforming it from mere written words into a day-in
and day-out way of life and managing as the manager carries out the objective.

There are several other reasons why the plans to support objectives
are vital, such as:

To determine how realistic the objective is. Will the plans, viewed
collectively, lead to accomplishing the objective? If not, the objective may
require changing, or new plans are needed to accomplish it.

To provide a timetable for action. Plans help the manager schedule
his time during the target period. When must certain actions be started
and finished?

To provide a control basis. Specifying an action step and a timetable permits the manager to determine if he is on schedule or if corrective action is necessary at various stages during the target period.

To determine resources required. Spelling out the how provides the basis and justification for the resources (money, manpower, equipment, time) that will be needed. Two different alternative methods of achieving an objective will require completely different resources.

To communicate and coordinate with others. Spelling out the action plans provides other departments and managers who may be involved with a need-to-know guide as to what may be required from them, or provided to them. Both are necessary for effective communications and coordination.

To determine authority. The way a manager plans to achieve his objective has a major impact on the authority he will require. Specific action plans provide the basis for determining the authority required.

LENGTH AND DETAIL OF PLANS

One of the more difficult questions to answer in the abstract is how long plans should be and how much detail should be included to support the objectives. Experience indicates that plans run the gamut from only a few words to support a major objective to several pages. Both are probably extremes. A good general rule is that plans should be as brief as possible but sufficiently detailed to serve the purposes outlined in the preceding section—and especially to permit testing the objective for realism.

Edward J. Green, a leading authority on corporate planning, offers the following suggestions: (1) Support objectives with a minimum of paperwork, (2) don't try to do all the planning in writing, and (3) improve individual coordination and communications.

One large corporation well known for its successful planning instructs its managers as follows:

> The company's growth could cause substantial increases in the number of plans and in the number of pages of text and exhibits to be reviewed. In order to keep this total within manageable limits it is essential that managers make every possible effort (1) to keep the length of their plans to a minimum without omitting significant information and (2) to use every possible means to facilitate the reading, appraisal, and review of the plans.
>
> For maximum effectiveness at all levels plans should be—
>
> *Results-oriented.* Where possible, information should be expressed quantitatively and related to results.

Specific and concise. Information should be (1) highly selective, (2) stated as succinctly as possible, and (3) limited to truly significant facts, problems and action steps.

Brief—use words sparingly. Wherever possible, figures should be used in place of words. Words should be used only for (1) descriptions, such as of plans, environments, premises, opportunities, problems, and action steps; (2) explanations, such as of changes and variances; and (3) appraisals. Language should be terse and where practicable, telegraph-style sentences should be used.

Devoid of repetition. Unnecessary depth and detail should be avoided. This pertains particularly to information previously presented in plans, monthly letters, or weekly reports, which reviewers can reasonably be expected to know.

Repetition should also be avoided within the various sections of plans.

STEPS IN PROGRAMMING OBJECTIVES

The four generally accepted steps for programming out an objective are:

Stating the objective clearly.
Identifying alternative means of accomplishing the objective.
Weighing the alternatives and selecting the better ones.
Programming the better alternatives.

Stating the Objective

Note must be taken here that the ease and effectiveness of planning out the objective depends upon the prior structuring of an objective, which is clearly stated and as specific and measurable as possible. Take, for example, the following objective written by one manager:

Effect a significant increase in the efficiency of my unit by July 1, 1977, without any increase in labor or materials cost. Fifty percent of the increase to be achieved by December 31, 1976, and the remainder by July 1, 1977. The increase in efficiency to be measured comparing the current year's volume and costs with the preceding year.

While this "objective" is replete with numbers and dates, there is no way the manager can plan to achieve it because he hasn't stated what it is that he plans to accomplish. The use of the weasel word "significant" nullifies the objective.

In contrast, let's examine a better objective written by a sales manager. In this case, the objective is stated as:

Increase sales gross margin (the profit on the factors he controls) of my area by 2 percent by 8/1/77 and maintain at that level for remainder of 1977.

This objective is clear, specific, and measurable. It requires the manager to achieve a definite profit level. He can now proceed to the next step in programming his objective.

Identifying Alternatives

A manager usually has several different means or alternatives by which an objective might be achieved. His job at this stage is to identify all that are possible. Thus the sales manager mentioned before might identify the following alternatives for accomplishing his profit objective:

Add more salesmen.
Increase size of territory.
Add more P.O.S. (point of sale) materials
* Decrease costs of small accounts.
Generate more advertising and promotion.
* Increase number of sales calls.
Open new accounts.
Decrease travel and entertainment costs.

* *After analyzing, the sales supervisor decided to pursue these alternatives.*

The enlightened manager who recognizes the value of multiple inputs will at this stage actively seek out the ideas and recommendations of his subordinates. He'll recognize that the greater the number of alternatives identified, the better his opportunity for successfully achieving the objective.

Weighing and Selecting Alternatives

Normally, it is neither possible nor desirable to pursue all the alternatives that were identified in the preceding stage. Thus the manager's job now is to evaluate each possible alternative and select those that will lead more efficiently and effectively to achieving the objective.

When weighing the alternatives, the manager must consider factors such as the money and people required, payback on investments, time required, demands of other departments, impact on employee relations, duration of the benefits gained, and other pertinent factors that may influence the value of the alternative.

After the sales supervisor had evaluated all of his alternatives he selected the alternatives shown by the asterisks in the preceding list.

Figure 18. Plans to achieve objectives.

SUPERVISOR: Harry Lasta

OBJECTIVE #1: Increase sales gross margin of my area by 12 percent by 8/1/77 and maintain at that level for remainder of 1977.

Major Action Steps	J	F	M	A	M	J	J	A	S	O	N	D
1. Decrease cost of serving small accounts.												
1a. Identify all customers not purchasing $5000 per month.	◄											
1b. Determinate sales potential of each target customer.		◄										
1c. If potential less than $5000 transfer to jobber.		◄	◄									
1d. Inform customer and schedule jobber visit with customer.				◄								
1e. If potential is $5000 develop cooperative sales promotion program.					◄							
1f. Implement 1e.						◄						
1g. Evaluate and report results.							◄					
2. Increase minimum calls per salesman to 12 per day.												
2a. Analyze work methods of "High Call" salesmen.	◄ ◄											
2b. Identify salesmen with less than 12 calls placed.		◄										
2c. Analyze territory and order of calls.			◄									
2d. Determine best routing of calls.						◄						
2e. Determine most effective realigning of all territories.				◄ ◄								
2f. Implement plans.					◄							
2g. Evaluate and report results.					◄							

January–December

These are the alternatives he will program out, step by step, indicating a timetable for the completion of each major step.

Programming the Alternatives

Figure 18 illustrates a popular format for programming objectives. In this example, the sales manager has programmed out the two alternatives he decided to pursue. Each of the other alternatives he might have selected would be programmed out in similar fashion until the total plans have been formulated for accomplishing the objective.

EVALUATING THE PLANS

Realism again becomes a key word when evaluating the adequacy of plans to achieve objectives. Both the manager who recommends the objectives and plans and the executive who must review and approve them should examine the plans in the following light:

Is it reasonable to expect that the plans as written will result in achieving the objective? If not, either the objective or the plans must be reworked until the question can be answered in the positive.

Have all practical alternatives been identified and evaluated?

Has a definite timetable been identified and evaluated?

Have the plans been expressed in a manner that permits measuring progress in accordance with the timetable?

Are the plans clearly understandable by others who will be involved in carrying them out?

Do they optimize the return on the resources required?

CONCLUSION

The manager has now determined *what* he is going to accomplish (his objectives) and *how* he is going to achieve the objectives (his plans). Now he must determine *how much* resources will be required (his budget).

15

ACTION STEP 9

Allocating Resources

In this step, the manager must identify the resources he must have to carry out his objectives and plans. Traditionally, this process has been referred to as budgeting. However, for reasons that are discussed later in this chapter, the better approach requires the process to be labeled "resource allocation." As we shall see later, this is more than a mere change in words

POPULAR MISCONCEPTIONS

Of all the questions raised by the dramatic growth of management by objectives, few are more indicative of disorganized confusion than those relating to the position and role of budgets in an MBO system. The following are just a few of the situations I faced recently.

Company A: The president indicated that the company had been operating with MBO for two years and now believed that it was time to implement a budget system.

Comment: Budgets are an integral part of an MBO system and the company could not have been practicing MBO without them.

Company B: This company followed the practice of approving budgets during February of each year and then having its managers write their objectives during the ensuing six months.

Comment: The budget is on the wrong end of the planning and objective-setting process. Budgets should conclude, not begin, the process. There is little basis on which to approve the budgets unless the objectives and plans have been formulated.

Organization C: Every two years the head of a Canadian government department is required to submit and defend the budget for his operations at a "budget justification" meeting. He asked if it would be a good idea to also have his objectives and plans prepared and available for the same meeting.

Comment: Objectives and plans are the only way the budget can be justified. Without the objectives and plans, the budget cannot be tested for realism.

Company D: The senior management team was thoroughly convinced that it was operating under an MBO system simply because all operations were covered by operating expense and capital budgets.

Comment: Budgets are only one part of an MBO system. By themselves they're usually a sterile exercise in compiling numbers—an exercise in futility.

Organization E: The head of this social agency had issued instructions to his managers that the budget should cover only the objectives of each manager. Any subject that was not covered by an objective was not to be included in the budget.

Comment: Budgets cover more than just objectives because the latter are usually limited to priority matters. Routine matters are not covered by objectives, but the cost of the routine *is* reflected in the budget.

Organization F: In the early days of its MBO installation, this organization had three different budgets intended to serve three different purposes: financial planning, motivation, and control.

Comment: One budget, properly designed and constructed, should serve all three purposes.

All the above situations reveal a rather alarming amount of misconception and confusion regarding the role of budgets. Also, they indicate the failure of many organizations to update the traditional approach to budgeting to make it compatible with an MBO system. The resulting void has had a major impact on the effectiveness of the MBO efforts. Budgets have a key role to play, but only when this role is thoroughly understood and budgets are placed in their proper position are they effective. Otherwise, they operate to the detriment of MBO.

TRADITIONAL BUDGETING IS OBSOLETE

The impact of 20 years of widespread practice of management by objectives has brought about dramatic changes in the traditional practice of management. Many parts of the management process have been rendered obsolete,* including the traditional view of budgeting and its relationship to planning.

Commonly, budgets have been looked upon as a plan or estimate of future income and expenses. They were heavily oriented to control. An excellent example of the traditional approach to planning and budgeting is illustrated by the following case involving a university chancellor.

The date is July 20, 1976, and one of the chancellors of a large university is conducting his annual planning session for the year 1977. He announces that the total budget for 1977 for all units under his direction will be $10 million allocated individually as follows:

Director of housing	$ 2 million
Director of program development	1 million
Director of communications center	3 million
Director of residence halls	1 million
Director of testing program	2 million
Chancellor's office	1 million
	$10 million

The 1977 budgetary figure represents a reduction of 10 percent from 1976 levels in accordance with a mandate from the governor to increase the productivity of all state activities by a comparable amount.

The chancellor provides the following ground rules to department heads for their guidance when preparing their plans for 1977:

Emphasis will be on increased productivity.

There will be no lessening of quality standards.

Budgetary allocations will be adhered to strictly, both in total and by individual units.

Final budgets are due on September 1, 1976.

The chancellor concludes the meeting with a pep talk about the satisfaction derived from doing a job well under trying circumstances.

Each of the directors submitted his/her budget, and the final budget was assembled on September 1. It reflected the following:

* For an in-depth treatment of this impact see Dale D. McConkey, "MBO—Twenty Years Later, Where Do We Stand?" *Business Horizons*, August 1973.

Director of housing	$ 2 million
Director of program development	1 million
Director of communications center	3 million
Director of residence halls	1 million
Director of testing program	2 million
Chancellor's office	1 million
	$10 million

The chancellor commended his staff for their planning expertise.

As with most traditionalists, this chancellor has made several telling mistakes, all of which will decrease his effectiveness as well of that of his organization. First, his approach precluded any but a cursory participation on the part of his managers. They parroted back to him what they assumed were predetermined figures and what their boss wanted to hear. Second, he deliberately refused to establish any competition among his managers for the available capital. Those who had been guilty of operating inefficiently in the past were given the same consideration as those who had been breaking their backs and operating in a highly effective manner. Thus emphasis was placed on spending the money made available, not on optimizing results. Third, the chancellor has positioned the budget on the wrong end of his so-called planning process. He's assigned a cost allowance to each manager without first giving any consideration to priorities and what *should* be done during the year. Fourth, in the chancellor's approach, controlling took priority over motivating managers to greater accomplishment.

UPDATING THE PURPOSE OF THE BUDGET

The purpose and role of budgets must undergo considerable updating if budgets are to perform their required role—and it is a most important one—within an MBO system.

Budgets must be primarily viewed as the planned allocation of resources to the manager's objectives. This is more than a change in definition! It involves an entirely new way of looking at budgets and their role.

Also, it requires viewing the very role of management in a new light. The true role of a manager can be seen as optimizing the return on the resources entrusted to him/her. It is the total optimization of all of a company's resources (capital, people, plant, and equipment) by all of its managers that, in the last analysis, determines the success of the organization. Resources available to an individual manager are always limited in a healthy organization. A company that doesn't establish competition for its resources is a sick company, as is a company that has more resources than it knows what to do with. Therefore, an effective planning and budgeting approach should always promote competition among its managers for the available resources. Except in those rare instances where exigencies of the moment may dictate a different priority, the available (and always limited) resources should be awarded to the manager who can justify a return of 12 percent on those resources in contrast to another manager whose objective will return only 8 percent.

The revised definition and approach to budgeting means that the formulation of objectives and plans precedes the preparation of the budget, that objectives are based on a priority of needs of the organization, and that each manager is given the opportunity to compete for the available resources by demonstrating what he/she will do with the resources if they are awarded to him/her. Thus from an MBO viewpoint, budgets in their simplest form are the quantification in dollars and cents of what the objectives and plans of all managers viewed collectively mean in profit and/or loss for the target period.

Now let's return to the university chancellor and examine how he could have used the MBO approach to optimize his results.

His first remedial step would be to begin his process earlier in the year, say in January or February of 1976, when preparing plans for 1977. This earlier start will permit additional dialog between him and his directors and among the directors themselves on major points on which they must coordinate.

Next he would not begin his briefing by assigning each of the directors a budget allocation. Instead, he would provide his directors with the ground rules within which they would do their planning. These ground rules might include the following:

> Emphasis will be on increased return on the resources used.
>
> Each director will submit specific objectives covering the major results he/she plans to achieve.
>
> All objectives must be supported by concrete plans for achievement.
>
> All plans and objectives must be justified to the maximum extent possible.
>
> One overall organization objective is to lower total expenditures by the maximum extent possible consistent with contribution.
>
> First draft of objectives and plans is due by March 15, 1976.
>
> Final allocation of resources will be based on the relative merits of each director's objectives and the priorities of the overall organization.

In this revised approach, the chancellor has given each of his directors an opportunity to compete for the available resources. In effect he has said,

"Tell me what you should be doing during 1977, justify it, and then we'll determine how much of the resources you will be awarded." Now he's practicing a motivational approach to planning.

THE UPDATED VERSION IN PRACTICE

The rightful position of budgets can be seen by viewing the format of a typical profit plan for an organization operating under MBO. Figure 19 is a simplified version of the profit plan constructed under a motivational approach. The budget flows from objectives, not vice versa.

Figure 19. Position of the budget in a profit plan prepared under the "motivational" approach.

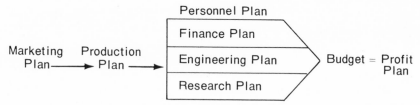

The manager in charge of each of the six major functions prepares his operating plan, containing his objectives and plans to achieve them. The operating plans are coordinated with all managers on a need-to-know basis. Then a budget is prepared. The budget thus flows from the objectives and plans.

SOURCE: Dale D. McConkey, "The Position and Function of Budgets in an MBO System," *The Business Quarterly,* Spring, 1974.

This format clearly indicates the budget in its proper position. This positioning promotes what is commonly referred to as the motivational approach to profit planning. The manager begins his planning with practically unlimited opportunity to optimize results. He knows that his results are limited only by his ability to justify the contribution he can make. He doesn't begin his planning with a budgetary constraint. Figure 20 illustrates the position of the budget in a "fiscal" approach to planning. The objectives flow from the budget.

THE PLANNING SEQUENCE

The relationship of budgeting to planning and the role budgets should play can be illustrated by following the step-by-step sequence of the preparation of a profit plan for a particular year. The calendar year 1976 will be used in this illustration.

Figure 20. Position of the budget in a profit plan prepared under the "fiscal" approach.

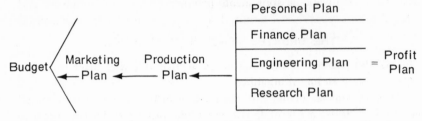

The budget is enunciated first and then objectives and plans are written to support the budget. Objectives and plans thus flow from the budget. This is an outgrowth of the "fiscal" approach to planning; that is, revenue was projected, then costs were projected, and the difference constituted the objective.

SOURCE: Dale D. McConkey, "The Position and Function of Budgets in an MBO System," *The Business Quarterly*, Spring, 1974.

Step 1. The top management of the organization issues what is commonly referred to as "the call for the profit plan" for 1976. Typically, this call is issued by the chief executive officer to each of the officers reporting to him. The call will contain the following information, to be used as guidance for lower-level managers as they prepare their "operating plans" (objectives and plans to achieve them):

The overall objectives of the organization for 1976.

An analysis of the outside environment as it may impact on the company's operations in 1976; for example, the competitive picture, the economy in general, the industry picture.

The priorities of the company during 1976.

The major assumptions on which the 1976 overall corporate objectives have been based.

The ground rules to be followed by lower-level managers when preparing their operating plans.

A timetable for preparing the operating plans.

The manager should already have an approved long-range plan—commonly covering five years—for his department. This, of course, provides him with considerable guidance as he prepares his 1976 plans and objectives.

Step 2. Each officer and department head completes the necessary analysis and coordination with other managers and then submits his operating plan covering all his operations for 1976. In essence, the operating plan will include the objectives recommended for the target period, the plans by which each of the objectives will be achieved (sometimes referred to as "programming the objectives"), and "ball park" numbers as to what the objectives and plans mean in terms of revenues, expenses, and rates of return, plus capital required. In effect, each of these managers is preparing an estimated budget covering his planned operations. It is emphasized that the manager prepares this budget *after* determining what he plans to accomplish. He does not begin his planning with a set of budget figures handed to him from above.

Step 3. This step comprises the analysis of the operating plans for all the officers and their consolidation into a total profit plan for the organization. (See Figure 19.)

The operating plans of all the officers and departments will be subjected to a penetrating financial analysis, and a consolidated budget will be prepared for the total company.

The president and his staff will review the total profit plan for consistency with company objectives, ground rules, and priorities. (The president's staff in this case may include the financial officer, the top planning manager, and other staff specialists. In some cases it may include a budget committee.)

The president may discuss with each of his officers the officer's operating plan and suggest revisions or complete changes.

A consolidated budget is prepared reflecting the changes resulting from the discussion. Resources are allocated to the objectives based upon how well each manager competed for the available resources and the priorities which have been set for the target period.

The consolidated budget is compared with the overall objectives of the corporation for the target period.

If the consolidated budget is consistent with the corporate objectives, the operating plans are approved.

If the consolidated budget is not consistent with the corporate objectives, one of two approaches will be followed: (1) The operating plans will be returned to the officers for additional analysis and efforts to try to bring them up to the corporate objectives, or (2) the operating plans—if considered valid—are accepted and the corporate objectives are adjusted accordingly.

Additional comment is in order with respect to the preceding paragraph. The hallmarks of an achievement-oriented manager are a willingness to take the necessary time and effort to arrive at well-formulated objectives and plans in the first place and unwillingness to adjust the objectives downward unless there is absolutely no alternative action he can take to prevent the downward adjustment.

Thus when all the individual operating plans do not add up to the overall corporate objectives, the first recourse should not be to lower the overall objectives. First, complete emphasis should be devoted to leaving the objectives at their present levels and second, all possible alternatives for overcoming the void should be pursued.

Step 4. Figure 19 indicates that preparation of the budget is the concluding part of the profit plan. This is an accurate portrayal when the profit plan is viewed for a particular target period, say one year.

In a very real sense, however, there is never a "conclusion" to the planning process: It is a continuous, ongoing part of the job of all managers. Once the profit plan has been approved, it is not filed away to be removed from the files and read sometime in the future. It must be looked upon as a viable, living document that the manager uses as the major guide for his day-to-day actions. Actual performance against the plan will be evaluated as the year unfolds. Certain revisions will be necessary during the year to keep the plan realistic. The experience gained with the plan during one year will serve as the basis for much of what is included in the profit plans for subsequent years.

Thus the planning process should be considered as a continuous circle or loop in which:

Objectives, plans, and budgets are prepared for a particular target period.

The objectives, plans, and budgets are approved and the manager begins operating under his plan.

Results are evaluated against plan continuously during the target period and at the conclusion of it.

The entire process is repeated, beginning with the preparation of objectives, plans, and budgets for the next target period.

CONCLUSION

Budgets have a key role to play in the MBO system, but they are not an end in themselves. Once properly viewed and constructed, they provide a valuable vehicle for controlling or monitoring; however; their primary thrust should not be for control purposes. The primary thrust of budgeting must be to motivate managers to optimize their results. Control is a secondary, later consideration and should come about as a byproduct, not as the main product.

The transition from "control" to "motivational" budgeting necessitates not only a change in the positioning of the budget but also a rather radical change in the position and orientation of the budget director. Traditionally, he/she has been a member of the controller's staff and as such has had a "financial-statement orientation" of looking backward at what has already happened. He/she must start considering himself/herself as a member of the management team looking ahead. A backward orientation implies control. A forward orientation permits the motivational approach.

The transition is not easily made. It requires a radical departure from decades of training and practice that emphasized the definition of the budget director as one who looked at corporate life through a rearview mirror where he/she often saw little but controls, reports, and variances. Unfortunately, even today, only a few schools of business approach budgeting from an MBO, motivational approach.

The motivational approach to budgeting requires that:

Competition for resources be emphasized.

Results not be predetermined by beginning the planning process with budgetary allocations.

Each manager be permitted and encouraged to demonstrate the contribution he/she is capable of making, before resources are awarded.

Budgets should flow from objectives. Objectives should not flow from budgets.

Management by objectives, properly implemented and directed, is a potent means for motivating managers to greater performance. MBO is an achievement-oriented approach. The role of budgets must be one that capitalizes on the motivational qualities inherent in the system.

16

Coordinating with Other Managers

THIS IS THE SECOND TIME so far in the objective-setting steps that the necessity for major coordinating has arisen. The first was back in Step 2, when the manager was required to effect preliminary coordination with all other managers with whom his operations are involved. He used the information gathered in Step 2 as part of his "intelligence" base for proceeding through the subsequent steps.

The second major coordinating effort takes place in Step 10. This can be looked upon as an "insurance" step, as it is the step in which the manager ensures that all necessary and final coordination has been effected with the other managers before the former begins carrying out his objectives. For example, the production manager must ensure that his objectives and plans as now structured are compatible and consistent with those of the marketing manager; the personnel manager must ensure that what he plans to do meets the needs of all other managers for whom he must provide personnel services; and the manager in charge of the management information system must coordinate with other managers in like fashion.

ANSWERING THE CRITICAL QUESTION

The effectiveness of this coordinating step will depend in large part upon how well each manager answers several questions, such as:

1. Have I identified all other managers in my coordination network, those with whom coordination *must* be effected?

2. Have I effected the necessary communications and coordination with each manager in my coordination network?

3. Do my objectives and plans adequately reflect the results of this coordination?

4. Do my objectives and plans contain any gaps, places where I have missed doing something that I should?

5. Are there any overlaps in my objectives and plans, instances in which I may be duplicating something another manager is doing or something that is really part of another manager's responsibility?

6. Do other managers with whom my operations are involved agree that my objectives and plans as written will carry out my responsibility to them?

7. Will the objectives and plans of other managers carry out their responsibility to me?

ASSISTANCE IN COORDINATING

Each individual manager has the primary responsibility for coordinating his objectives and plans with all other managers. However, the enlightened manager will avail himself of several valuable resources as an aid when coordinating in this step.

Often there is one or more persons (commonly a director of planning services) and, more and more, an MBO adviser (at general staff level) who are responsible for fitting together all the pieces of the jigsaw puzzle (objectives and plans) to ensure that they constitute a big picture (the total plan for the organization). The manager should welcome this source of assistance whenever he believes they can be of assistance.

COORDINATING WITH FINANCE

In today's highly competitive climate in which "the numbers" play such an important role, the manager should make a special effort to ensure that he has effected full coordination with the financial department. A major purpose of such coordination is financial analysis of all objectives and plans. As used here, the term "financial analysis" does not refer to the traditional bookkeeping task of making certain that all numbers add up to the correct sum. Financial analysis must go far beyond mere bookkeeping to be effective. A competent financial analyst will play a key role and make a decided contribution if he/she analyzes and makes recommendations as to whether all cost and revenue components have been included in the data, what other alternatives have been considered, what the financial impact of these alternatives would be, plus or minus, and what additional alternatives are available for increasing profitability above the level that might be generated by the plan as now written.

Financial analysis has two important roles to carry out: (1) to ensure that all items of expense and income have been included and are properly reflected and (2) to determine that all possible alternatives have been considered and that the profit opportunities of each have been clearly identified. Two brief examples will illustrate these two functions.

Example 1. The proposed plan indicates that an increase in sales of 3,000 units will result in a profit increase of $50,000. The financial department must work out a complete profit and loss statement on this point. It must trace these units from the initial purchasing of raw materials through the complete process to the point at which they are sold. The financial analysis may show that the purchase of raw materials for the additional 3,000 units will permit the purchasing department to effect additional economies through volume discounts and that projected profits are understated. Or the analysis may show that profits are overstated because producing the additional units will require extensive overtime work or capital additions that will increase depreciation charges. Analysis may indicate that the plan should be pursued, even though the projected profit must be reduced, because selling the additional units is a low-cost method of opening up new marketing areas for future years. When all this has been spelled out, the financial analysis must conclude with a statement of the profits the company can reasonably expect from the sale of the 3,000 units under the conditions provided for.

Example 2. The plan submitted by the marketing director projected an increase in profits of $100,000 by increasing the national advertising allowance by 2 percent. The marketing director's previous experience had been primarily in advertising-oriented positions—as an account executive for a large advertising agency and more recently as a corporate director of advertising. Like most managers, he tended to emphasize and have the most faith in the techniques with which he was most familiar. As a result, his marketing plan placed most of the chips on advertising as the likeliest route for increasing profitability.

A detailed financial analysis not only cast serious doubt on the ability of increased advertising to generate the projected profit but also raised the question whether other alternatives—changes in the wholesale pricing structure and the economics of a different distribution method—might not generate profits above those projected for the increased advertising. The plan, along with the questions raised by the financial analysis, were returned to the marketing director for review. A financial review of the second version of the marketing plan supported his new proposal to revise the distribution channels, so that the company handled this expensive selling through brokers instead of selling direct to small accounts. This change, along with a lower sales price made possible by not serving the many small accounts, resulted in projected savings equal to the original target without increasing the advertising expenditures. To illustrate the benefits possible from a different combination of alternatives, the financial analysis might have shown that profits could be raised above the figure specified in the original objective by changing the distribution method, lowering the price, and undertaking some or all of the proposed advertising increase.

COORDINATING TECHNIQUES

A combination of one or more of the following techniques is commonly used for effecting the coordination:

1. Individual discussions with the other managers involved in which the highlights of each manager's objectives and plans are discussed.

2. Exchange of written copies of each manager's objectives and plans. I suggest that some means be used to call the attention of each manager to key sections in which the other managers are involved; for example, underscoring in red or actually stating what is required of the other managers.

3. Group meetings in which each manager briefs the others as to what he plans to do and what he will require from other managers. The value of this technique increases in situations in which each of several managers may have responsibility for part of a highly integrated operation.

CONCLUSION

Coordinating has always been a major part of each manager's responsibility. Step 10 provides the vehicle for helping him/her perform this responsibility.

17

ACTION STEP 11

Tailoring Authority

AUTHORITY is another essential ingredient of objective setting; authority permits the delegation to be carried out. Regardless of the skill and thoroughness with which the preceding parts of the process have been handled, no delegation takes place if the subordinate is not granted the authority to accomplish his accountability. The authority required for effective delegation of accountability is characterized by several attributes.

1. There must be a transfer of power from the superior to the subordinate. Authority must be considered synonymous with the power to act.

2. Authority must be specific enough for the subordinate to proceed without fear of exceeding his authority or having his actions reversed. Instances involving the use of poor judgment where consequences would be highly detrimental to the organization would be an exception, of course.

3. Authority should be granted in advance (for the target period) rather than on an ad hoc basis so that the manager may plan his future course of action more effectively.

4. Authority should be spelled out in writing to facilitate understanding between superior and subordinate and among other persons who may be involved as the manager carries out his accountability.

5. Normally, authority should be delegated to the lowest possible organizational level where all information necessary for decision making and action comes together or is available.

Note: This chapter has been adapted in part from an earlier book by the author, *No-Nonsense Delegation*, AMACOM, 1974.

6. The authority delegated must be publicized to all persons who may be affected or involved in the action.

7. Above all, the degree of authority must equal the extent of the subordinate's accountability. It must be consistent with the manager's objectives and plans to achieve them.

COMMON MISTAKES IN DELEGATING AUTHORITY

Although few managers would question the wisdom of granting a subordinate sufficient authority to perform his job, the principle often is violated in practice. Some of the commoner violations follow.

Commensurate authority. Frequently, the catchall phrase "He enjoys authority commensurate with the job" is used to describe the manager's authority. However, this is often a myth; the definition is so general that little if any actual authority may be transferred. Quite often the words mean "Take the action and I'll let you know whether or not I agree with you." As the word "commensurate" is subjective and means different things to different people, it provides no guidance to anyone. It must be defined in specific terms.

The premise that a manager should enjoy authority commensurate with his job is sound. However, the premise must be translated into practice. It acknowledges the need for authority, with the understanding that additional, more specific, authority grants are forthcoming. These specific grants must be made as early in the game as possible to prevent the manager from proceeding at his own peril or amid confusion. Naturally, the specific authorities granted will be influenced by the competence of the incumbents, the magnitude of the problems, their accountabilities, and the circumstances.

An excellent illustration of the weakness and danger inherent in the words "commensurate authority" is the labor relations manager who served as chief negotiator for his company for negotiating collective bargaining agreements. In actual practice, the "commensurate authority" he enjoyed meant that he had full authority to meet with the union and receive and discuss its demands. However, he was required to call headquarters before making any but the most routine concessions. He soon fell into the habit of using this requirement as a crutch and excused himself to "call the boss" whenever negotiations got particularly sticky.

Anyone who has negotiated a labor contract knows that often there comes a time when the contract can be settled then and there. However, if the negotiator is not authorized to settle at that moment of receptivity, the negotiations may drag out for weeks. This particular negotiator was never able to take advantage of the magic moment. The union representatives knew he was only a messenger boy and instead of being willing to settle, they usually tried to get more. Also, the labor relations manager had no opportunity to plan his strategy and tactics to settle at a particular figure because he never knew what figure headquarters would agree to.

Ratification. As the term implies, ratification involves an after-the-fact approval of an action by the manager's superior. It is undesirable, for at least two reasons, as a means of securing authority. The subordinate proceeds at his own peril without any concrete idea as to whether his boss will approve the action. And the boss is forced to approve the action—frequently by condoning it—or to overrule his subordinate. It is eminently better for both parties to have the authority delegated in advance.

Symptomatic of this weakness is the boss who tells his subordinate that it really isn't necessary to spell out specific authority, that the two of them will resolve the authority question as the delegated project proceeds. Very often the boss actually is saying that he doesn't want to share his authority or that he likes to keep his finger in the pie by having his people constantly check back with him.

Accountability without authority. Most people are willing to let their subordinates share with them in performing the work; however, a proportionate number are not always willing to give up some of their authority. In other words, they want and seek help with the chores but are reluctant to share the power, influence, and status that accompany authority. Reluctant bosses are great developers of followers, but they seldom become known as a leader of leaders; leadership goes with authority.

Authority survives the action. Authority means not only that the superior grants it *before* the action but also that the superior supports it after the action. A president delegated authority to a vice-president to replace any department head who was incompetent. The vice-president decided that a particular department head would have to go. Because of the key nature of the job to the company, the vice-president mentioned his plans to the president, whose reaction was, "It's your show, use your own judgment." The vice-president terminated the substandard department head. However, without informing the vice-president, the president contacted the department head and arranged a clandestine meeting with him. Later, the president called in the vice-president and proceeded to hint at several reasons that he believed the vice-president had erred. Subsequently, the vice-president was never convinced that he had the authority to run his own show and he checked with the president before making any but the most routine decisions.

The continuing-support phase means the superior must (1) make sure the subordinate understands what is expected of him; (2) help the subordinate reach his objectives by providing information, staff assistance, and tools as needed; and (3) give him advice, counsel, and correction without taking away any part of his accountability and authority.

Authority is personal. As authority must be tailored to accountability, it follows logically that authority also must be personal. It must be based on such differences as accountability, competence, and circumstances surrounding the delegation. A manager operating a plant thousands of miles away in a foreign country will require a different authority from that of his local counterpart, who is only a few miles away from the boss. Standard schedules or manuals of authority can impede the performance of an aggressive manager with ambitious accountability; the same authority would be more than enough for a less qualified manager. Tailoring of authority to match accountability is discussed later in this chapter.

SECURING AUTHORITY

Authority usually is spoken of as something the superior grants his subordinates. This thinking places the initiative on the superior's shoulders. For purposes of tailoring authority to accountability it is better if authority were looked upon as powers recommended by the subordinate to the superior and approved by the latter. This transfers the initiative to the subordinate, where it belongs. How often have we heard a subordinate gripe about his lack of authority and then learn that he has never recommended that his authority be increased?

Subordinate managers would be well advised to keep reminding themselves that they—not their superiors—are most affected by success or failure on their jobs. They must take the initiative in removing any obstacles to performance, including being sure they get all necessary authority.

The boss, as his contribution to setting authorities, must remember that the more latitude he grants his subordinates—both in terms of allowing them to participate in establishing their authority and in the amount of the authority—the more committed and motivated his people will be to do a better job. Once more it's a matter of allowing managers to help determine their own destiny.

REVISING AUTHORITY

Whenever authority is granted in advance—and it should be to the maximum extent possible—provision must be made for revising the authority as necessitated by changing circumstances. Objectives and plans may not work out as scheduled. Managers may be able to handle more or less authority than was first anticipated.

Methods for revising authority range from the informal to the formal. In most instances heavy reliance is placed on the subordinate to recommend changes whenever he feels they are needed; this is desirable as it places the initiative on the manager, where it belongs. Frequently, changes are initiated by the superior on the basis of his own observations.

The more formal approach is practiced by a large company in the floor-covering industry. This company conducts formal quarterly reviews with its managers to evaluate performance as compared against objectives. During these reviews, a standard item on the agenda is a review of the authority granted to each manager. Thus each manager knows he will have a minimum of four times "in court" each year at which he may request changes in his authority.

Regardless of how diligently and how well a company sets the authority for its managers, situations will develop that are not covered by the delegated authority. Even the chief executive officer of an organization, the manager with more authority than anyone else, must on occasion turn to his executive committee or the board of directors to resolve questions about his authority.

The goal when establishing authorities should be to cover all the anticipated actions the manager will be required to take during the target period. These should be closely tailored to individual accountability by providing the subordinate with an active opportunity to recommend the authority he will require and then approving it before he begins carrying out his job.

CONCLUSION

This step covered the authority each manager requires to carry out his objectives and plans. Authority is a major action vehicle for bringing life to these two areas.

18

Tailoring Feedback to Objectives

ONE OF THE PRIMARY responsibilities of an effective manager is to maintain the greatest possible control over the destiny of his operation, even in the face of changing events and circumstances. Conversely, an ineffective manager is one who permits his operation to get out of control when change occurs. A manager's objectives and plans will remain viable and dynamic (that is, responsive to change) only if (1) the factors that exert a major impact on the manager's operations are clearly identified, (2) a monitoring procedure is established to detect and measure the impact of changes in these factors, and (3) the manager takes corrective action at the earliest possible time to cope with the changes as they are detected.

It is unfortunate, and indeed contradictory, if the provision for change is not built in because MBO itself is essentially a major change agent. Failing to provide for change treats the manager's objectives and plans as something static and carved in stone. Management is dynamic, and events and circumstances will change during the target period. The impact of these changes must be dealt with if the manager wishes to maintain control over his destiny. This chapter covers the major monitoring, or control, aspects of an MBO system.

THE FIVE MONITORING AND CONTROL AREAS

The initial tailoring of feedback to each individual manager can be very time-consuming and laborious when it is being done for the first time. It is, nevertheless, a mandatory step, one that will be eminently worthwhile in future years.

Although a manager requires many types and categories of information, there are five areas in particular that the manager must control under an MBO system. He must have control of *assumptions,* of *objectives,* of *plans,* of *resources,* and of the *routine.*

CONTROL OF ASSUMPTIONS

The proper use of assumptions will provide the manager with a valuable early-warning alert, but only if he has positioned himself to capitalize on it. Unfortunately, this is one of the more commonly neglected control points. As noted earlier, it is not possible to establish objectives (which always cover a future period of time) without basing them on major assumptions that are formulated during the objective-setting process. The assumptions on which the objectives and plans are based must be clearly stated, recorded, and tracked continuously during the target period to determine if they are valid.

To illustrate, let's assume that a manager's objectives are based on six or seven major assumptions, which he has formulated. Let's assume further that he is a marketing product manager in charge of product X. One of his major assumptions provides:

It is assumed that the total market for product X is 10,000 units during 1977.

Naturally, wherever this assumption has entered into his 1977 planning, he has predicated it in relation to market potential. We'll now assume that his objectives have been approved and that the target year 1977 has started to unfold. On March 1 of 1977 he examines the assumption in light of the latest available information and finds that the total market potential is probably closer to 8,000 units. This immediately flags the manager that his objectives are based on an assumption that is not coming true. This also tells him that a new assumption is called for and that he must formulate a new assumed total market potential. Even more importantly, it tells him that he must revise one or more of the following: objectives, plans to achieve them, or resource allocation. Any time an assumption proves to be wrong (and they frequently will) one or more (sometimes all) of these three components must be considered for revision. This is the first method by which the manager keeps his objectives and plans updated and realistic at all times.

It should be noted that assumptions can act as the early-warning system described above only if all assumptions *have been clearly stated, have been recorded, and are constantly monitored.*

CONTROL OF OBJECTIVES

Objectives must be measurable to the maximum extent possible; otherwise control becomes practically impossible. Consider, for example, an objective that reads:

> Make a substantial increase in the efficiency of my department by September 1, 1977.

The use of the highly subjective word "substantial"—frequently referred to as a weasel word—makes it impossible to measure performance on the objective and thus to control performance on it. Additionally, it is not possible to lay out plans to achieve the objective because no two people would agree as to the end result being sought.

Now compare this with the following well-worded objective for a plant foreman:

> By July 1, 1977, reduce scrap costs in department by 10 percent and maintain at that level during the remainder of 1977.

MBO requires that meaningful feedback be tailored to the individual objectives of the line manager. Figure 21 illustrates the result of this five-step method, which includes:

Step 1. Statement of Objective.

Step 2. Definition of the measures to be used for monitoring performance.

Figure 21. Tailoring feedback to delegated accountability (example: a plant foreman).

1. Objective	2. Performance Measure	3. Frequency of Report	4. Distribution	5. Form
By July 1, 1977, reduce scrap costs in department by 10% and maintain at that level during remainder of 1977.	Total costs of raw materials and direct labor for units that cannot be reworked. Additional costs of units that can be reworked. Analysis of absorbed burden.	Weekly	Foreman Production superintendent Plant accountant Quality assurance manager Inventory control manager	SR-10

Step 3. How often the feedback will be provided, determined primarily by the frequency with which the manager is in a position to take remedial action.

Step 4. A determination, on a need-to-know basis, of who should get copies of the report.

Step 5. A description of the form in which the report will be presented (the simpler, the better).

The result of this part of the tailoring process assures the manager that he is receiving meaningful feedback designed primarily for his use. The same data may be used for other purposes—for example reporting to higher-level managers—but the emphasis is first on the manager's needs.

CONTROL OF PLANS

The step-by-step plans by which the manager has decided to achieve his objective serve as another excellent means of control. However, they will serve this purpose only if they are prepared in enough detail; that is, they are broken down into several distinct action steps, and a timetable for completion of each step has been agreed to. For example, the plan that supports the following objective of a corporate budget manager is worthless when it comes to using it to establish controls:

Objective	*Plan to Achieve*
By December 31, 1977, have completed the corporate operating plan for 1978 and distributed to divisional managers for final approval.	Discuss with division Controller and managers what their plans are for 1978.

This manager didn't construct his plan in enough detailed steps and failed to establish interim target dates or a timetable for use during the year. He won't know until the target period is over—and there's no time left to take any corrective action—whether or not he's achieved his objective. Interim measuring, correcting, and revising during the target period have become impossible.

Figure 18 in Chapter 14 illustrates how an objective should be planned out by action steps to permit the establishment of interim control.

CONTROL OF RESOURCES

Little need be said here about control of resources. The function and use of budgets and budgetary control were covered in Step 9. However, it should be reemphasized that budgets should be viewed as the allocation of resources to objectives—in other words, the budget is tailored to the objectives and plans. Also, budget reporting must follow good principles of responsibility accounting, with all status and variance reports going primarily to the manager who has the responsibility for the objectives and plans.

CONTROL OF THE ROUTINE

Normally, objectives cover only the more important or priority parts of the job during the target period. As indicated earlier, controls are then established to monitor performance on these priority objectives.

This leaves for consideration the control or monitoring of the more routine parts of the job that aren't covered by objectives. Thus an important policy decision at this point is to determine how much control is desirable or necessary over this routine. Practice varies widely. Some organizations insist upon complete control of objectives and leave control of the routine to the discretion of the individual manager. Other organizations demand that both the priority and the routine be controlled rather tightly.

One practical way—but one that must be used with considerable discretion lest violence be done to effective delegation—is to reduce the priority actions to objectives as has been recommended in this book and then tailor controls to them. Next, the routine parts of the job are embodied in standards of performance.

The basic difference between objectives and standards of performance in this context is that objectives concern priority matters and are self-liquidating (they usually end when the target period is reached), while standards of performance cover routine matters and may continue from one target period to the next without being changed. Examples of standards of performance are:

1. Performance is satisfactory when the reject rate is maintained at a maximum of x percent of production volume. (A production manager)

2. Performance is satisfactory when selling costs do not exceed x percent of sales. (A sales manager)

3. Performance is satisfactory when the monthly report of operations is distributed within the first five working days of each month. (A management information manager)

Once these standards of performance have been established, they are controlled by the exception principle; that is, action is taken when the standard is not met.

CORRECTIVE ACTION AND REVISIONS

It should be obvious that the feedback report itself is not the end being sought. What is being sought is the *action* that the report should cause to happen—corrective action to help the manager stay on target or, when necessary, to permit the revisions to assumptions, objectives, plans, or budgets so that they are always realistic and being followed.

Before concluding this section, note that a competent MBO manager doesn't take revisions lightly, especially downward revisions from previously established levels. Before ever considering a downward adjustment in his objectives, he first considers leaving the objective at the same level and exploring every possible alternative for correcting whatever unfavorable variance may have occurred. In fact, the two hallmarks of a competent MBO manager are, first, willingness to devote the time and effort necessary to establish realistic objectives in the first place, and, second, to be completely unwilling to lower the objective unless he has first pursued every possible way of meeting the original objective.

19

ACTION STEP 13

Repeat the Cycle

STEP 13 is the step that, hopefully, all managers will be in a position to complete because it indicates that the MBO system has been sufficiently successful to justify continuing it. The necessity for this step also emphasizes the ongoing nature of MBO.

Considerable time and effort will be required the first time the manager works through the steps in the objective-setting process. There is no way this can be avoided. The time and effort are well justified because the manager, in effect, is building a well-constructed foundation on which to base the future operations of his unit.

In subsequent years, however, less time and effort should be required to complete the objective-setting process. Much of what the manager did during the preceding year will be available for his use next year. Usually, only updating is required—the wheel doesn't have to be reinvented. For example, unless there has been a major addition or deletion to the manager's job, his responsibility and key results areas will usually not change. Unless there have been major changes reflected in the environmental analysis, much of the manager's situational analysis will remain pretty much the same.

Another aid to the manager in future years is what Edward J. Green refers to as the pigeonhole approach to updating objective-setting and planning information. Green, chairman of Planning Dynamics, Inc. and a well-respected authority on corporate planning, recommends that each manager continuously maintain a pigeonhole file to be used when completing the objective-setting process in each subsequent year.

The pigeonhole file works this way. Assume that a manager has just begun operating with his approved objectives and plans for the current year. He knows that a year from now he must again complete the objective-setting process, and he wants to prepare for next year as much as possible while the current year is under way. Using a looseleaf notebook or a series of folders, he sets up a pigeonhole file for each subject or step in the objective-setting process. During the year as he comes across pertinent information or questions, he files the material in the appropriate file. Thus when he sits down next year, he has already completed much of his necessary homework. He doesn't have to start from scratch.

20

Objectives Versus Plans
—at Various
Management Levels

THE QUESTION often arises as to how a higher-level manager goes about planning or programming how his objective will be achieved without dictating to his subordinates and locking them into predetermined courses of action. A corollary question is, What do the objectives and plans look like (what is their content) at various levels of management? To answer these questions, it is necessary to draw a distinction between what might be called unit objectives and position objectives.

Several managers, and often several levels of management, must play a part in achieving *unit objectives*. For example, say that a sales department as a total unit must sell 10,000 items. Several sales managers must contribute to achieving this objective, as illustrated in Figure 22. In contrast, position objectives must be achieved primarily by the individual manager himself.

UNIT OBJECTIVES

The objective-setting process and the flow chart (Figure 11) covered earlier indicate that once the manager writes his objective (Step 7), he must then formulate plans to achieve the objective (Step 8). While this is technically correct, it can lead to misunderstanding if the level of management is not considered. For example, the president is primarily accountable for the eight or so top, overall objectives of the corporation. Certainly he doesn't sit down and lay out all the plans by which the top corporate objectives will be achieved. He does, however, *ensure* that the plans are formulated by lower-level managers. This distinction is important. Higher-level managers *ensure* that the plans are developed. Lower-level managers *develop* them.

Thus the plans by which higher-level objectives will be achieved essentially comprise the objectives of lower-level managers. This is illustrated by the simplified example of the sales department shown in Figure 22—a sales department with three levels of management.

In this example, we'll assume that the sales vice-president has as his objective the sale of 10,000 items (this is a unit objective for the entire sales department). As noted previously, the sales vice-president doesn't

Figure 22. Simplified planning of unit objectives.

personally develop the plans by which this objective will be achieved. He *ensures* that the plans are developed and, as illustrated by Figure 22, the plans by which the objective will be achieved are largely the objectives of the two regional sales managers reporting to the vice-president.

Next we move down one level to the regional sales manager— another "ensuring it's done" level. The plans by which the regional sales manager will achieve his regional objective are the objectives of the division sales manager—the lowest level of management. Finally, the division sales manager, as the lowest level of management, will have detailed plans as to how his objective will be achieved.

Another example of unit objectives is the production department in which the highest-level manager is the production vice-president and the lowest-level managers are the production foremen. It is these foremen who will actually plan out how the actual production objectives will be achieved. All other levels of management between the production vice-president and the foremen are "ensuring it's done" levels.

Finally, tracing through the same approach in a financial department will serve to further illustrate the relationship between unit objectives and plans by levels. Assume that one of the top corporate objectives covers profit—which it invariably does. One of the several ways in which the financial vice-president and his managers can contribute to profitability is to provide more accurate and timely information for use by all managers for decision-making purposes.

The financial officer formulates as his unit objective the improvement of the information provided to managers. This will be an overall but specific, umbrella-type objective that those reporting to the financial officer will play a part in achieving. Assume that the following managers report to the financial vice-president: treasurer, data processing manager, and controller. The plans by which the vice-president will achieve his objective will be essentially the objectives of the three managers reporting to him.

Although the subject is covered in more detail in a later chapter on administration of an MBO system, one point is worth repeating here. Unit objectives should be consolidated, not compiled, as they move up the line. The difference is simply this. In consolidation, only selected portions of lower-level objectives and plans are transmitted up the line. In compilation, all the objectives and plans of the lower level move up to the next level, where they are added to the information at that level, and so forth for each succeeding higher level. Compilation results in a papermill, and the higher-level managers receive an excessive amount of detail that they do not need and should not want.

POSITION OBJECTIVES

If it weren't for position objectives, all levels of management above the first level would exist only to ensure that the lower levels did something. In other words, the objectives of these higher levels would be limited to adding up the objectives of the managers reporting to them to arrive at objectives for the unit. This unenviable position is avoided by the manager in charge of a unit having both objectives for the unit, plus objectives for his position. His position objectives are unique to him. He not only establishes these objectives but also formulates the plans by which they will be achieved. His lower-level subordinates do not play a major role in achieving these position objectives.

A good example of position objectives is the responsibility for subordinate effectiveness. Only the manager to whom the subordinates report can have this as his objective. He must personally structure objectives and plans to bring about increased effectiveness of his subordinates. The objective is unique to his position. An objective unique to a president is one dealing with acquisitions. Establishing sources of financing is one commonly unique to a treasurer.

The following example shows possible subjects of objectives that are unique to various levels of management within a financial department:

> *Treasurer*
>   Cost of capital
>   Return on investable funds
>
> *Credit and Collection Manager*
>   Bad-debt level
>   Aging of accounts
>
> *Data Processing Manager*
>   Machine-utilization level
>   Personnel-utilization level

Another example of objectives unique to a position is frequently found in smaller banks. Often, the president is "Mr. Outside," and the executive vice-president is "Mr. Inside." In this kind of organization the president serves primarily in a customer relations role—for example, contacting potential new customers, entertaining customers, and creating a favorable image of the bank generally. The executive vice-president actually manages the operations of the bank, usually as the chief operating officer. Thus while the president, as the top officer, will have final accountability for the unit objectives of the entire bank, he will also have unique objectives covering his "Mr. Outside" role.

TYING IN UNIT OBJECTIVES

Some people espouse the idea that it should always be possible to draw a direct line between the objectives of lower-level managers and the top objectives of the corporation that the lower-level objectives are supposed to be supporting. This would be highly desirable in theory because it would ensure 100 percent compatibility and coordination of all objectives. However, this is rarely possible in practice.

Often, the lower we move down the management ladder, the more difficult it becomes to establish a direct relationship between unit objectives and the top objectives of the corporation. This is especially true in a steep organization structure in which there may be eight levels of management between the chief executive officer and the first-line manager. In lieu of what could develop into a useless exercise in line drawing, it is usually preferable to concentrate on ensuring that the objectives at each level are directly supportive of or beneficial to achieving the next higher level of objectives.

21

Writing
Measurable Objectives
for Staff Managers

THE ADVANCED APPLICATIONS of management by objectives now permit
the staff manager to write measurable objectives, to measure rather finitely his contributions compared to his objectives, to receive deserved
recognition in the process, and to take his proper place as a member of
the profit-making team. Concurrently, the staff manager's organization
receives value due for its money and begins to eliminate the management
void that has existed since World War I.

This void has been most costly and resulted from the failure to measure staff managers and hold them accountable for achieving specific,
profit-oriented results. The key to solving the problem lies in writing
measurable objectives for those managers working in the so-called staff
departments or functions of personnel and labor relations, public relations, finance, law, research and development, engineering, purchasing,
marketing services, industrial engineering, and others.

WRITING MEASURABLE OBJECTIVES

The paramount difficulty in writing staff objectives is overcoming the
long-practiced misconception that they cannot be measured. Under MBO
they can and must be measurable. To admit otherwise would be tantamount to agreeing that 20 to 40 percent of the average company's per-

sonnel budget is being expended on staff functions that can't be measured and that companies, therefore, must rely upon some form of divine guidance to make certain they are receiving value due for these tremendous expenditures. It should suffice to say that a company would be extremely reluctant to approve such amounts for any other type of project without first determining the rather finite measurements by which its return on investment would be gauged.

Take, for example, an organization whose general and administrative expense budget, exclusive of items such as interest on debt and other nonpersonnel items, approximates $2 million—a not uncommon situation. Further, assume that the percentage of the staff costs of this figure is only 20 percent. Thus we are talking about $400,000 for the costs of staff managers and the matters they recommend, secure approval of, and ultimately control. Let's relabel this expenditure of $400,000 to change its cost classification and to illustrate the measures that would be required if it were, for example, a request for new equipment.

Before the company approves the expenditure, it would want to know, at the very minimum, the details of how, when, and for what the money would be used; the advantages of the new equipment over the old; the financial worth of these advantages; and the return on investment for the $400,000.

Assume that a production manager walks into his boss's office and asks for $400,000 to buy new equipment; he tells his boss that it is impossible to determine or measure what return the organization will receive on its two-fifths of a million dollars of investment. Imagine what would happen in this particular organization! In the first instance, no production manager worth his salt would ever make such a request. In the second instance, and in the unlikely event he did, his request would be turned down out of hand, and his name would be moved to the bottom of the promotion list. If the company continued to retain him in employment, he would probably spend his next few weeks attending classes on basic business techniques for the student manager. Yet a company is guilty of exactly this when it approves the same expense for staff managers who have objectives or responsibilities that are considered incapable of being measured.

The charge that staff objectives could not be measured was valid prior to MBO because at best they were "for motherhood and against sin" types of objectives. They often read as follows:

> To attain and maintain the highest possible degree of quality (for a quality control manager).

To provide expert financial and accounting advice (for a financial manager).

To design a product of the greatest consumer appeal at the lowest cost of production (for a design engineer).

To formulate and recommend programs that will promote employee interest and morale (for a personnel manager).

To purchase raw materials and supplies in accordance with specifications (for a purchasing manager).

To advise and counsel the company's managers in the preparation of both short- and long-range plans as an aid in achieving the company's objectives (for a planning manager).

To support the production department by providing well-thought-out recommendations on matters such as operational layout, work flow, and manufacturing processes (for an industrial engineering manager).

To enhance the company's image in the eyes of the buying public by securing the placement of publicity favorable to the company in media such as newspapers, magazines, radio, and television (for a public relations manager).

DETERMINING STAFF'S MISSION

The staff manager must give considerable thought to his true mission in the organization before he can write worthwhile objectives. The failure of the staff manager to make this determination usually will result in his compiling a list of routine activities that he plans to pursue. For example, the true mission of an advertising manager is not to formulate and administer advertising programs; the real job is to help generate sales by the type, manner, and cost of the advertising effort he or she completes. In similar fashion, the mission of the research manager is not to spend money carrying out research activities but to add to sales and profits by developing new products or improving old ones. An industrial engineer's job is not to conduct efficiency studies but to help increase production output. In all three examples a distinct demarcation must be established between merely pursuing activities and achieving specific results. Two examples will illustrate the importance of this difference for a staff engineering manager.

In the first example, the engineering manager considers his mission as being "to provide engineering services to the operating divisions." When he writes his so-called objectives he will undoubtedly end up with a lengthy list of activities designed to carry out his mission; it would be all but impossible to arrive at any other type of objectives because he has cast his mission as an activity. In the second example, the engineering manager states his mission in terms of the results he must achieve to justify his existence. His mission states that he is accountable for "effecting savings in plant and equipment costs through achieving X, Y and Z results." An actual engineering objective covered by the second example reads as follows:

"Reduce design engineering and manufacturing cost ratio to total equipment and rebuild cost from present 17.3 to 15 percent without reducing quality of design and manufacture of equipment."

Thus before staff managers can consider writing meaningful, measurable objectives, they must arrive at an understanding of their true mission. Failure to do so will result in objectives that are not specific and not responsive to the real needs of the organization.

FROM QUALITATIVE TO QUANTITATIVE OBJECTIVES

Before the extensive use of MBO it was usually believed that line managers should have quantitative objectives—those dealing with numbers such as sales figures, cost levels, ratios, return on investment, quotas, and profits. For the most part, staff managers who dealt in intangibles did not have quantitative objectives but only qualitative ones in which the manager tried to state as specifically as possible what he was going to accomplish. Even though it is still necessary for the staff manager to rely sometimes on specific, qualitative objectives, staff objectives are moving more and more to the quantified type. Following are two examples that illustrate the movement from qualitative to quantitative objectives. The first one is a general corporate objective; the second is a specific staff objective:

Example 1: A general corporate objective. Companies have long appreciated the value of having a quality reputation for their products. It builds customer confidence, sales, and profits. Thus companies frequently established an objective dealing with product quality. It usually read along the following lines:

"Our objective is to achieve the number one quality reputation for our company within the industry."

At best, this was a qualitative objective and, while highly laudable, it could not be measured. No definition of quality had been agreed to and it was not possible to determine when or if the objective ever was reached. It was a "for motherhood" type of objective. Before it could become a meaningful objective in accordance with MBO it was necessary to define what the objective meant and how it was to be measured. The period of roughly the past eight years has seen organizations make dramatic strides in solving both the definition and measurement problems. This was accomplished by including in the objective *those specific conditions or indicators that must be met when in the judgment of management the objective had been satisfactorily accomplished.* With this technique, the preceding quality reputation objective is now restructured as follows:

> Our objective is to achieve the number one quality reputation for our company in the industry. This objective will be accomplished when:
>
> 1. The number of field service calls does not exceed x percent.
> 2. The in-plant reject rate is x percent or less.
> 3. Warranty costs are less than x percent of sales.
> 4. Labor and materials cost for rework does not exceed x percent.
> 5. The company's product is rated in the first two positions at least eight out of ten times in the monthly issues of *Consumer Highlights* magazine.

Example 2: For a staff manager. The same procedure, as illustrated in the preceding example, will be now applied to a personnel manager's accountability for training and development. His mission is not to "conduct training and development programs," but to actually train a certain number of employees according to standards that will achieve certain specified results. Prior to MBO, this manager's qualitative objective probably read:

> "To formulate and conduct training programs to ensure the availability of trained personnel to meet the company's manpower requirements."

As was the case in the first example, this objective suffers from the lack of definition as to what was meant and some method of measuring whether or not it is accomplished. It moves from qualitative to quantitative status when it is restructured as follows:

> To meet manpower requirements of the company by formulating and conducting training programs that will achieve the following results:
>
> 1. A replacement has been trained and is qualified for promotion for each job at salary level 15 or above.
> 2. Three graduate mechanical engineers are capable of promotion to the senior level.
> 3. Twelve foremen have completed and achieved a grade of 80 or better in the course Basic Supervisory Techniques for Foremen.
> 4. At least four stationary engineers have completed the necessary training and have secured the license for first class.

5. Twenty clerk-typist trainees have completed typing course A and are able to type copy at the rate of at least 50 words per minute.

Here again, this example illustrates how a general, qualitative objective can be highly quantified and made into a meaningful, measurable objective. This procedure will be illustrated further with a few brief examples for other staff managers.

Credit manager. This manager's true mission is to generate increased sales by extending credit and collecting accounts receivable. Both functions can exert a significant impact on profits. If he is too strict when approving credit, he can cost the company increased sales. On the other hand, a larger amount of bad debts may result if credit is extended too loosely. He can cost the company money that it could earn from interest if collections are not made on time. Thus the conditions he must meet, to adequately perform his job, might be spelled out as follows:

The credit manager will have performed his job in a satisfactory manner when:

1. Credit limits have been established for all accounts.
2. Credit applications are approved or disapproved within two days of receipt in 98 percent of the cases.
3. Accounts receivable are collected within 30 days for 60 percent of outstanding receivables and 45 days for 38 percent of receivables.
4. Bad debts do not exceed 2 percent of sales for the year.
5. No loss of sales results from the above.

Development engineering manager. The qualitative objective for this manager usually would dwell upon his responsibility for designing and developing products and processes. His true mission is to enhance profits by the manner in which he runs his function, and his profit-contributing role is clear when spelled out as follows (many development projects require more than one year to reach fruition, and usually the objective covers more than the one-year period used in this illustration):

The manager of development engineering will have performed satisfactorily when he achieves the following results:

1. Development costs are within a plus or minus 5 percent of budget for 98 percent of projects.
2. At least three new products reach the commercial stage and each achieves the sales and returns specified by company policy.
3. A savings of at least $50,000 is realized through the improvement of present products. This saving may result from reductions in labor, materials, or equipment.
4. Move Project A to a position where a go or no-go decision may be made by September 1.

In summary, often a staff objective can be changed from a qualitative type to a quantitative one by first deciding the specific result desired and then describing the specific conditions that will have been met when management considers the requirements of the objective to have been satisfied.

MAKING OBJECTIVES SPECIFIC

Although it is desirable to quantify staff objectives as much as possible, it is not always possible or prudent to insist upon complete quantification.

In terms of being prudent, it is more worthwhile to the company to approve an objective of considerable importance even though the objective can be quantified to a lesser degree than it is to approve an objective of lesser worth that can be quantified to a greater degree. Assume, for example, a financial manager having responsibility for financial forecasting and forms control. It is more difficult to quantify an objective covering financial forecasting than one covering forms control. If the company insists upon extensive quantification, the financial manager might be prone to recommend an objective, and a highly quantified one, that provides that he will reduce the cost of printing forms by 5 percent. He doesn't recommend an objective for financial forecasting because it would be more difficult to structure.

In this example, the insistence on extensive quantification has cost the company money. The savings from not printing forms may have equaled a few hundred dollars while the loss through not pushing improved financial forecasting may have cost thousands of dollars or more. The same reasoning is applicable in the instance of a personnel manager who recommends an objective to reduce by x mills the unit cost of paper cups used in the cafeteria but doesn't recommend an objective covering a much-needed compensation plan because the latter is more difficult to quantify.

Nor is it always possible to completely quantify staff objectives. To insist upon complete quantification in those instances in which it is not possible will not result in better objectives; instead, it will result in much-wasted effort by staff managers as they try to do the impossible. As a result their faith and value in the MBO system will suffer. Like many facets of the management process, there are no clean-cut and ironclad rules as to the dividing line separating overquantification from lack of quantification. This is a matter that each organization and its managers must decide. However, there are a few proven ground rules that, when followed, will help to make any objective more specific in terms of definition and measurability.

Results not activities. Staff managers can improve their objectives appreciably by wording an objective in terms of the result they plan to achieve rather than the activities in which they will engage. It is far better to describe results, even though the result itself may not be capable of one hundred percent accuracy in definition, than to talk about activities. Examples of both are:

> *Activity:* To conduct market research studies to improve the sale of company products.
> *Result:* To select by July 1 three test markets for testing new Product B.

Who, what, and when. Another technique for making an objective more specific is to make certain it includes a clear statement of what is going to be accomplished. These are the three salient points of any delegation and should certainly be included in the objectives of an MBO system, which essentially is a system for delegating the responsibility for results through all levels of management.

Relative terms. There is a tendency, especially concerning staff objectives that cannot always be quantified completely, to lapse into the expediency of using relative terms to describe results. Words such as "adequate," "sufficient" and "reasonable" are poor substitutes for more descriptive ones; they lead to countless misunderstandings and make measuring practically impossible. Consider the word "sufficient." What does it mean? Does it mean the same to all people? Can the magnitude of results be measured? Is it a sufficient standard against which to reward or discipline a manager? Can it be used to prepare a financial plan?

All relative terms should be replaced with more precise ones even though the more precise words still may fall short of complete precision. For example, instead of using the relative word "reasonable," state the result within parameters; even wide parameters are preferable to a relative word. Examples:

> *Poor:* To achieve a reasonable improvement in the time required to prepare and distribute the monthly report of operations.
> *Better:* To reduce by 5 to 15 percent the time required to prepare and distribute the monthly report of operations.
> *Poor:* To effect as much reduction *as possible* in the cost of operating the law department.
> *Better:* To reduce the cost of operating the law department by 10 to 30 percent.
> *Poor:* To direct the quality assurance function in a manner *sufficient* to meet anticipated needs.
> *Better:* To improve product quality by recommending inspection procedures designed to detect 80 percent of substandard products.

Note that none of the alternatives listed under "better" is perfect; however, the statements are infinitely more valid as objectives than the ones that included relative terminology.

CONCLUSION

Management by objectives provides the staff manager with the vehicle and opportunity for gaining acceptance of his function and recognition of his contributions. MBO provides the opportunity only. The degree to which the manager capitalizes on this opportunity depends in large part on how adept he becomes in structuring measurable objectives. To accomplish this he must first determine what his true mission is within the organization (for what is he really accountable?) and then translate this accountability into specific, realistic, and measurable objectives that play their proper role in achieving the objectives of all other departments and the overall objectives of the organization.

22

Differences Between Staff and Line Objectives

THE ABUNDANCE of MBO literature notwithstanding, there is a definite dearth of material on the differences between writing staff objectives as contrasted to writing objectives for line managers. Most writers devote little time or attention to these distinctions and appear to proceed on the erroneous basis that if differences do exist they are so slight and exert such a small impact that they need not be considered when structuring the final objective.

Doubtless the failure to accord adequate recognition to these distinctions—and sometimes they are subtle ones—accounts in part for the difficulties often encountered by the staff manager when he sits down to write his objectives. This failure is responsible for much of the confusion and feeling of inadequacy on the part of the staff manager's superior when the latter must review and ultimately approve the subordinate's objectives. Very often this confusion results in the superior's approving staff objectives that should never see the light of day. Equally often, the final result is a group of sloppy, unrealistic, and nonmeasurable objectives that give MBO a kick in the teeth and lend additional credit to the misguided premise that measurable objectives cannot be written for staff managers.

Although objectives, if properly structured and applied, are as applicable and beneficial to staff managers as they are to their line associates, there are a number of basic differences that must be observed. Certain of these differences apply during the preparatory work leading up to writing the objective, while others concern the method and form of actually structuring the objective. The final result sought for both line and staff managers must be realistic, measurable, and profit-oriented objectives.

NUMBER OF OBJECTIVES

It is frequently necessary for the staff manager to have a greater number of objectives than the line manager. This results from the multiplicity of accountabilities for which the staff manager is responsible. For example, one can secure a fairly accurate measurement of a sales manager (line) by reviewing his performance on two objectives: the dollar revenue he generated and the amount he spent to reach the revenue figure. A measure of equal validity can be realized by reviewing a production manager (line) in light of the volume he produces and the unit cost at which the volume was produced. Both of these rather easy measurements are possible because in both instances the primary accountability of their jobs can be expressed in one or two objectives even though both line managers will usually have other objectives of a secondary nature.

This is decidedly not so with the average staff manager. Take, for example, the job of a typical financial manager who may well be responsible for major functions that include accounting, budgeting, data processing, treasury, and financial analysis. An evaluation of how well he accomplished his data processing objective would give no hint as to how well he accomplished his treasury objective. Similarly, outstanding achievement of the budgeting objective would provide no clue by itself as to what results were realized on the accounting objective. The same is true for a lawyer who may be a hotshot at settling claims but who falls down on his objective of providing labor law counsel to his fellow managers. Similar reasoning applies to a research manager who performs admirably if he were considered only on his basic research objective but not on his applied research objective.

The experience of many different organizations substantiates that the overall performance of a line manager can be measured with a fewer number of objectives.

LENGTH OF OBJECTIVES

Just as the staff manager requires a greater number of objectives to adequately measure his performance, his objectives usually require more detail and are therefore more lengthy.

Unlike a profit center manager (line) who has short, concise objectives such as (1) increase sales by 10 percent, (2) realize pretax profit of $2 million, and (3) achieve a return on investment equal to 14 percent before taxes, the staff manager must usually go into considerable detail when defining his objective in such a way that it will be measurable. Because he may not be able to make liberal use of concrete numbers, he must be as specific as possible when describing the results he is going to achieve. The staff training and development responsibility of a personnel manager will illustrate this point. He cannot merely state in his objective that it is "to conduct a development program." This would not be specific and could not be measured. Instead, he must spell out those results that will have been achieved when this objective is considered accomplished. His objective likely will read along the following lines: "My training and development objective will have been accomplished when (1) twenty clerk-typist trainees have successfully completed the beginner's typing course and are qualified for assignment, (2) five computer programmers have completed course B and have passed the practical and written examinations, and (3) a program has been formulated and recommended in final form to the president providing for the training of a qualified replacement for each manager above salary Level 14."

TIMING

Line managers participate in the annual objective-setting process from the first day; staff managers must necessarily wait until some future time. The length of time they must wait is crucial to the effectiveness of their objectives because the earlier the staff manager can begin working on his objectives, the better they will be. Since much of the staff manager's objectives will depend upon the line objectives and what is required of him to support the line, he must receive initial guidance from the line. This does not mean that the staff manager should be forced to wait until all line objectives have been discussed and approved. All line managers should give him a copy of the first draft of their objectives and a copy of each additional draft. Since objectives usually progress through two or three drafts, the staff manager is able to participate in the objective-setting process at each step. It is infinitely better than waiting until all line objectives have been approved and then springing the line objectives on the staff manager at the last minute. Usually companies that work that way have not yet brought staff into the MBO approach.

Up to this point the discussion has concerned those objectives the staff manager must structure to support line objectives. There is another broad, important subject area for staff objectives in which the staff manager can clearly take the initiative without waiting for any cue from the line. This category includes those objectives the staff manager should structure to improve his effectiveness within his own department—objectives that require no coordination with line operations. Examples are the treasurer who recommends an objective to increase the yield from 5 to 6 percent on funds available for investing, and the industrial engineer with an objective of reducing his manpower costs by 5 percent on certain recurrent projects. Each staff manager has these "personal" objectives, which he can and should pursue enthusiastically.

PROJECT-ORIENTED

As contrasted to many line objectives that tend to be broad and all encompassing (for example, a profit objective that requires the manager to coordinate and bring together all the components that contribute to profits), the objectives for staff managers frequently are project-oriented; that is, they deal with a narrower, specific action. This has been found to be especially true with research and engineering managers and with other technically oriented staff jobs.

Project orientation leads to another difference with staff objectives: the target periods for accomplishing the objectives are shorter than for line objectives. The experience of Scully-Jones and Co., manufacturers of tool holders, is a good example. This company approves a schedule of proposed starting and completion dates for each of its design and engineering managers. Research and development performance has been redefined in terms of personalized, short-term goals. The company reports that the change has brought about improved work quality and that completion dates of projects have become more realistic.* Similar experience has been echoed by research, design, engineering, and development managers in roughly 50 companies.

Examples of project-oriented objectives with short target periods are:

Determine appropriate procedures for measuring chemical changes to fiber surfaces by October 1.

Complete bill of material for major project "A" on July 1 and then release to production.

Complete physical reorganization of laboratory by August 15.

Maneuver project D to a make-or-break decision by October 1.

Reduce frozen assets to $100,000 by June 15.

Reduce tardiness rate to 3 percent by April 1.

* *The Manager's Letter*, AMACOM, May 20, 1967.

STRUCTURING

The staff manager's objectives must be structured in a manner that will ensure that his total performance is evaluated.

To illustrate, let's select the job of a purchasing manager whose major responsibilities include procurement, value analysis, warehousing, vendor relations, sales of surplus, and direction of purchasing department. One of the principles for writing objectives is that they should address themselves only to priority matters, not routine ones. In this particular case it is assumed that the purchasing director, after analyzing priorities, recommended and secured approval for four major objectives: procurement, warehousing, sales of surplus, and value analysis. He did not recommend objectives relating to direction of his department and vendor relations, both of which are important functions. As these latter two functions do not appear on his list of objectives, he probably won't be measured on them during the year or at the end of the year unless some major problem develops. This undesirable condition would be even worse if a manager in charge of nine major functions had only three objectives; only one-third of his accountability would be reflected by his objectives. How, then, can the manager's performance be measured with respect to those functions for which no objectives have been written?

One obvious answer is to require the manager to have at least one objective for each major function for which he is accountable. This alternative has definite disadvantages. First, requiring an objective for each function results in a set of objectives in which priorities range from very high to none. If this method were practiced by all managers in an organization, such a long, hodgepodge collection might well detract management attention from its high-priority, bread-and-butter objectives.

Second, the longer the list of objectives, the more time and administrative routine required to police and administer them. Each time an objective is approved, a measure must be determined and a feedback technique established to monitor it; thus the paperwork costs have begun. While there is no magic number of objectives, apparently the fewer the better.

The second alternative is to write objectives for priority matters and to adopt a simple technique for keeping track of other functions. A number of companies set up a secondary list of measuring indexes—labeled "standards of performance" or "performance indicators"—which are easily administered. The manager writes objectives covering his priority matters and lists the other segments of his responsibility as standards of performance. For example, if a purchasing director is required to place all orders within three days after receiving a purchase requisition, this would become a standard of performance, not an objective. Similarly, a financial manager's standard of performance might be to distribute a certain accounting report within five days after the close of an accounting period.

The number of standards of performance usually ranges from six to ten depending upon the breadth of responsibility of the job and the amount of control the company considers necessary.

INTERIM REVIEWS

Almost all well-run MBO programs provide for interim reviews, at least quarterly, of the manager's progress. Most of the major objectives of line managers (for example, revenue figures, production volume, unit costs, sales costs) are broken down in the budget by months and quarters. Thus when the time arrives for a quarterly review, these breakdowns clearly show where the line manager should stand at that point if he has met his objectives to date. This is not true for the objectives of staff managers. Usually there are no natural breaking points, so these must be provided for by the staff manager in structuring his objectives.

Take, for example, an industrial engineer whose objective for the year requires him to lay out a complete plant. If this objective is not broken down into the particular segments he must accomplish by the end of each quarter, management must wait a full year in order to accurately judge his achievement. Under an effective MOB system the annual objective of this manager would be divided into segments as follows:

Layout of Department A
Complete by April 1
Layout of Department B
Complete by July 1
Layout of Department C
Complete by October 1
Layout of Department D
Complete by November 1
Layout of Department E
Complete by December 31

TWO BOSSES

All enlightened managers would frown on a person's having more than one superior, yet the staff manager often must serve two masters. One of his bosses is the person to whom he reports; the other is the manager to whom he must provide service or advice and counsel.

The research manager in charge of both basic and applied research finds himself in this unenviable position. On the one hand, he is responsible almost solely to his immediate superior for the basic research part of his job while, on the other hand, he may be servicing several other managers to fulfill his responsibility for applied research. Thus he must structure his applied research objectives in such a fashion that he can secure the concurrence of both his fellow managers and his immediate superior. This task can be very difficult, especially if his boss is not in sympathy with or knowledgeable of the applied research needs of the other managers. The line manager's job in this regard is usually much less trying, as he must please one boss and usually on a narrower range of subject matter.

COMMUNICATIONS

The very meaning of "line and staff" would imply differences in communications for the staff manager. "Line" refers to the way in which orders flow down the line (to and through line managers), while reports and recommendations flow up the line (through and to line managers). It is almost an axiom that line managers must be kept informed in view of their direct relationship to the primary functions of the company and its mission. For example, it would be rare if the marketing department were not informed of some production problem bearing on production's ability to fill orders or for production not to be quickly apprised of a cutback in planned sales and orders.

Unfortunately, the same cannot always be said when it comes to staff departments. Often they are not informed of these major changes or, if they are informed, often get the word later. This does violence to the MBO approach, requiring as it does that the efforts (objectives) of all managers—both line and staff—be closely aligned and meshed to achieve the overall corporate objectives. A concerted effort is required by all managers in the organization to ensure that staff managers are continually informed on all matters about which they need to know. When communication weaknesses do occur, the staff manager should take the initiative in bringing them to light.

CHANGING OBJECTIVES

Under a successful MBO system objectives should be changed from one target period to the next, not necessarily in subject matter but in the degree or form of the task. This criterion helps ensure that objectives change in keeping with the changing priorities of the company and that various programs are terminated promptly once the need for them has been satisfied. It is especially applicable to staff objectives because the need for changes is much less obvious than is the case with line.

For example, when a company changes its profit target from one million dollars in 1976 to one and a half million dollars in 1977, it is apparent that line objectives dealing with sales revenue and production volume and costs must change to meet the revised overall objective. The need for change is not so apparent for staff objectives dealing with subjects like training, safety, community relations, and vendor relations. Often, there is a tendency to continue these programs in a rather routine manner without examining them for possible changes precipitated by changes in the profit objective. In all cases where the staff manager recommends the same objective from one target period to the next, he should clearly indicate that it is the same objective and be required to explain why it continues to be applicable.

DELIBERATION REQUIRED

Perhaps the greatest difference between writing staff objectives and line objectives is the extent of the deliberation required on the part of staff to zero in on meaningful objectives, especially to determine the subject matter of the objectives. Much of the staff manager's deliberation requires his trying to determine the real reason why he and his job exist in the first place. A financial manager isn't there merely to keep books. He's there to contribute to profit or some other objective, such as reducing the amount of time required to place feedback reports in the hands of other managers to aid them in making better, faster decisions. Similarly, a purchasing manager isn't retained merely to buy the materials required to run the business; he's there to make a profit contribution, such as getting the best quality materials and the best vendor service at the lowest possible price. An industrial engineer shouldn't be accountable for conducting efficiency studies; he should be strictly accountable for effecting certain cost reductions or achieving other tangible results.

It is this mental wrestling on the part of the staff manager that is necessary to determine his real mission and then translate it into specific objectives, which require added deliberation. Contrast this with the more self-explanatory and easily discernible mission of the line manager. It is rather obvious that the sales manager is there to sell and the production manager is there to produce. Thus while the job title itself will usually suggest the subject matter of objectives for line managers, this is decidedly not true for the staff manager. He first must probe, discuss with other managers, and then decide the subject matter.

AUTHORITY TO ACT

The staff manager is often plagued by a lack of knowledge with respect to what authority he may have to carry out an objective he has recommended. This matter is usually spelled out in considerable detail for the line manager. The lack of clearcut authority is especially troublesome to the staff manager in light of the "two bosses" situation discussed previously. I suggest most strongly that if there is any confusion whatever in the staff manager's mind about his authority, he endeavor to resolve it before his objective is approved. At the very minimum, he should include as an adjunct to the objective a statement of the authority he believes he has or will require to accomplish it. In writing attainable objectives the person responsible *must* have the proper authority and control over the objectives. Otherwise, he may well fail to attain them because of matters outside his control.

CONCLUSION

Objectives and the whole management by objectives system are as applicable to the staff manager as they are to the line manager. Staff managers can and should be included in the objective-setting process both for the benefit and progress of the individual manager and for his company as a whole. The staff manager who would make his maximum contribution should:

1. First appreciate and understand the differences required to structure staff objectives as opposed to line objectives.

2. Determine the subject area of his objectives for the particular target period.

3. Structure realistic, measurable, and attainable objectives.

4. Secure confirmation of his accountability and authority.

23

Performance Evaluation

PROBABLY one of the better statements attesting to the importance of performance evaluation or appraisal to the MBO system was provided by management consultant Arch Patton when he said:

> When we talk about "appraising the manager's performance," we are really discussing the management of the enterprise: setting corporate objectives, allocating responsibility for their accomplishment, assessing relative individual attainment of these goals, and rewarding or penalizing executives in these terms. If even one link in the chain is weak, the entire process suffers. This is particularly true where individual performance appraisal is concerned, for people and their efforts make the difference between outstanding and poor corporate performance around the world.*

The wisdom of Patton's comments becomes clear when we look at several of the reasons for measuring or evaluating managerial performance:

As a means for motivating the achievement-oriented manager;

As the basis for rewards (salary increases, incentive compensation, service awards, time off, and promotions);

As the basis for discipline (static job status, demotion, discharge);

As a guide for individualized training and development requirements.

Even a casual review will reveal that these reasons go straight to the heart of what makes a successful management group. They are the make-or-break aspects of an organization's progress.

---

* "Does Performance Appraisal Work?" *Business Horizons*, February 1973, pp. 83–91.

Note: This chapter has been adapted in part from the author's book *MBO for Nonprofit Organizations*, AMACOM, 1975, pp. 74–81.

Assuming that the importance of these matters has been correctly gauged—and I suggest that most top managers would agree with the ranking—it would seem that a company would settle for no less than the best possible evaluation approach.

DEFECTS IN THE EVALUATION PROCESS

There are several reasons why the evaluation approach of many companies is not the best available. First, much of the difficulty results from the traditional approach to have all of us attempt to qualify ourselves as pseudo-psychologists and sociologists when we evaluate our subordinates. Instead of insisting that we evaluate our subordinate managers on the basis of the concrete results they achieve (or fail to achieve) the personality-oriented traditionalists would have us rate our people on such nebulous—and almost irrelevant—factors as how well they get along with their people and the status of their health. While trite, the way a person parts his hair probably continues to be a key evaluation factor in more organizations than we would care to admit.

Another defect in the process is that we often attempt to measure performance without first determining how and what we are measuring; that is, we try to measure without having first established a standard against which the measuring will take place. Expressed another way, if we are to measure a manager's effectiveness, we must first decide and agree on some definition of "effectiveness." For example, one of the factors most commonly found on managerial appraisal forms is: "Degree to which the manager is cost-conscious." There is no way in the world a manager could be evaluated on this factor unless his superior had first determined that for the manager's particular job, for the particular evaluation period, under the particular circumstances that prevailed, the spending of x amount of money was an acceptable standard for a cost-conscious manager.

A third obstacle to effective evaluation is trying to compensate for the inadequacies of the evaluation process by making it replete with long, complicated recording forms and high-sounding words and requiring an excessive amount of time and effort for the superior to rate the subordinate. The watchword of this school would appear to be: Make it big, pretentious, and time-consuming, and it will at least sound effective.

Another problem, and this one should be labeled "Myth Number 4," is the much-advocated, but meaningless theory that the evaluation process should be used solely for development purposes and never, but never, should rewards such as salary increases be connected with the process. Who do we think we're kidding? When we evaluate a manager and discuss his evaluation with him, it is patently ridiculous and actually dangerous to purposely ignore the question always uppermost in his mind; namely, "Yeah! I hear you boss, but what does it mean to my paycheck?"

As managers we make the biggest mistake when we base the future of both the organization and its managers on any evaluation process that isn't the best and most accurate we can make it. When we use an inadequate measuring device, chances are we are rewarding the undeserving, failing to recognize the real performers, and as a result not giving our organizations the value to which they are entitled from our stewardship.

IMPROVING THE EVALUATION PROCESS

Fortunately, there's nothing magic or complicated about correcting the problems. Basically, we need to adopt an approach to evaluating managers that is based on (1) acceptance that managers must be measured on the results they actually achieve, not on what they say they will do, not on the amount of time and effort they expend, and certainly not on their ability to win a popularity contest; (2) establishment of standards (key results and objectives) against which performance will be measured; and (3) actual measurement of results achieved against the standards and linking of rewards, discipline, and other personnel actions to the level of performance indicated by the measurement.

The performance of all managers must be measured, and it must be measured in a highly sophisticated manner that ensures accuracy and equity. Organization health depends upon it. How then, can this be accomplished?

MEASURING BY OBJECTIVES

This approach provides that each manager will have an approved set of objectives that he is responsible for accomplishing during the measuring, or target, period. Most commonly, these objectives are set and reviewed on an annual basis. They constitute the manager's concrete job description and statement of accountability for the period under consideration.

There is little doubt that the better method for setting objectives is the one in which the objectives are drafted and recommended by the individual managers and then approved by their superiors. Once approved they become (1) the manager's directive of required action and (2) the standards against which he will be measured—and rewarded or removed.

SPECIFIC OBJECTIVES A MUST

The word "standard" implies preciseness or a specific nature. Hence if objectives are to serve their intended purpose, the importance of making them specific cannot be overemphasized. If they are general or nebulous, they fail as a standard and effective measuring becomes impossible. An example will illustrate this point.

Assume that both a division head and his department head were shortsighted enough to set an objective that reads: "The division manager's objective is to make a substantial improvement in the efficiency of his department during 1977." This alleged objective is subject to so many interpretations and misunderstandings that there is no way to evaluate when or if it has been reached. Contrast that objective with one that reads: "Reduce the cost of operating his division during 1977 by $100,000 without eliminating any of the 12 major services currently provided."

THE RATING PROCESS

Once the commitment has been made to measure by results, the actual rating process becomes both more accurate and more meaningful, and the entire process is facilitated. The only form needed is simple, usually one page long, which is vertically divided in half. At the beginning of the measuring period (for example, January 1 for the year 1977), the left side of the form contains a list of the specific objectives the manager must accomplish during the measuring period. Both the subordinate and the superior are thoroughly familiar with these objectives, and both agree as to the specific meaning of the objectives. Figure 23 is a results-oriented evaluation form.

At the end of the measuring period (for example, December 31 for the year 1977), the superior moves to the right side of the page, and opposite each objective writes in the results that were actually achieved by the manager during the measuring period.

Once the form has been completed, the manager's performance becomes obvious and few mental gymnastics are necessary to determine how effective he was. The left side of the form says, "Here's what he should have done." The right side says, "Here's what he did." This, then, becomes the basis for discussion with the manager.

The discussion with the manager who has been rated this way will be dramatically different from interviews based on traditional appraisals. Instead of not knowing what to expect, chances are the manager will know almost exactly how he has performed before the boss even opens his mouth. After all, the manager knows exactly what was expected of him and certainly has been keeping track of his own progress toward those objectives.

Thus the appraisal interview has become job-centered rather than personality-oriented. Instead of wasting time sparring with each other over immaterial factors, both superior and subordinate can get right down to brass tacks and constructively discuss the results and ways to improve them. Neither the boss nor the manager is ill at ease because they do not have to discuss personalities and nebulous factors that almost always prevailed with traditional measuring. A few simple, easily applied checks can quickly tell an organization how effective its evaluation process is. Those organizations that rank low on the audit would be well advised to get their measuring house in order. The most important of these checkpoints include:

Extent of use. Once completed, what are the ratings used for? Are they merely filed, or are they constantly referred to for the purposes mentioned earlier?

Orientation. Do the ratings concentrate on measuring results actually achieved, or are they oriented to personality factors that bear little resemblance to the results for which the manager is being held accountable?

Length of recording form. While the number of uses to which the rating is put will exert an impact on the length of the rating form, it is questionable whether any results-oriented rating form need consume

Figure 23. Results-oriented evaluation form.

| Objectives | Measure | Results Achieved | | | |
| | | Quarters* | | | Total Year |
		1st	2nd	3rd	
1. Improve by 10 percent number of qualified applicants referred for job openings.	1. At least three qualified candidates referred for each job opening.	T	O	T	Achieved in 97 percent of cases.
2. Increase by 15 percent number of qualified welders during 1977.	2. Number of persons completing basic welding course #5.	O	T	T	17 completed course.

*Codes facilitating management by exception: T = On target. No action necessary
O = Off target. Action necessary

Figure 24. Comparison of "traditional" and MBO appraisal methods.

	Traditional	MBO
Frequency	Usually annually (if at all).	Usually quarterly.
Emphasis	Traits.	Results vs. objectives.
Subordinate's frame of mind	Mental block (doesn't know how "traits" will be evaluated).	More positive (feedback has told him how well he's doing).
Suggestions for improvement	Poor receptivity (much has been based on his traits).	More positive (much has been based on his job performance).
Tie-in to rewards	Rewards usually not directly tied in.	Rewards are usually tied directly to results.
Summary	Little connection to results.	Results-oriented.

more space than the front and back of one piece of paper. Longer forms should be reviewed to make certain that quantity isn't being substituted for quality.

Specific versus general. It is mandatory that all ratings be completed in language that is as specific as possible. All ratings should describe specific accomplishments, not hopes, aspirations, and effort expended.

Connection with rewards. Does the management group have the conviction that the good and bad things they will receive from management life are determined primarily by the evaluation process, which in turn reflects the positive results they contribute or fail to contribute to the progress of the enterprise? If not, it's doubtful that the best performers will ever really appreciate the merits of the measuring process.

Correlation with reality. The acid test of all measuring processes must be the degree to which the ratings jibe both with the results managers achieve and with the competence of managers. If, in actual practice, the glowing words on a rating form are not matched by a manager's real performance, the measuring process is inadequate. Ratings must do more than indicate that 90 percent of the managers are warmhearted and true-blue.

TRADITIONAL VERSUS MBO APPROACH

Figure 24 compares the major difference between traditional performance evaluation and the MBO approach. Note several significant differences, chiefly the frequency of the reviews and the move away from orienting to the person and personalities to a job-centered orientation that emphasizes results.

QUARTERLY VERSUS ANNUAL EVALUATIONS

Figure 25 shows the major advantages of quarterly reviews during the target period. Two major changes in emphasis will be evident. First, the time orientation has moved from a past one to a future one. Second, the whole review takes on a more positive, motivating approach.

PURPOSES OF INTERIM EVALUATIONS

Interim evaluations and dialog between the superior and subordinate contribute to increased managerial effectiveness in several ways, if the content of these reviews includes these points:

1. Review progress against objectives.
2. Take corrective action on problems and variances at the earliest possible time.
3. Review remainder of the target period for realism.
4. Revise objectives and plans and resource allocations as necessary to preserve realism.
5. Evaluate authority to determine whether it is sufficient.
6. Discuss what the boss should be doing to help but isn't doing.
7. Discuss what the boss is doing but shouldn't be doing.

Figure 25. Advantages of quarterly reviews during target period.

ANNUAL APPRAISAL AND INTERVIEW	
Emphasis	*Disadvantages*
Past year's performance	Emphasis is on past; nothing can be done about it. Oriented more to a chewing out. Discourages dialog. Provides limited opportunity for boss to help subordinates.

QUARTERLY APPRAISAL AND INTERVIEW	
Emphasis	*Advantages*
Past quarter's performance and plan for future quarters	Emphasis is on the future; something can be done about it. Oriented more to a positive planning and review session. Encourages dialog. Enhances opportunity for boss to help subordinates.

EFFICIENCY VERSUS EFFECTIVENESS

The words *efficiency* and *effectiveness* are often used interchangeably; this is a mistake when it comes to evaluating performance. They mean two completely different things; for example:

> *Effectiveness:* Were the objectives achieved?
> *Example:* Was the 12 percent sales increase or the 5 percent cost-improvement objective met?

> *Efficiency:* How were the objectives achieved?
> *Examples:* Did the manager follow acceptable management practices and policies? Did he plan or "luck" his way into achieving the objectives? Did he make the best use of his resources? Were his actions consistent with the longer-term health of the entity?

Although considerable emphasis must be given to the results actually achieved, we cannot completely ignore the means used. For example, it is entirely possible over the short range for a production foreman to achieve spectacular results by browbeating his employees to the point of exhaustion. Clearly, over the longer term this would be disastrous. A sales manager could achieve his annual sales volume objective by convincing customers to build up large inventories of the product. But sales would suffer next year when customers sold from their ample inventories instead of reordering.

Balancing effectiveness and efficiency is one of the toughest jobs a manager will face in the evaluation process. If he errs on the side of efficiency, he may be substituting subjective evaluation relating to method for the more objective evaluation of results achieved.

An in-depth treatment of this subject is provided by Harold Koontz, noted author on manager subjects, in his book *Appraising Managers as Managers.* *

A WORD OF CAUTION

I recently listened to a speech by a well-known management theorist who advocated bringing MBO into a company "through the back door" by installing MBO initially for performance appraisal. Hopefully, not too many of his listeners heeded his counsel because he, probably unwittingly, was leading them into one of the more serious pitfalls in MBO. MBO should

* New York: McGraw-Hill, 1971.

never overemphasize performance evaluation. This is negative! The paramount thrust of MBO should be to provide the manager with an aid for increasing his effectiveness and thus optimizing his results. This is positive!

The natural result of placing too much emphasis on evaluation are comments (spoken or unspoken) from subordinates, such as: "The boss isn't being honest with me. He says that MBO is a total system of managing to help me achieve better results. However, in practice he's utilizing MBO only to get me to set standards on my performance so he can hang me when I don't meet them."

When implementing MBO it is usually better if results-oriented evaluations aren't formally introduced until two or three years have passed. This helps keep positive emphasize on the system as a way of managing rather than having it generate distrust and fear because the manager is worrying about being evaluated while he is learning how to apply the system.

24

Compensating Managers for Results

PARABLE: Once upon a time there was a dumb jackass standing knee-deep in a field of carrots contentedly munching away. A wise farmer wanted the jackass to pull a loaded wagon to another field but the jackass would not walk over to the wagon. So the wise farmer stood by the wagon and held up a bunch of carrots for the dumb jackass to see. But the dumb jackass continued to contentedly munch away on his own carrots.

MORAL OF STORY: *Jackasses do not work for carrots.*

UNDERLYING the approach to managerial compensation followed by many companies is the implicit assumption that well-educated managers usually can be coaxed into doing that which even the dumb jackass will not do. But the majority of managers cannot be coaxed. This observation has led to the frequently espoused premise that managers do not work for money. The premise should be expanded to provide that managers do not work for money *when the jackass effect is inherent in a compensation plan.*

The jackass effect is present in any compensation plan when the plan is not formulated and administered in a manner that preserves and furthers the only two objectives of meaningful compensation. These objec-

Note: This chapter has been adapted from the author's article "The 'Jackass Effect' in Management Compensation," *Business Horizons*, June 1974.

tives are, first, to promote and attain equity and, second, to motivate for better performance.

Equity is attained when a manager's compensation is based on the results he has achieved and is related to a comparison of these results with the results achieved by all other managers in his organization. The motivation objective requires that the manager be convinced that extra effort and achievement on his part will result in extra compensation. He must believe that his efforts will be recognized and rewarded. The manager must know this in advance of expending the efforts—not after he takes the action.

THE JACKASS EFFECT IN PRACTICE

The jackass effect commonly assumes five forms in actual practice:

Compensation is on the wrong end of the action.

The manager's accountability is so nebulous that his performance cannot be measured.

An ineffective evaluation method is used.

The compensation plan acts to level all managers into a group rather than to recognize variances in individual performance.

Compensation is separated from performance.

The Wrong End

Too often, compensation plans are formulated in a manner that causes a manager to take some action and, after the action is completed, someone determines how much the manager should be paid for the action. In this approach, compensation is treated almost solely as something that follows the action. It is not unlike an owner who tells a contractor to build a house and, after the house is completed, the owner tells the builder how much he will be paid.

Compensation cannot act as a motivating force unless its future impact is well known *prior* to the action. This prior knowledge, which the manager must carry with him while he is accomplishing the action, is the key to motivating him to better performance.

An excellent example of having compensation on the wrong end of the action is a large Eastern food company. It has a "discretionary bonus" plan for its managers. Practice indicates that the word "discretionary" is used advisedly. At the end of each year, the president and a few of his advisers sit down and determine which of the managers will receive a bonus and how large each payment will be. There are no established eligibility criteria to decide which managers will receive payments, and there is no formula for determining how much each of the lucky ones will receive.

Surprises abound when payments are doled out each year. Managers are surprised at their selections, and the amount each receives is a surprise. The company's plan could be aptly labeled "The Surprise Approach to Compensation." Managers cannot be motivated when they have no advance knowledge of who will receive payments or on what basis the payments are calculated.

MEASUREMENT AND MEASURING TOOL

Only one valid basis for rewarding managers exists—the quality of their performance. The jackass effect exacts its toll when accountability is delegated in a way that performance cannot be measured and when the measuring tool (managerial appraisal or evaluation) is not geared for judging the actual results.

Measurable accountability is not estabished when the traditional job description is used to delegate the accountability. Traditionally, rather feeble attempts were made to assign this accountability in the form of a job description. Too often, however, job descriptions were overly general statements of activities that the managers should pursue. No emphasis was given to the specific results the managers should achieve. Usually, the descriptions required the managers to keep busy without specifying the end results of all the effort. Thus the managers' accomplishments could not be measured with any degree of accuracy because there was no measuring scale.

Figure 26 provides an excellent illustration of a commonly used performance evaluation form that does not measure how well accountability has been carried out. It records only the superior's perception of the degree to which the subordinate possesses the personality traits listed on the form. There is no correlation with the actual results achieved and thus no basis for determining what compensation the manager should receive. This approach is usually adopted as a last resort when no measurable accountability has been fixed and there is nothing tangible to measure.

The Great Leveler

PARABLE: Once upon a time there were six jackasses hitched to a wagon pulling a heavy load up a long steep hill. Two of the jackasses were not achievement-oriented and decided to coast along and let the others do most of the pulling. Two others were relatively young and

Figure 26. Example of traditional performance evaluation form.

Factor	Excellent	Above Average	Average	Below Average	Poor
Degree of cost-consciousness		X			
Grasp of function	X				
Initiative		X			
Decision-making ability	X				
Application	X				
Judgment		X			
Health	X				
Appearance	X				
Loyalty	X				
Gets along with people		X			
Develops subordinates			X		
Work habits		X			
Contribution to company's progress	X				
Potential for advancement		X			

Rated by

Reviewed by

inexperienced, and had a difficult time pulling their share. One of the remaining two suffered from a slight hangover from consuming fermented barley the evening before. The sixth jackass did most of the work.

The wagon arrived at the top of the hill. The driver got down from his seat, patted each of the jackasses on the head, and gave six carrots to each. Prior to the next hill climb, the sixth jackass ran away.

MORAL OF THE STORY. *Never be the sixth jackass if everybody gets six carrots.*

John Jones and Bill Smith are plant managers in the same company and each is currently earning $14,000 a year. The worth of their jobs has been evaluated by commonly accepted job evaluation techniques. The evaluations reveal that the two jobs are practically identical and, therefore, the following salary ranges have been established for both:

Salary Increase Schedule

Minimum	$12,000
Step 1	12,800
Step 2	13,700
Step 3	14,600
Step 4	15,600
Maximum	16,600

What happens under this plan if Jones contributes ten times as much as Smith during a particular year? What is the maximum increase in salary the outstanding producer can be granted over that of the other manager? Clearly, the maximum increase is $2,600 (the difference between their present salaries and the maximum of the range). In actual practice it would be even less, probably $1,600 (the difference between Jones's present salary and Step 4). Thus for making ten times the contribution of his counterpart, Jones receives only a routine merit increase. Such a small salary increase would not be equitable to the high-performance manager, nor would it motivate him to continue his high performance.

Another problem resulting from utilizing only straight salaries is that every salary increase becomes a fixed cost and the manager will continue to receive it in the future regardless of the level of performance he maintains. To illustrate this point, take the above case in which the manager receives a salary increase of $1,600 for his outstanding performance. What happens next year when the manager's performance is only average? Usually, it is not advisable to reduce the salary of a manager. Thus he will carry into future years a salary payment that he earned for his performance for only one year.

Obviously, the typical straight-salary plan is not sufficiently dynamic and flexible to accommodate the differing circumstances that can and should exist in a management group. About the only way to achieve any flexibility in a straight-salary plan—to recognize varying performance levels—is to vary the amount and/or frequency of salary increases. Even this small amount of flexibility is not fully utilized by many organizations. As a result, it is usually advisable to add an incentive compensation plan to the salary plan. Incentive plans are discussed later.

COMPENSATION SEPARATED FROM PERFORMANCE

PARABLE: It came to pass that high unemployment among jackasses was visited upon the land, and the sixth jackass returned to climb the hill again. The hill was climbed and the driver said to the sixth jackass, "Let's sit down and discuss your performance. We'll have an appraisal interview on how well you climbed the hill."

The sixth jackass wondered where his carrots were. Noting the puzzled, eager look on the sixth jackass's face, the driver explained that
the purpose of the appraisal interview was to improve hill climbing.
The carrots would be discussed at some time in the future. The sixth
jackass ran away again.

MORAL OF THE STORY: *Never be the sixth jackass when it is not certain there is food at the top of the hill.*

For years, the traditionalists have advocated that superior–subordinate discussions about the subordinate's performance should be clearly
separated from any discussion concerning how much compensation the
subordinate will receive for his performance.

The premise frequently advanced in favor of making the separation is
that the injection of an emotional issue like compensation into a discussion
on management development would cause the less attractive subject of
development to be neglected. In principle, the argument sounds plau-
sible. As a practical matter, however, it has yet to be demonstrated that
the manager is able to forget compensation when his performance is being
discussed. On the other hand, it has been repeatedly demonstrated that,
no matter what is said during the performance interview, the manager is
saying to himself, "Yeah, boss, I hear you talking, but what does it mean
to my paycheck?"

Thus attempts to omit the subject of compensation often have an effect the opposite of that intended. The deliberate skirting of the subject of
compensation causes it to be spotlighted in the manager's mind; frustration and a lack of trust often result.

OVERCOMING THE JACKASS EFFECT

Major policy changes and decisions are necessary in most organizations if
the jackass effect is to be overcome and if equity and motivation are to be
built into managerial compensation. The magnitude and impact of these
changes will bear a high degree of correlation with the extent to which the
organization is mismanaging its compensation program.

Equitable compensation that truly motivates better managerial performance requires an integrated "building block" approach in which each
of the following components, or blocks, is present in the right balance:

The establishment of clear-cut, measurable accountability.

The use of a measuring system (appraisal or evaluation) which effectively determines how well the accountability has been carried out.

The adoption of a dynamic compensation plan that recognizes wide swings in managerial performance.

The establishment of the greatest possible direct tie between performance and rewards.

The words "integrated" and "balance" are used advisedly because compensation must be practiced as a system of interrelated parts. Too often, compensation has been looked upon in the very narrow sense as comprising only the monetary payments; the other necessary components have been omitted or slighted. Effective compensation requires a broader perspective which views compensation as outlined above.

If one or more of these components of the integrated system fail to play their proper roles, the system is damaged—equitable. motivational compensation will suffer. For example, if measurable accountability has been established but the evaluation or appraisal methods are not sufficiently reliable to measure specific achievement against the accountability, there is no basis for rewarding the manager. Similarly, it is not possible to evaluate achievement unless measurable accountability has first been established.

Clear-Cut Accountability

The only true basis for compensating a manager is to first assign him accountability for achieving specific results. His accountability must be expressed in specific terms that can be measured later to determine how much and how well he accomplished his tasks.

The more effective compensation systems require that accountability be spelled out in the form of specific, measurable objectives that the manager must achieve during a particular target period. The following are specific, measurable objectives for a general manager of an operating division for a particular year:

Achieve pretax profit of $5 million.
Achieve sales of $60 million.
Achieve a return on investment of 12 percent.
Reduce average monthly inventory by 11 percent.
Complete phase 2 of management development program.

In this example, the vague, general nature of accountability has been avoided. Instead, the division manager's accountability is now expressed in specific, clear-cut terms that can be measured and used as the basis for meaningful compensation. These objectives will be used later to illustrate how the remaining parts of the compensation system are carried out.

Measuring Performance

Once clear-cut accountability has been established, the next step is to measure the extent to which the accountability was achieved—to evaluate managerial performance. Here again, the traditionalists failed to consider the system's nature of compensation. Because the accountability was vague and general, the traditionalists did not (and could not) follow a results-oriented approach to measuring; instead, they fell back on evaluating the manager on the basis of effort expended. The traditional approach usually took the form of the previously described evaluation procedure, which emphasized personality traits. Obviously, it all but completely ignored examination of the critical question of what specific accountability was delegated to the manager. This approach to evaluating performance must be eliminated if effective compensation is to be achieved.

Table 1. Results-oriented performance evaluation.

Objectives (At beginning of year)	Results (At end of year)
Achieve pretax profit of $5 million.	$6 million
Achieve sales of $60 million.	$65 million
Achieve return on investment of 12 percent.	13 percent
Reduce average monthly inventory by 11 percent.	11 percent
Complete phase 2 of management development program.	Completed

Table 1 is a good example of results-oriented evaluation. The evaluation incorporates specific, measurable objectives for the division manager. In this approach, the manager's performance is measured against each of the objectives for which he was accountable during the preceding year. The culmination of this matching of performance against objectives serves as the basis for determining how much compensation he should receive. This approach is consistent with one of the cardinal rules of performance evaluation—that performance appraisal must be sufficiently valid so that the results may be used for compensation purposes.

Rewarding Performance

Now that accountability has been established and performance on that accountability has been measured, the next step in the integrated system is to reward the performance in a way that promotes both equity and motivation.

While the importance of certain parts of a total compensation package such as stock options and pensions should not be minimized, they are not treated here because they are not directly related to individual performance. That is, the value of a stock option is not dependent upon individual performance but upon how the investing public prices the stock, and all managers share equally in pension benefits. Two forms of compensation can and should be tied directly to individual managerial performance: salary and incentive payments.

Normally, direct compensation that is limited to salary payments is not sufficiently flexible and dynamic to recognize the wide swings or differences in performance among a group of managers. The cases of John Jones and Bill Smith, the two plant managers described earlier in this article, are vivid testimony to this premise.

Equity and motivation can best be served by utilizing both salary payments (fixed compensation) and incentive payments (variable compensation). With this approach, these direct payments can be viewed as resulting from two sources: salary payments and incentive payments.

Salary payments are rates paid for "holding down the job." The manager will always receive his salary, regardless of whether or not he receives incentive payments. The approaches and techniques for establishing salary rates are too well known to dwell upon here. It will suffice to say that an enlightened compensation policy should provide for the payment of salaries based on the going rate for a particular managerial job based on a national average for that job. The rate should be examined at least annually to ensure that it remains current.

Incentive payments are made, in addition to salary, on the basis of how well a job is accomplished. Because incentive payments are a variable form of compensation and are paid according to how well the manager performs, they provide the greatest possible opportunity to recognize any level of performance that the manager achieves (or fails to achieve). They permit compensation to be tied directly to performance on an individual basis.

If the manager's performance is below par, he receives no incentive payment—only his salary. If his performance exceeds par (his objectives), he receives above-par incentive payments. For a year in which his performance was outstanding, he will receive commensurate incentive payments. All incentive payments are truly variable and based upon his varying levels of performance. Following is an illustration of how the division general manager discussed earlier would be normally paid under an incentive plan.

The weighting problem. The first requirement is to establish the relative weight of each of the manager's objectives *prior* to the target year in which he is to carry out the objectives. Prior weighting of the objectives is critical; only by making known the future impact of compensation prior to the action can compensation exert an influence on the action as it occurs. The objectives of the division general manager might be weighted as shown in Table 2.

Table 2. Applying point weights to objectives.

Objectives	Possible points
Achieve pretax profit of $5 million.	50–100
Achieve sales of $60 million.	30–80
Achieve return on investment of 12 percent.	40–60
Reduce average monthly inventory by 11 percent.	20–40
Complete phase 2 of management development program.	10–20

The importance of weighting objectives cannot be overemphasized, nor should the difficulty be minimized. It is one of the more difficult chores in formulating an incentive compensation plan, one that has caused many organizations to avoid using incentive compensation in favor of less effective but easier-to-develop compensation approaches. One of management's top-level responsibilities is to solve problems, not walk away from them.

An an illustration, how should the manager in the simplified example in Table 2 be evaluated and rewarded if he overachieves his profit objective? Or if he overachieves both his sales and profit objectives but fails to meet his objective for return on investment (ROI)? Or if he achieves all three objectives covering sales, profit, and ROI, but is able to do so because he completely neglected his inventory reduction and management development objectives?

Obviously, the compensation policy and plan must provide for evaluating the manager on his overall performance on both quantitative factors (effectiveness—were the objectives accomplished?) and qualitative factors (efficiency—how well were the objectives accomplished?). It would be self-defeating to evaluate a manager only on effectiveness (for example, he exceeded his sales objective by 15 percent) without also looking at his efficiency (achievement of the extra 15 percent by concentrating on easy sales of fast-moving products with a high cost of goods sold but with low profit margins).

The balance must be preserved by clearly indicating in advance— through the step-by-step plans or programs that should always support major objectives—how and in what proportion the objectives will be achieved. Therefore, when the target period is over and the performance is being evaluated, it is possible to determine whether the manager used good planning to achieve his objectives or whether he achieved the objectives through questionable management practices.

Another policy decision is to define "minimum" performance to qualify for extra compensation. Must all objectives be achieved? If not, which objectives must be, and in what proportion? Must an increase in the sales objective be accompanied by a corresponding increase in profit and return on investment?

The normal award. As each of the points shown in Table 2 is translated into incentive payment dollars (using future accomplishment as the determining basis) the manager is provided with the option of determining at what level of accomplishment he wants to work during the target period, or, expressed differently, the amount of compensation he wishes to earn. It is possible to obtain this advance knowledge about objectives (and the effects on performance that it can help bring about) by using what is commonly referred to as the "normal award" for achievement of objectives. The normal award can be defined simply as the amount of incentive compensation (commonly expressed as a percentage of base salary) that a manager can expect to receive when he fully achieves his objectives. Table 3 shows a normal award schedule for various levels of managers.

Obviously, the schedule or curve is constructed to increase the amount of the normal award at the higher levels of management. This reflects the greater potential of higher-level managers to make a more substantial contribution to profits and to show greater responsibility for broader and more critical planning, decisions, and action.

Table 3. Normal awards at various salary levels.

Salary level	Normal award percentage of base salary
$12,000	15%
20,000	20
30,000	25
40,000	30
50,000	35
–	–
100,000	50
–	–
200,000	65

Assume that the normal award for the division general manager is 35 percent of salary and that his salary is $25,000. Two assumed levels of performance will be used to illustrate the compensation he would earn. In one case, he just achieves his objectives (par performance). In the second case, he exceeds his objectives (above par performance). The number of points he earns in both cases are shown in Table 4.

Table 4. Points earned at various performance levels.*

Objectives	Possible points	Par		Above par	
		Results	Points earned	Results	Points earned
$5 million profit	50–100	$5 million	50	$5 million	60
$60 million sales	30–80	$60 million	30	$60 million	33
12 percent ROI	40–60	12 percent	40	13 percent	44
Inventory reduction of 11 percent	20–40	11 percent	20	11 percent	20
Phase 2—management development program	10–20	Completed	10	Completed	10
Total			150		167

* In this example, the increased points are calculated on a one-to-one basis proportionate to the degree to which performance increased. Many companies accelerate the amount of the award at a higher rate once par performance has been achieved.

Following the "par" example used in Table 4, the division manager would receive 150 points for achieving his objectives. His normal incentive award at this point would be 35 percent of his salary, or $8,750. He would receive additional incentive compensation for the degree to which he achieves above-par performance.

Once the normal award concept is adopted, the company must turn to a policy decision regarding the amount of the reward for more than 100 percent achievement of objectives. This policy should provide at least a one-for-one reward for the degree to which the objectives are exceeded. Translated into an actual example, this policy might provide payments to the manager according to Table 5.

Table 5 may be extended indefinitely; its most important feature is that for every percentage increase by which the manager exceeds his objective, his incentive payment should be increased by at least a commensurate percentage. The amounts are expressed both as a percentage of salary and in absolute dollars, since some companies relate incentive payments to the manager's salary and other companies establish absolute dollar levels that are not related to salaries. If all salaries have been es-

Table 5. Rewards for more than 100 percent
objective achievement.

| Percent of objective achievement | Incentive payment amount | |
	As percent of base salary	In absolute dollars
100	10	x dollars
110	20	$2x$ dollars
120	30	$3x$ dollars
130	40	$4x$ dollars

tablished on an equitable basis, the former method is usually preferable, since it results in proportionately higher payments made to holders of higher-level jobs.

Some companies limit maximum incentive payments to a certain percentage of salary. For example, the maximum payment a manager may receive is equal to 30 percent of his salary. Others use an open-ended method under which the amount of incentive payments is unlimited. The latter policy is more conducive to motivation because it emphasizes to the manager that his compensation is limited only by his accomplishments. The first policy does not provide the manager with real financial motivation to exceed his objectives by more than the point at which his compensation stops. However, for the first year or two of a new plan, to prevent incentive payments from running away while the plan and the objective-setting process are being debugged and refined, it may be well to establish a payment limitation. This limitation can be removed when the plan is operating effectively.

The benefits. The use of the weighting points and the normal award curve provides two major benefits to the manager, both of which bear heavily on equity and motivation. First, by knowing the weights prior to beginning the target year, he is able to calculate how many points he will earn at various levels of performance. For example, he knows that he will receive 30 points for achieving sales of $60 million (Table 4). If he desires to earn more points, he knows he must sell more than $60 million. He can make this decision prior to beginning his action for the target year. Second, he knows that his incentive compensation depends upon his own performance and that he has practically unlimited opportunity to earn additional compensation.

Neither time nor the purpose of this chapter permits the treatment here of the methods for establishing the total incentive fund for an organization as a whole or of the methods for distributing portions of the total fund to various departments and divisions. It should be noted, however, that the total monies available for awarding an individual manager may be heavily influenced by the performance of the total company, his particular division or department, and, ultimately, by his own performance.

THE IMPACT OF OUTSIDE FACTORS

One of the more complex issues that must be considered when applying an incentive formula is how to handle the impact of outside factors over which the manager has no control. These outside factors can operate to enhance or impede his performance. For example, a few years ago a flu-like epidemic in the East caused a substantial and unanticipated demand for a leading brand of cough drops. The sales manager for this product was able to greatly exceed his sales objective. This raised a question with respect to his incentive compensation. Should he receive additional compensation for the additional sales that did not result from his managing and planning but from factors outside of his control?

While there is no easy or "right" answer to this question, two general approaches are commonly followed. The first is to include a "windfall gain or loss" provision in the incentive plan. In this approach the manager's superior (and ultimately the incentive compensation committee consisting of outside directors) endeavors to isolate and evaluate the major factors over which the manager had no control. The manager's incentive compensation may be adjusted according to this evaluation. A less desirable alternative is to consider only the results achieved without attempting to evaluate the why. The manager's incentive sinks or swims according to the final tally.

The second approach is to evaluate the results achieved in light of the step-by-step plans developed by the manager to support his objectives. The purpose of this evaluation is to determine whether he planned (managed) his way to the results or whether he was just lucky. Evaluation of the planning process also permits an assessment of the impact of unfavorable outside events.

Regardless of which approach is used, the provisions and operations should be explained as completely as possible to all eligible managers before—not after—the target year begins.

Tying Compensation to Performance

If the equation "performance equals rewards" is to be valid, it is necessary to emphasize the interrelated nature of the two. This includes eliminating the arbitrary practice of separating performance appraisal interviews and compensation interviews. One of the traditional reasons advanced for making the separation goes to the heart of the old, ineffective performance evaluation approach based on personality traits. These were frequently used to justify almost any salary increase granted by a superior to a subordinate. For example, if a superior wanted to justify an increase for a subordinate, he would rate the subordinate as being excellent on all factors being rated. It was difficult to quarrel with the rating because it was not determined by objective results.

Thus the traditionalists thought they could eliminate this stacking of the deck by separating the two interviews. However, any validity this reasoning once enjoyed has now been negated by the increasing use of performance evaluation based on results. Measuring based on the specific results achieved makes it difficult to stack the deck to justify a whim or unjustified wish.

If performance is to truly equal rewards, increased emphasis should be devoted to discussing compensation as a natural and necessary part of the performance appraisal interview.

> PARABLE: Once upon a time a farmer had six jackasses and a barn full of carrots, which he kept under lock and key.
>
> At the end of a day of wagon pulling, the farmer looked back over the day's performance of each jackass. To one of the jackasses he said, "You did an outstanding job; here are six carrots." To four of the others, he said, "Your performance was average; here are three carrots." To the remaining jackass he said, "You didn't pull your share of the load; here is one carrot."
>
> Another day of wagon pulling dawned. The top jackass, having been properly rewarded, began the day in high spirits. The thoughts of the remaining jackasses were consumed with how they might earn more carrots through their efforts that day. The farmer had carrots available, but they had to be earned.
>
> MORAL OF THE STORY: *Jackasses do work for carrots!*

25

Avoiding the Pitfalls

MBO's RAPID GROWTH in the past 20 years has been accompanied by significant problems, but these problems were caused by the weaknesses of the managers who applied the systems, rather than by any inherent weaknesses in the MBO system. This premise is amply substantiated by the following list of 20 ways to kill even the best MBO approach. To managers considering adoption of an MBO system, the list may be helpful in planning; for companies that have already embraced MBO and have experienced only limited success, it should serve as a debugging checklist. For still other organizations that latched on to MBO as a showpiece or because someone else had it, the list will be a handy guide to killing the effort much more rapidly so that they can proceed, without too much delay, to picking another pig in a poke.

Of all the potential pitfalls that tend to trap the uninitiated or the unwary, two general ones stand out in particular. One is *adopting in ignorance*—deciding to adopt MBO without really understanding what it involves and how it works. The second is *implementing in haste*—trying to implement too much, too fast. Note that many of the specific pitfalls covered in the remainder of this chapter are the logical result of these two general, major pitfalls.

Consider MBO a Panacea

Don't be fooled by those cautious souls who insist that there is no such thing as a panacea. MBO must be one in light of the legions of businessmen, educators, consultants, writers, soothsayers, and others who travel around the country chanting MBO's virtues. Believe them when they say that MBO will accomplish wondrous things all by itself, that the quality of management is incidental, and that MBO's strengths make even an incompetent manager look great.

Those persons who are bent on killing MBO shouldn't muddle their thinking by listening to the countless successful managers who point out that an effective MBO system presumes a competent management in which each major part of the management process is playing its proper and balanced role.

Tell 'em Their Objectives

Here is the real key to killing MBO: Instead of trusting your subordinates to develop meaningful objectives for themselves, then taking the time and effort to discuss the objectives with them, write the objectives yourself and hand them out to each of your subordinates. Be certain to impress all managers with the fact that these are "their" objectives and that they are to break their backs to accomplish them. Follow this up with frequent pep talks during the year.

In this way, you'll save the weeks of effort usually required for dialogs between superior and subordinates to establish effective objectives. One Wisconsin company president has become so adept at this efficiency technique that he can set and distribute objectives for all his managers in just a few hours, and he firmly believes that this one-man show is good MBO.

This technique removes a manager's motivation and commitment to carry out his objectives. As one noted authority on organizational effectiveness suggests, the real value of MBO is participation in the objective-setting process, not the objectives themselves.

Leave Out Staff Managers

Include only line managers in your MBO system. Leaving out staff managers can be justified on the basis that they are concerned only with intangibles that can't be measured and that they are employed only to provide service, advice, and counsel to the elite corps of line managers. Don't hold staff managers accountable for profit-oriented results. Instead, let them sit around their offices waiting for line managers to seek their advice or to be asked to perform some service for line. Above all, maintain the traditional wall between the two groups by stressing that line managers are responsible for making the profit decisions while staff can only recommend.

Ignore current studies that show that, on an average, 20 to 40 percent of the total manpower budgets of most companies is allocated to staff management and its activities. Pass up all opportunities provided by MBO to include all managers—whether they are staff or line—on the profit-making team. Be content, in the name of hollow tradition, to leave 20 to 40 percent of your managers out in left field and to overlook any contributions that they are capable of making to profits and progress. Thwart their development by not giving them specific responsibilities and account-abilities.

Forget that measurable objectives can be written for every job. Ignore the fact that while it is easier to write objectives for certain jobs, the results of all managers can be measured, using objectives as the basis.

Delegate Executive Direction

If you are the chief executive officer or some other top-level executive and are responsible for giving system direction, don't spend too much of your own time on this chore. Instead, delegate full responsibility for directing MBO to your personnel manager, planning director, or assistant. Tell him/her to report back to you once in a while to tell you how things are going. Delegating in this fashion will save both time and worry. Time will be saved because you won't have to devote any of it to directing the system; worry will be eliminated because the system soon will be regarded as just another personnel or planning gimmick and will die of its own accord.

Without exception, every successful MBO system has borne continuously, from its very first day of implementation, the clear and unmistakable mark of the chief executive officer. So if you want to make a quick killing, delegate responsibility.

Create a Paper Mill

Everyone knows that a successful business operates on paper, so don't let your MBO system operate without a plethora of paper and paperwork. Pick someone who loves paperwork to administer the system and insist that everything be reduced to writing and that several copies of each document be prepared. Use a tricky form for every detail of the system. In fact, be imaginative in developing new and more complicated forms. If necessary, steal ideas and forms from other organizations. Don't forget, the more forms and paperwork you require, the more impressive it will appear to others who haven't yet implemented MBO. When your operating managers complain that all the forms and procedures are interfering with their managerial efficiency, just answer, "Nothing worthwhile ever comes easy!"

Finally, don't be misguided by managers with successful systems when they tell you that MBO should be as simple and as free of paperwork as possible.

Ignore Feedback

Treat feedback to a manager on how he is performing either as a luxury that can't be afforded or as information that is necessary only at the top level of the organization. To make feedback all but impossible, see that charts of all accounts, the budget, and any reports to managers are prepared on a different basis and that any feedback that does exist is prepared in a standard format not tailored to individual objectives.

Finally, don't practice any semblance of responsibility accounting in which the right kind of information is given to the right manager for proper decision making and control. If some manager is brazen enough to request this feedback information, merely tell him that it is his participation in the objective-setting process that is important, not how well he carries out the objectives. Overlook the proven facts that feedback is an absolute prerequisite to a successful MBO system and that the more achievement-oriented a manager is, the more he is interested in feedback on his performance.

Emphasize the Techniques

Don't be overly concerned about end results. Instead, insist that all managers become highly skilled in the techniques and methods of MBO and see that there is an abundance of techniques and methods on which they must concentrate. Cook up more every time the already-long list appears about to exhaust itself. Keep your managers so busy mastering the techniques, procedures, and skills that they won't have time for analysis, thinking, and planning. Remember, busy minds are happy, fruitful minds.

Also spend countless hours in meetings and training sessions designed to get managers so enamored with conceptualizing the system that they never get around to applying it. If discussions start to lag, devote several more meetings to discussing the minute differences between goals, objectives, standards of performance, and results. Expand these categories, if necessary, to prolong the discussions.

Above all, don't believe the successful MBO practitioners when they try to convince you that the most effective managers are analysis-oriented, not method-oriented.

Implement Overnight

Don't bother devoting the three to five years of effort normally required to make a successful MBO program; do it overnight without the required training or orientation. Then you'll be all set to sit back and reap the system's benefits—which will never come. Particularly if you're in the upper level of management, don't waste time schooling yourself and your managers in the concept, mechanics, rationale, pitfalls, and continuous adaptations of MBO to your organization. Jump right into the water—after all, no one ever learned to swim until he got wet.

Don't worry that you're succumbing to one of the primary pitfalls of MBO by trying to move too rapidly, biting off too much at one time, and not laying a proper foundation for the continuous growth of the program. Rationalize your precipitous implementation on the basis that your organization is unique and can succeed in accomplishing in a few weeks what it took other organizations an average of at least three years to accomplish. Give yourself plenty of credit—until your program falls apart—that the ability to move with dispatch is the real mark of your ability as a topflight manager.

Fail to Reward

Place blind faith in the axiom "Man does not live by bread alone," and give your managers only minimal amounts of bread while expecting them to consistently turn in superior results. Adopt as standard practice the old across-the-board approach to compensation in which everyone receives just about the same increase each time, regardless of the wide differences in contributions. Don't compensate personnel on output or contributions, but rather on the basis of efforts—regardless of results—or what they say they can do. Don't hurt anyone's feelings—regardless of his lack of competence—by not granting him a salary increase or promotion. Treat compensation as a human relations tool, not as a means of promoting equity and motivation. The impact of your actions will show after the initial speeches and flag waving have died away and your managers begin to wonder whatever happened to the second part of the performance-equals-rewards equation.

A logical outgrowth of the failure to reward is the allegation that MBO is only another means of pinning people down to specific objectives, then disciplining them when they fail to measure up. A well-functioning MBO system is accompanied by so many benefits that this allegation is overshadowed and placed in its proper perspective; however, in the absence of equitable rewards, it assumes a dominant position.

Have Objectives but No Plans

This is a beautiful way to murder MBO and it's very simple to practice: Just have managers spend their time formulating highly acceptable and needed objectives, then don't require them to formulate realistic plans to make the objectives become an actuality. Leave this to divine providence.

An alternative approach is to have managers write long, detailed plans to support their objectives, then don't test them for realism. Judge the realism of the plans on the basis of length, thickness, or weight; don't devote too much attention to quality.

Stick with Your Original System

Never waver from your chosen path. After considering all the various MBO approaches and as many actual programs as possible, select the one that you believe is best for your organization, then stick with it, come hell or high water. Refuse to be swayed by experience or by those who champion changes from the original version. Ignore those persons who believe that "your" system, especially in its early stages, must undergo constant change and tailoring to make it more effective. It's your system, so do as you wish. Many years later, after your program has been laid to rest, you can look back with pride in the knowledge that it was your system and you weren't hoodwinked into changing it. Your system died as it was born, undisturbed by the cry for change.

Be Impatient

Become firmly convinced of the wisdom of those who suggest that all good managers are impatient. In fact, go them one better—be highly impatient to realize the benefits of MBO. Install MBO this year, then be unhappy this time next year if sales haven't tripled and profits doubled. If MBO is half as good as you've heard it is, expect these minimal results, at least.

If your plans don't materialize, quickly lose faith in MBO and damn the consultant or associate who sold you on it. Minimize your part in it by commenting that you weren't sold on it in the first place but only went along because of your policy of always being willing to try new things. Whatever you do, don't be willing to accept modest improvements each year as experience is gained until each of the modest improvements culminates in significant overall progress. This would defeat your purpose of trying to kill the system.

Quantify Everything

Insist that only highly quantified objectives will be approved. Demand that the results of each objective be stated in absolute dollar figures so that they can be measured with 100 percent accuracy at the end of the target period, then sit back and watch the feverish activity that you've generated, especially among staff managers who deal in objectives of an intangible nature.

Watch carefully the quality and potential value of the objectives that are recommended. Watch, for example, as your personnel manager submits a highly quantified objective to reduce the cost of the employee magazine by $100 but fails to mention the need for a new salary and wage program, or as the financial manager submits the highly quantified objective of reducing duplicating costs by $1,000 but neglects to recommend a much-meeded management information system for which an objective would be more difficult to structure. Watch all these things happen as the pennies pile up but the dollars never seem to appear.

Stress Objectives, Not the System

Devote only minimal time to the system itself—its rationale, operation, applications, and pitfalls. Instead, have your managers begin to write objectives immediately after you have given them a brief explanation of the 10 to 12 qualities of an effective objective. Refuse to be bothered by their questions about how their objectives will fit into or operate under the system. Tell them that they are to concentrate on writing objectives and that you will take care of the total system. Treat them in the same manner as you would a production line worker who spends his entire working time placing a nut on a bolt without ever being able to visualize what the total machine is like.

Don't waste time worrying about what may happen as a result of your managers' not knowing why they are writing their isolated objectives. Just continue to make them expert objectives writers. If they question you or demonstrate a lack of interest, just paraphrase the line from *The Charge of the Light Brigade:* "Yours is not to question why." That battle was lost, too.

Dramatize Short-Term Objectives

Operate on the premise that if you take care of the present, the future will take care of itself. Disseminate this philosophy until all your managers become imbued with it.

Always have some form of long-range plan, but don't dissipate your efforts worrying about it. Concentrate on making yourself look good today; some other person may be sitting in your chair tomorrow. Try to get promoted at least once every three years and watch your replacement go crazy coping with the problems of your old department.

Develop a thick skin so that you won't be concerned when your maintenance manager turns in a spectacular record this year by postponing all necessary maintenance, when your first-line foreman reduces per-unit costs by 300 percent by driving the employees to the point where all of them strike at the beginning of next year, or when your sales manager increases annual sales by 400 percent by overloading customer warehouses with products that will spoil before they can be sold. In other words, pooh-pooh the wisdom of never mortgaging the long-term future to look good today.

Omit Periodic Reviews

The more successful MBO systems feature periodic reviews, usually at quarterly intervals, during the target period. The purposes of these reviews are to measure performance, to review the validity of the original objective, and to take remedial action if necessary while there is still time left during the target period.

MBO can be dealt a lethal blow by omitting these reviews. Neither the supervisor not his subordinate will know how the other is performing until the final review at the end of the target period, when there will be no opportunity to take corrective action. Without interim reviews on a formal basis and according to a definite schedule, any detection of varying performance will be as much a matter of luck as of plan.

Omit Refresher Training

Many organizations do a highly commendable training and orientation job when MBO is first installed. The training, though, ends at that point, and managers who are new to the system are left to secure their MBO training through a combination of osmosis and hit-or-miss tutoring by the older hands, who may or may not be competent teachers. Changes and refinements to the original program are handled in much the same way.

This is an excellent way to kill MBO, since the first three years following the installation of an MBO system constitute a period of continuous tailoring of the system to the unique requirements of the organization. After three years, the original installation may have been changed by as much as 50 percent, and only the most informal training has been conducted on the changed portion.

Don't Blend Objectives

Another way to emasculate MBO is to fail to coordinate all objectives. After all, one of the basics of MBO is the requirement that each manager write his own objectives. Carry this one step further and treat all

objectives as completely individual matters. Don't spend the time necessary to ensure that each manager's objectives are complementary to the
objectives of other managers and that all objectives support the overall objectives of the organization. Permit each manager to write objectives as
the spirit moves him. Remember, the important thing is that all managers
write objectives.

Those who would kill MBO in this way should not be surprised to
find that the sales manager has an objective to sell 20,000 units while the
production manager's objective is to produce only 10,000 units, or that
the personnel manager's objective is to plan and hold a company picnic
while the main plant is on strike.

Be Gutless

Avoid expressing your own objectives in specific terms. Otherwise,
you might be pinned down later if you don't accomplish them. The fact
that your subordinates must take their cue from you as to the kind and extent of the objectives they recommend shouldn't disturb you excessively.
By forcing them to stand on their own feet without excessive guidance or
babying, you're helping them to develop.

Also, fail to establish priorities. As long as all your managers are busy
doing something, their time is well spent. Get upset only when they
spend two or three days a week on the golf course; make them return to
the shop and spend all their paid work time doing something.

Be extremely reluctant to remove any manager whom MBO spots as
incompetent. If your other managers seem upset by your failure to take
action, explain to them that not everyone can be a chief and that every organization with a social conscience has its own little Indian reservation.

Finally, be overly cautious about making decisions. Take a long time
for each decision, or you might make a wrong one. And blame the reduced tempo of your organization on everything but poor decision making
on your part.

Refuse to Delegate

This is another excellent way to kill MBO. Refuse to believe that the
entire MBO system depends on a continuous and successive delegation of
accountability for results for everything from overall corporate objectives
to the objectives of first-line supervision.

There are two reasons why managers don't delegate: Either they are
ignorant of how to delegate or they are afraid to delegate. You can create a
third reason simply by refusing absolutely to delegate. Why should you
allow someone to run something for which you are going to be held ac-

countable? Why let one of your subordinates get some of the glory? Why reduce your indispensability in the eyes of your superiors? Why should you spend time training people for more responsibility? In short, why delegate in the first place?

You can let your subordinate write his own objectives, but be certain that he confines them to routine matters. Then overcontrol him, give him detailed orders and instructions, and never allow him to use his own judgment.

MBO stops at those levels where delegation doesn't take place, so push this for all it's worth if you want to destroy your MBO program.

IGNORANCE OR DESIGN

All these pitfalls pose serious stumbling blocks to the success of MBO. Of course, no manager actually starts an MBO effort with the goal of destroying it. However, the injurious impact to MBO is the same whether the manager fails through ignorance or design.

MBO is a tough, demanding management system that requires highly competent managers to operate it. By paying attention to the problem areas discussed here, they can increase the effectiveness and value of the MBO systems that they have implemented or plan to implement.

26

Administration
of the System

AS POINTED OUT earlier, the administration of the management by results approach should be made as simple as possible. The principal administration requirements are assigning the responsibility for administration, recording the objectives, controlling the status of objectives, and preparing reports to management.

ADMINISTRATIVE RESPONSIBILITY

A clear distinction must be made here between the *executive direction* of the system and the *administration* of it. Because MBO is a total way of managing the company—it's *the* way by which we manage—the executive direction of the system must rest with the senior line officer, usually the president. It cannot be delegated because this would be tantamount to the president's delegating his entire responsibility for managing the company. The same is true for all other heads of units within the company, with respect to their own units.

At Corporate Level

Administration of the MBO system, on the other hand, involves tasks such as the pulling together and consolidating of all objectives and plans, monitoring the planning schedule, preparing status reports, and related activities. For the corporation as a whole, this responsibility is usually handled by the director of planning services, an MBO adviser, a top manager in the financial department, or an assistant to the president. The title is not important as long as the person is competent. It is especially important that he/she not place himself/herself in the position of appearing to give executive direction to the program. This is a job of administration only.

At Lower Levels

Administration within departments and other units is usually delegated to one of the staff managers or to a special assistant if the unit is large enough to justify this latter job. A competent executive secretary can handle this assignment if proper training has been provided. Often, again depending upon the size of the unit, this need be only a part-time assignment.

RECORDING THE OBJECTIVES

Although objectives need not be recorded in any particular shape or form, follow-up and control are facilitated by having all managers adopt a uniform format. Figures 27 through 31 illustrate the forms currently used by several companies. Especially convenient is the split page favored by United Air Lines (see Figure 30). The objectives are recorded on the left, and the actual results are listed opposite them on the right-hand side. In this way, the complete story for each objective is readily discernible.*

Figure 18 illustrates a form in popular use for recording the individual objectives and the plans and schedule for accomplishing the objectives. It consolidates considerable information on one piece of paper.

CONTROL OF STATUS

In keeping with the fondness of many managers for the presentation of data, it is possible to develop an objectives control chart (adapted from the familiar production control chart) to record the status of progress continuously. In such a chart, the objectives are listed vertically down the left-hand margin and the target dates horizontally across the page. Thus the chart provides a handy means of recording results as of any desired date and so controlling progress toward each objective.

Other companies merely establish a tickler file of significant dates contained in the objectives proper. Then when a particular date arrives, the status of the objective is automatically reviewed and recorded. Re-

* Figures 27–31 appear at the end of this chapter.

gardless of which method of follow-up is used, it must be borne in mind that the important reason for it is to provide management with the necessary intelligence on which to base its decisions, including those aimed at corrective action.

The bulk of the status reports discussed so far are designed primarily for control by managers below the top level. The president would have a laborious job indeed if he had to review the objectives and results of each manager. (One exception to the rule is the president of a rubber company who personally keeps tabs on the objectives of his top 200 managers.) Normally the individual manager's objectives are filed with his superior, who is responsible for controlling and evaluating them. For example, a department head will be personally concerned with the objectives of his division heads, each of whom, in turn, will review those of the managers reporting directly to him.

In keeping with the doctrine of management by exception discussed earlier, another method of keeping tabs on the status of results is merely to make a list of all objectives that have not been reached by the end of the target period and present it to the superior for action. In this method the superior doesn't, and shouldn't, concern himself with those objectives that are on target and proceeding smoothly. Using a list such as this, a vice-president of sales, for example, can get a quick picture of the status of results accomplished by his managers without having to review each and every objective of each manager. Similarly, by having a regular status list of exceptions, the president will have a ready and convenient method of evaluating the accomplishments of all his officers.

Usually, only the officers' objectives will be retained by the president since these, when combined, spell out the company's overall goals and the action necessary to achieve them. Below the officer level we find the detailed plan of delegation that each manager has made to reach the sum total of his/her objectives.

Consolidating versus Compiling

Objectives should be consolidated, not compiled, as they move up the line. Some companies have created a paper mill by not heeding this counsel. Compiling refers to the practice of simply adding all the paperwork (objectives and plans) from one level to that of another level as it moves up the line. Compiling results in higher levels of management receiving an excessive amount of lower-level detail and material, data in which they shouldn't and can't be involved.

Consolidation, in contrast, requires that only selected, key information be moved up the line from lower levels. For example, the president receives primarily the objectives and information relating to the officers reporting to him. The vice-president of sales receives only the material relating to those sales managers reporting directly to him, not from managers four levels down in his department.

REPORTS TO MANAGEMENT

The various types of reports used by top management in controlling and evaluating results are the crux of management by results. They answer the three necessary whats: what has happened, what is happening, and what management must make happen if objectives are to be realized. Depending upon the nature of the objective and the manner in which it is capable of being expressed, they provide management with interim opportunities to effect action, together with an evaluation of the actual results achieved after the target period has ended.

The B. F. Goodrich Company uses a simple method for reporting the results attained. The form used for each manager is divided into two parts vertically (see Figure 28). On the left-hand side are the objectives for which the manager is responsible. On the right-hand side are the results actually achieved—both for six-month periods and for the year as a whole. This form presents the complete picture for review by management. While simplicity does have decided advantages, the method requires a rather detailed analysis by the superior. Perhaps more desirable from the standpoint of the average top management, therefore, is the method of reporting used by Reynolds Metals Company at its plastic films plant in Grottoes, Virginia. The plant has four basic books for administering and following up its objectives:

1. A "black book" lists the yearly objectives of plant and department heads, together with performance standards for measuring progress in attaining them.

2. A "red book," issued monthly, provides information on profits, return on investment, cost reduction, methods improvement, conversion efficiencies, quality, inventories, and current cost data. The purpose of this book is to show department heads their current standing in relation to the specific objectives (recorded in the black book) that they set at the beginning of the year.

3. The monthly "blue book" gives individual reports and schedules. Included are condensed balance sheets and operating statements, P&L by major product lines, details of expenses, numbers of employees and payroll amounts, summaries of inventories, and a worksheet showing how inventory, cost of sales, and variance relationships are reconciled. This

report is used to inform plant, division, and corporate management of the plant's financial condition.

4. A monthly "gray book" offers detailed comparisons, by type of expense and cost center, of actual monthly costs against budgeted allowances. The book also contains expense ledger detail, plus excess scrap and materials-usage data, and a total conversion cost. The variable budgeted allowances are individually computed each month and added to the current fixed amounts for a sound monthly spending allowance. The purpose of this information is to give detailed cost performance data to individual managers responsible for the plant's cost elements and so put the responsibility accounting technique into use.[1]

State Mutual Life Assurance Company of America reduces its quantitative goals to writing, and follow-up is achieved through the quarterly management control report. The first part of the report summarizes the company's overall earnings. Next, the earnings are broken down according to individual insurance operations, group insurance operations, return on investment, and various subdivisions under these major headings. As reported in *Business Management:*

> In all cases, the earnings reports are divided into three columns—earnings in the current quarter, earnings in the year to date, and earnings in the year to date as compared with what was planned. Thus, this last column gives State Mutual's top management a ready indication of whether or not the company is achieving its quantitative goals.
>
> In addition, the reports show what expenses the company is incurring. Expenses are listed both by line of business—e.g., group term insurance, group permanent insurance—and by department—e.g., administrative, legal.
>
> The frequency of these reports should also be emphasized. They provide management with information about earnings and expenses in sufficient time for it to make revisions, if necessary.[2]

Budget control reports are another means of follow-up, especially useful for those objectives that have been quantified and expressed in units corresponding to accounting and budgetary units. While the usual budget reports will not provide all the necessary follow-up information in the most convenient manner, they will serve as one of the sources of control required by a company. Moreover, in companies that emphasize responsibility accounting, much of the information needed for control and

[1] Adapted from *The Manager's Letter*, AMACOM, September 20, 1964.
[2] "Long-Range Planning," February 1965.

follow-up will be available as a matter of course, and special reports will not be necessary. If responsibility accounting has been accepted as a key tool for all levels of management, chances are that it will already apply down to and including the first level of supervision.

Responsibility accounting is designed to provide each manager with the data he requires for effective performance in his job—data that are prompt, pertinent, accurate, and clearly understandable. Information is keyed to individual needs; that is, it is made available only to those managers who are in a position to profit from it. In other words, the aim is to build the accounting system around the organization so that the necessary facts and figures are supplied to the proper manager in the form most useful to him or her. This tailoring process serves three major purposes:

1. It feeds back information to the responsible manager, pointing out the effects of his past performance and spotlighting important areas for future attention. Because of the nature of responsibility accounting, in all cases the manager has the authority to take the necessary action.

2. It enables higher management to evaluate each manager's effectiveness against objectives and to take any indicated steps promptly.

3. Each senior executive receives information concerning the performance of his subordinates, who in turn receive information regarding each of their subordinates. Each manager also is kept up to date on his own performance.

Thus the regular accounting and budget reports will reflect progress made toward quantified objectives having to do with costs, income, production and sales volumes, rates of return, and related indexes. Also, they will provide much-needed information for measuring qualitative objectives. Follow-up will obviously be facilitated if target periods are set to correspond with a company's accounting periods.

In short, paperwork can be held to the minimum. Wherever possible, in fact, special reports designed only to implement the management by results approach should be avoided or, where necessary initially, discontinued at the earliest possible time.

Figure 27. Sample objectives and results for district manager of a large Midwestern brewing company.

197x Goals	Accomplishments
1. Achieve a 9% increase in total packaged beer sales in district, and 4% increase in total draught beer sales. COMPLETION DATE: Dec. 31, 197x	6.2% increase in packaged beer sales and 3.8% increase in draught beer. Reached predetermined goals in four of seven markets. Wholesaler change accounts for slight decrease in sales in market C.
2. Secure or retain 100% distribution in each market in district. COMPLETION DATE: Dec. 31, 197x	Retained 100% distribution in markets D, F, and G; market E increased from 97% to 100%; market B increased from 95% to 98%; market A increased from 72% to 91%; and market C from 80% to 84%.
3. Convince wholesalers D, E, and G to construct adequate POS storage facilities. COMPLETION DATE: July 1, 197x	POS storage room constructed by all three wholesalers. Completed by June 1.
4. Convince wholesalers A, C, and E to adopt the key account program. COMPLETION DATE: May 1, 197x	Key account program adopted in market A in March and in market E in June. New wholesaler in market C has agreed to adopt plan early in 197x.
5. Replace three delivery vans at wholesaler E and one delivery van each at wholesalers A and C. COMPLETION DATE: Dec. 31, 197x	Wholesaler E replaced two delivery vans, with third to be delivered in February 197x. Wholesaler A replaced one van, but no replacement at wholesaler C due to wholesaler change.
6. Persuade wholesaler C to add one driver-salesman and one draught beer specialist to his personnel. COMPLETION DATE: June 1, 197x	Goal deleted due to change in wholesaler in market C. Will reinstitute goal for 197x.
7. Convince each wholesaler in district to establish and maintain regular weekly sales meetings to introduce new merchandising and POS programs, sales promotions, etc. COMPLETION DATE: July 1, 197x	Regular weekly sales meetings were established by each wholesaler by end of March. Meetings were maintained throughout the year, except in market C, where wholesaler was changed. Meetings there will be resumed as soon as feasible.
8. Have every wholesaler truck in district painted to company specifications. COMPLETION DATE: Dec. 31, 197x	Succeeded in having eight more trucks painted to company specifications, leaving three that are still not properly identified. If current plans are continued, all will be painted by end of 197x.

197x Goals	Accomplishments
9. During 197x, work at least one full day with each wholesaler field representative in the district. COMPLETION DATE: Dec. 31, 197x	Was able to work with over 80% of the total field representatives. Found this to be very rewarding. Will continue this goal in 197x.
10. Give the district representative training and responsibilities that will assure his being ready to assume a district manager assignment by end of year. COMPLETION DATE: Dec. 31, 197x	Through planned program of training, the ADM, Richard Roe, is now capable of DM assignment. Throughout the year, worked at least one week per month at the same market location with ADM to train and observe his development.

197x Goals Added	Accomplishments
April 197x: Train and develop the two heirs of previous wholesaler C (dec'd. 3/20). Make recommendation by end of year to replace or not. COMPLETION DATE: Dec. 31, 197x	By August, was evident that heirs were not capable of running the business. Recommended that wholesaler be changed. Submitted recommendations and papers on suitable replacement in October. In conjunction with division manager, effected the change as of November 1.

Are there other significant facts about this employee or his accomplishments that are not adequately covered elsewhere?

The district manager was faced with an unusually difficult situation in market C early in the year when the wholesaler died after an illness of several months, during which time the business was badly neglected. The two sons, although active in the sales end of the business for several years each, had never been involved in the financial or management decisions. There was doubt as to their maturity and ability. The district manager spent many hours and days of his own weekends working with these two men in an attempt to train and develop them. When he became convinced that it was a hopeless task, he was successful in persuading them to sell out the business; he found a stable, experienced, and financially secure replacement to buy them out, and concluded the wholesaler change with a minimum loss in terms of sales. With less diligent care on the part of the district manager through his advice and insistence on good management principles in a rapidly deteriorating situation, the company could have suffered a serious setback in this important market. The above effort did not deter him from the attainment of goals affecting the other markets in the district.

Served as United Fund Drive chairman for his county in 197x.

What is your current estimate of this employee's capacity and ambition for future growth? Does he have potential for advancement? (Include any suggestions for his self-development.)

During the past year, this employee was in a position to show that he can effectively operate under pressure in a difficult situation. Has ambition and drive. Recommended him as assistant to area director to further his training and advancement opportunities. Employee to budget his work to allow timely preparation and submission of required reports.

Immediate supervisor _____ *Date* _____

Reviewed and approved by _____ *Date* _____

Employee _____ *Date* _____

Figure 28. Position objectives form, B. F. Goodrich Company.

TYPES OF OBJECTIVES

An individual manager's list of objectives should represent a balanced management job. The following list includes examples of management areas that should be considered wherever applicable:

 I. *Marketing Objectives*
    (e.g., sales, operating income, industry position, and expense targets).
 II. *Production Objectives*
    (e.g., quality, productivity, and cost targets).
 III. *Financial and Control Objectives*
    (e.g., inventory turnover ratios, credit, and employment cost targets).
 IV. *Personnel Objectives*
    (e.g., organization, development, and motivation of personnel).
 V. *Research, Development, and Technical Objectives*
    (e.g., product and process improvement, new product development projects).

THE PROCEDURE

1. Each eligible executive is to prepare a list of proposed objectives for his position and submit it through customary channels to his division head.
2. The immediate supervisor is to review the proposed objectives in a meeting with the executive and agree on a final listing. The division head will submit two signed copies of this form to the director, organization development.
3. The lists of objectives will be reviewed by the president, the executive vice-president, and by the appropriate group vice-president. If it is felt that a list needs further study or clarification, it will be returned to the division head for that purpose.
4. The immediate supervisor will retain copies of the objectives in his files and will review them at least twice during the year in interviews with the individual executives. Interviews should be carefully planned in advance to cover all the listed objectives, should emphasize the compensation opportunities of our "reward and penalty" principle of incentive compensation, and should include a discussion of the steps to be taken to reach those objectives not currently on schedule.
5. If circumstances require a revision of an individual's objectives during any year, such revision should be made and the director, organization development, notified of the change.
   It is expected that changes will not be numerous. However, there may be occasions when it is profitable to add an objective or eliminate one that is no longer appropriate.
6. At the end of each year, a date will be established for the submission of final evaluations of performance along with bonus recommendations.
7. The use of this position objectives form for positions not included within the executive incentive compensation group is encouraged. Its use offers important advantages in addition to administration of compensation.

POSITION OBJECTIVES FOR PROFITS ACCOMPLISHMENT

FOR THE PERIOD BEGINNING _____ AND ENDING _____

Pos. Obj. No.	Statement of Position Objectives	Target Date(s)	Periodic Performance Check (Deficient, Adequate, Superior)	
			Date _____	Date _____
1.				
2.				
3.				
7.				
8.				
9.				
10.				

THE POSITION OBJECTIVES PROGRAM

The program has two important functions:

—It is a management technique for reaching a mutual understanding of each executive's responsibilities through the development and assignment of specific individual goals.

—It establishes an objective basis for compensating executives according to their individual contributions to division and corporate results. Although there are several factors that determine the funds available for bonus distribution, an individual's achievement of his annual objectives is of major importance in deciding the amount of his bonus reward.

PROPER STATEMENT OF OBJECTIVES

Because of the major importance of the program, it is necessary that great care be given to the preparation of good objectives. The following guides are recommended:

1. At least six specific objectives should be established for each executive.
2. Those objectives are to include the individual actions and results most essential to achieving division and corporate goals.

THIS EXECUTIVE'S NAME: _____

POSITION _____

POS. LEVEL _____

DIVISION _____

Actual Accomplishment of Position Objectives (State Results as Specifically as Possible)	Performance Evaluation			Explanations and comments as to special difficulties, extenuating circumstances, windfalls, etc., affecting accomplishment against each position objective:
	Below Plan (Deficient)	Approx. on Plan (Adequate)	Above Plan (Superior)	

(Signed) _____

3. The objectives should define reasonably attainable, but reaching, targets; i.e., they must represent relatively optimistic goals, the accomplishment of which *will contribute significantly* to attainment of corporate and divisional objectives.

4. They should be stated in such a way that their performance can be clearly measured. This requires the use of precise and understandable terms, such as "Increase sale of X product line to 20% share of industry" or "Develop a fully qualified replacement for my own position."

5. The list should include both quantitative (How much?) and qualitative (How well?) objectives. Quantitative objectives are to be selected where applicable, *but at least several of each executive's position objectives should be qualitative.*

6. Although most objectives will be stated in terms of results to be achieved during the coming year, *it is important that long-range objectives not be overlooked.* These long-range objectives may have payoffs that will come at a time later than the year in question, but there should be specific subgoals established for that year.

7. Specific target dates for each objective (or steps toward the objective) should be stated.

Figure 29. Management performance review, The Reuben H. Donnelley Corporation.

Name _____   Date _____

One copy of this form is to be used as a self-review by the individual whose performance is being reviewed. It will help him in preparing for the review with his immediate superior. It is for his own use and is not to become part of the record. Another copy is to be prepared by the supervisor.

Part I PERFORMANCE STANDARDS		
1 *Major Performance Factors*	2 *Objective*	3 *Performance Achieved*
First, list factors which can be measured quantitatively (i.e., how much). Then list factors which can best be judged in qualitative terms (i.e., how well).	Set at beginning of period. (These should be discussed fully and wherever possible they should mutually be agreed upon.)	At end of period (ordinarily one year).

4 *Performance Evaluation* *		5 *Comparison of Results*	6 *Tentative Objectives*
Consider carefully, and record, any special circumstances affecting performance over which the manager had limited or no control before assigning the final evaluation for each factor		With preceding year for this position.	For next year's performance.
Eval.	Comments		
Overall			

In completing column 4, use following symbols: O—Outstanding; AS—Above Standard; S—Standard; BS—Below Standard; U—Unsatisfactory; TN—Too New to Rate (less than 6 months on the job).

* Base judgment on what is expected as standard performance, not on a comparison of individuals in like positions. "Standard" is defined as "satisfactory performance."

Part II
STRENGTHS AND DEVELOPMENT NEEDS

A major purpose of the interview will be to discuss and agree upon specific steps to be taken to improve performance.

In Part I you characterized the extent to which previously established performance objectives were met. Now, to prepare further for the interview, constructively review past performance in terms of the knowledge, skills, and personal factors which contributed most to success and those which prevented or significantly deterred success in meeting performance objectives. Consider such factors as:

Knowledge of Function	Appraisal & Development of Others	Application to Job	Sound Reasoning	Oral Expression
Planning of Work	Delegation of Authority and Responsibility	Ability to Promote Teamwork	Emotional Stability	Written Expression
Acceptance of Responsibility	Use of Money	Cooperation	Drive and Perseverance	Civic and Professional Interests

Based on consideration of these factors and others directly related to the job, comment on the significant strengths and development needs.

Major Strengths:

Development Needs:

During the interview a statement of agreed-upon plans for improvement will be completed. Be prepared to discuss ways in which the above strengths can be put to greater use and ways in which improvements can be made where needs are indicated.

Figure 30. Administrative performance evaluation, United Air Lines.

I. COMPLETED BY THE EMPLOYEE Performance Goals and Plans of Action for Each Major Responsibility	II. COMPLETED BY THE SUPERVISOR Results and Comments

These are the performance goals
and plans of action of: Approved by:

_____   _____
(EMPLOYEE'S SIGNATURE)   (DATE)

_____   _____
(SUPERVISOR'S SIGNATURE)   (DATE)

	From	To
Name	File No.	Job Title	Co. Add. Code

I. COMPLETED BY THE EMPLOYEE Performance Goals and Plans of Action for Each Major Responsibility	II. COMPLETED BY THE SUPERVISOR Results and Comments

Figure 31. Goal worksheet, Abbott Laboratories.

NAME_____   POSITION TITLE _____

DEPARTMENT_____   IMMEDIATE SUPERVISOR_____

DATE PREPARED_____   DATE PROGRESS TO
BE REVIEWED _____

I. MAJOR WORK GOALS	PROGRESS REVIEW
Brief description of the most important job goals, results expected, and specific measures or sources of information that will provide evidence of accomplishment.	Demonstrate accomplishment of goal or progress toward accomplishment.

II. MAJOR MAN GOAL

The most important self-development goal.

PROGRESS REVIEW

Evidence of accomplishment.

III. OTHER IMPORTANT GOALS

PROGRESS REVIEW

OVERALL COMMENTS

Date Reviewed

Has a revised goal work sheet been prepared?

Immediate Supervisor (Signature)

Employee (Signature)

27

Implementing MBO

MANY of the widespread, multifaceted applications of MBO have been resounding successes. The success of others is questionable. Still others have been outright failures. Why?

Very often the answer lies in how the system was implemented, especially how the critical preimplementation phase was handled. A study of implementation methods as related to successful operation indicates a high degree of correlation in over 300 different MBO installations. Organizations that understood the full import of MBO and took the time and effort required to implement it properly have enjoyed the maximum fruits of the system. Those that devoted only minimal time and effort to implementation have enjoyed success only commensurate with their efforts.

Organizations that endeavored to adopt and copy the system out of hand, and overnight, have usually failed. The strongest support for these conclusions is that not one single company studied, which had properly implemented the system in the first instance, has ever discontinued using it as its primary approach to management. Certainly, these organizations have modified and amended their systems as experience was gained, but the basic MBO system is still intact and being vigorously pursued. Thus it becomes of paramount importance to define implementation and to set forth its key components. Of equal importance is a complete understanding of the prerequisites that management must meet before it begins to implement the system.

There remains little question that the MBO system has received numerous black eyes it did not deserve. Almost all these black eyes should have been visited upon the managers who tried to adopt it without being competent to do so. Contrary to belief in some quarters, MBO is not a simple system. It has many principles, many nuances—some subtle, some overt—many virtues, and many pitfalls. All must be understood, appreciated, and practiced by the manager who would apply it successfully.

BEFORE IMPLEMENTATION

Much of the success of implementation should be based on two major decisions that must always precede implementation; namely, do we really understand what MBO is all about and do we want to adopt it in our company? Too many organizations, much to their later regret, have moved right into implementation without having considered these questions carefully. The chief executive officer and, hopefully, his senior officers will complete an exhaustive analysis before making these critical decisions. Their analysis will require finding definitive answers to several major questions, which are:

1. Do we really understand the full import of MBO as it would affect our organization? Do we understand how it operates, as well as its strengths, its pitfalls?

2. Is it right for our organization—are we willing to devote the time and effort, especially on the part of the chief executive, to make it effective (it probably requires a minimum of three years to reach 85 percent effectiveness)?

3. Are we ready for it? Have we met the three major prerequisites— proper management atmosphere, organizational clarity, and an effective management information system? If not, can we meet them before implementation?

4. Is this the best timing? Are operations so unstable presently that there would be an excessive number of distractions from the concerted effort required? Will sufficient executive and managerial time be available? Would another period be better?

5. Why do we want it, what will it do for our organization? Various aids are available to assist in this analysis phase. They include—again, as a very minimum—the following. First, there is reading. Several excellent books by recognized professionals are available, but check out the author before buying the book. Books that include actual case studies of company experiences are especially valuable, as the companies discussed can serve as the basis for further investigation. Time spent on researching and preparing a bibliography will be well worthwhile.

The experience of other organizations is an invaluable aid. Properly undertaken, this phase will provide an excellent basis for making a decision. Ask penetrating questions of at least six organizations that have practiced MBO for at least three years and insist on full answers. Are they really practicing MBO or is it merely window dressing? What have been their successes and failures? What impact did it have on their management group and overall company performance? For what purposes do they use MBO? What conditions prevailed in the company? Would they do it all over again?

Finally, bring in competent (repeat, competent) outside help on an ad hoc basis to answer questions and provide guides and checkpoints for your decision.

The ultimate question to be answered is: Are you certain of what you are getting involved in and are you fully committed to making MBO work in your organization? Only if this question can be answered in the affirmative, without reservation, should an organization move on to the implementation stage.

THREE APPROACHES TO IMPLEMENTATION

Figure 32 summarizes the three most prevalent approaches to implementation and outlines the major features that must be evaluated before selecting the appropriate approach for a particular organization. It will be noted rather quickly that the major differences in the three approaches revolve around the degree to which top management is sold on and committed to MBO, the speed with which implementation proceeds, and the numbers of managers and managerial levels involved at any given time. For example, in a company having an enthusiastic, highly committed top management, the implementation often is completed in one to two years and all levels become actively involved almost from the very beginning. In contrast, a company having a more conservative management may spread the implementation over three or four years and only a relatively few managers become involved in the beginning, with the number increasing gradually as implementation moves to succeeding levels.

EFFECTIVENESS OF EACH APPROACH

Figure 32 indicates that success is tied closely to the speed with which the implementation proceeds, with the lowest probable success accompanying implementation when all levels of management are brought into the system at the same time and the installation is compressed into a short time span. While several successful installations have been made in this fashion, they constitute the exception rather than the rule. In the main, the managers involved have been typified by the characteristic listed under the "Type of Management to Which Suited" category.

There are several reasons why the "All Levels at Once" approach enjoys a low probability of success. MBO is a way of life, it is a tough, demanding state of managerial thinking translated into action. Neither a way of life nor thinking can be changed in a precipitate manner. Time for both indoctrination and assimilation is required. Time also is required to understand the full import and impact of the system prior to trying to assimilate it—let alone trying to implement it. The time constraint impacts even on small companies with only a few managers and levels of management, a lesson learned the hard way by a small manufacturing and sales company in the Midwest. This company, with annual sales of less than $10 million and approximately 40 managers, crashed through an MBO installation in less than six months. Now, 18 months and many disappointments later, the company still is struggling to establish a believable base with its managers so that it can begin implementing MBO the way it should have in the first place. Their task is not easy because it requires overcoming the disenchantment of each manager multiplied by 40 times. Conversely, one of the larger of the Fortune 500 companies spread its implementation over six years, proceeding one level at a time, and now enjoys the full fruits of its MBO labors. Neither the time span nor the approach was 100 percent responsible for this failure and success; however, the senior managers who were intimately involved in these two cases attribute much of the result to these two features of implementation.

OUTSIDE COUNSEL

The extent of need for outside help increases with the speed with which implementation proceeds. Invariably in the "All Levels at Once" approach it is necessary to make extensive use of outsiders who have gained their experience working with other organizations. Naturally, one of the more potentially unfavorable results is that the outsider may be advocating adoption of a system and principles that, while successful for other organizations, may require considerable varying, revising, and adapting for another organization. Such tailoring requires time for investigating and analyzing. When this time is not made available, the result usually is a copycat plan with many of the pertinent decisions being based on expediency. An excessive amount of retraining and debugging time will be required later even if the implementation is successful. Usually it is preferable to take the additional time for implementation and as much as pos-

Figure 32. Guide for determining an implementation approach for MBO.

	APPROACH		
	One Level at a Time	One Department Only	All Levels at Once
General description	Implementation takes place one level (sometimes two) at a time starting at the top. Six months to a year is devoted to each level before moving to next level.	A "guinea pig" department runs a "pilot" test to decide whether or not MBO will be extended to other departments.	All levels of management are considered as a single group and MBO is implemented all at once for the entire group.
Type of organization to which suited	Large one with many managers and many levels of management. Many services. Geographically dispersed. Many client groups. Nonintegrated product or services.	Either large or small and of any type, but more frequently to larger ones with many diverse operations.	Smaller organizations. Few managers and few levels. Integrated service lines. Geographically concentrated.
Type of management to which suited	Emphasizes long-term growth. Methodical. Conservative. Not oriented to objectives.	Doubting Thomas. Little, if any, exposure to MBO. Often wedded to the past. Slow to try new approaches. Very conservative.	Gung ho. Homogeneous group. Objectives-oriented. Skilled at delegation. Accustomed to dealing with disciplines. Highly educated managers.
Time required by top management (during implementation)	Considerable but spread over a longer period of time.	*	Extensive, running several months. Considerable time also required later to debug the mistakes from moving very rapidly.
Time required by all managers (during implementation)	Average and spread over longer period of time.	*	Same, as above, for top management.

Top management commitment required	Average.	*	Full.
Implementation time required	Three to four years.	*	One to two years.
Advantages	In-depth understanding by each manager. More opportunity to debug as experience is gained. Each level becomes "teachers" for next level. System is more tailor-made to organization.	Mistakes are isolated. Provides "selling" tool for other departments. Results in a trained cadre of knowledgeable MBO managers.	Training duplication is minimized. Greater impact, faster. Higher immediate involvement of all managers.
Disadvantages	More time-consuming generally. Training is duplicated. Some levels are operating under MBO while others are not. Extensive top management time and effort are spent meeting with several levels. Temporary confusion and misunderstanding at lower levels if not communicated with.	Selection of right pilot department is critical. No assurance efforts are aimed to top needs of organization. Future MBO efforts will suffer unduly if limited experience is not successful. Usual risks from projecting from a small sample.	Few checks and balances on validity of objectives. Likelihood of autocratic actions to maintain pace. Blind lead the blind. Mistakes are multiplied. Likely to adopt a canned program rather than tailoring it. Usually requires outside help. Decisions based on expediency.
Outside help required	Average.	Minimal to average.	Extensive.
Dollar cost of implementing	Highest.	*	Lowest.
Probability of success	Highest.	Average.	Lowest.

* Depends upon which way the implementation proceeds after the "pilot" run, that is, one level at a time or all at once.

Source: Dale D. McConkey, "How to Succeed and Fail with MBO," *The Business Quarterly*, Winter 1974, p. 60.

sible solve the problems and fully answer all questions before proceeding to the next stage. This requires continual deliberation by internal personnel, but it is time well spent.

When outside counsel is retained, there is a strong likelihood that the company's MBO system will become linked too closely with the consultant and managers will therefore look upon it as the consultant's program rather than an internal product of the company. Any program that isn't regarded as being the product and creation of the organization's leader will suffer in effectiveness.

COMMITMENT

For managers to successfully achieve their objectives, they must be fully committed to and motivated for top performance. Much of the key to getting them into this frame of mind consists of ensuring they understand the whys and benefits of MBO, both to their organizations and to them individually. Extreme care must be exercised, especially in the early days, to avoid leaving them with the negative impression that the system is primarily a device for pinning them with set accountabilities as a means of checking on them and possibly "hanging" them later on. The entire implementation stage must be approached in a positive manner. If an attempt is made to teach them only the mechanics of MBO, which usually happens in a speedy MBO installation, they may well indict the system on this negative note. This is another compelling reason why the "One Level at a Time" approach is recommended for most installations; managers become better indoctrinated in the rationale of the system, and usually they can witness its benefits as the implementation unfolds. In the faster installations, they must rely on blind faith that the system is of benefit and will work. They don't have the experience of the succeeding levels of management above them.

TOP MANAGEMENT TIME

Time required by top management is a major consideration when deciding which of the three approaches to follow. The chief executive and all senior officers and department heads must devote a high percentage of their time and efforts to the installation. It cannot be handled by staff people or others acting in their behalf; their personal time and direction are required for success.

The time element compounds itself in the "All Levels at Once" approach. Not only must top management spend considerable time on the installation but the time must be spent in solid blocks (almost exclusive concentration solely on the installation while it is unfolding). Few top managers can devote their time without major problems arising in other areas of their operations.

Although the "One Level at a Time" approach will require greater total time—resulting from duplicating training sessions and meetings with the several levels of management—the time need not be concentrated in a short period; for example, top managers can work on other matters between the training sessions and follow-up meetings. This is one of the primary reasons why most companies select the more gradual approach.

ADDITIONAL CONSIDERATIONS

Several characteristics peculiar to various organizations place an additional premium on the speed and method by which implementation is pursued.

Foreign operations, especially those having a large number of managers, not all of whom are bilingual, require additional time and dedication. Again, it is imperative that all managers completely understand the rationale of MBO and be comfortable working with the system. Language problems per se, coupled with the subtle and not so subtle nuances of MBO, dictate that additional implementation time be devoted to these managers and that the whole of MBO be fed to them more gradually. One large international company took almost seven years to complete its implementation, but it has been a successful one.

Similarly, organizations with poor communications and ineffective management information systems must proceed more slowly. A system that provides managers with the quality of data required to make effective decisions in the first place and then, later, to measure the success of their efforts is an absolute essential to a successful MBO installation. One of the more prevalent pitfalls of MBO systems is the insistence that managers structure specific objectives and concrete plans for teaching them and then failure to provide the necessary feedback to these managers. No organization should proceed with an installation without giving the requisite attention to its management information system. This requirement argues strongly in favor of adopting the "One Level at a Time" approach. This provides the necessary time to tailor a management information system stage by stage, concurrent with each level of implementation.

Finally, the clearest possible organization must be structured. The salient feature of MBO is that the system comprises a 100 percent delegation for results; delegation poses the rather absolute requirement that the entity know who is responsible for what. Without exception, every MBO system unearths existing confusion as to job content and accountabilities of managers. Confusion must be resolved before proceeding to the next stage or management level during the implementation. Once more, this problem is handled more effectively in the "One Level at a Time" approach. The reason would appear obvious. If there is organizational confusion at the top, say at the officer level, this confusion will be compounded down the line as the officer delegates to each of his subordinate levels. Proceeding one level at a time permits the confusion to be resolved at the higher level before being fanned out through the organization by use of the delegation process.

IMPLEMENTATION TRAINING

Regardless of which implementation approach is followed, the training of the managers involved should include certain common ingredients.

The controlling rationale, especially during the first six months, should be to take small bites and digest each one completely before proceeding to the next. This is the foundation-laying stage and, much like constructing a building, a sound total structure cannot be built on a sloppy foundation.

Stage 1: Getting ready. This stage should cover both MBO as a system and the writing of effective objectives. An objective should never be written until the writer understands the system in which the objective operates. Violation of this premise almost invariably results in noncoordinated objectives written in a vacuum and carried out in isolation rather than as a proportionate part of department and company objectives. Both the system and the objectives are covered by a combination of reading assignments, discussion groups, workshop sessions, and coaching by competent leaders.

After two or three months of indoctrination, managers usually are prepared to start writing simple objectives. Emphasis should be devoted to getting managers accustomed to, and comfortable working with, objectives and learning the place of their objectives in the total scheme of things. Emphasis should not be on writing the best possible objectives. This can come later.

During the ensuing three months, the intent is to have each manager write increasingly complex objectives, each writing followed by an evaluation and coaching session, until he has become fairly adept at structuring meaningful, measurable objectives. Finally, he recommends a group of objectives on which he will operate and be measured during the second six months—the dry-run phase.

Stage 2: Operating under objectives. It is made clear to each manager that he is operating under MBO on a dry-run basis during these six months and that his future will not sink or swim on the basis of his results. He is still undergoing training and indoctrination.

A feedback method is established to measure his performance against each of his objectives. Both he and his superior receive copies. Halfway through this stage the manager and his superior hold a formal review (just as they will do in the future for each quarter of the year) to evaluate progress toward objectives, discuss any variances, and review the validity of the objectives for the remainder of the period. Necessary revisions are made to plans and objectives.

A similar review takes place three months later (at the end of the full year) and if managers are found capable, they begin actually operating under all facets of MBO. The implementation then moves down to the next level of management, and similar indoctrination is provided for them. The process continues until all levels are covered and the total management group has become a part of MBO.

The importance of effective communications is emphasized during this transition from one stage to another. If the fact that MBO is being adopted is treated as a deep, dark secret, the levels of management that have yet to be covered will likely build up fear and distrust of the system. Managers at all levels should be acquainted with the fact that MBO is being adopted, including any timetable, the reasons why (purpose), and the part they will play in the system. Progress reports should be issued periodically and senior managers encouraged to brief their managers from time to time as the installation unfolds.

AFTER IMPLEMENTATION

No one has yet made a bug-free or perfect installation. Nor will they! Therefore, the final phase of implementation takes place after implementation and goes on forever to one degree or another. It consists of continually evaluating the system for effectiveness and making the necessary revisions and improvements commensurate with experience gained.

Major departures from the original system are better handled by periodic educational meetings like those held when the system was first implemented. The quarterly progress review sessions also are an excellent, ongoing means for evaluating the system itself and making improvements.

Much of MBO is a state of mind—a way of doing things better and emphasizing continual improvement. Minds aren't changed overnight and neither will MBO be effective overnight.

CAVEAT EMPTOR

One note of caution is appropriate for those executives who may require outside assistance when implementing. The rapid growth of MBO has brought with it the usual camp followers, soothsayers, and peddlers of magic. They take the form of consultants, business educators, and educational management associations. A week seldom passes without another one publicly declaring himself to be an expert in MBO. And their ranks continue to grow, swelled as they are by the unqualified who read a few books on the subject, attend a session of two, and then hang up their shingles. Of such stuff experts and instant—but short-lived—heroes are made.

Those who may consider outside help would be well advised to seek definitive answers to these questions before making a selection:

1. Has he had at least five years of experience working with all phases of MBO? Hopefully he will have been a key manager operating in an organization that practiced MBO.

2. Has he made at least one full-scale MBO installation and then lived with it for a minimum of three years?

3. Does his experience include all phases of MBO treated as a total management system, or has he worked primarily with one or two facets of the total system, such as planning and/or evaluation of performance? The specialist is like a duck out of water when trying to advise on the many aspects of an initial installation.

4. Did he get the bulk of his knowledge from practical experience, or is he quoting from a book or some quoter of quoters?

5. Does he talk practical, operating language, or does he fill the air with definitions and high-priced terms? Does he preach or practice?

6. Can he give specific examples as to how each phase of MBO works?

7. Will he give you an introduction to the subject and a thick report of recommendations, along with a big bill, and then leave, or will he stay and work with you through the implementation stage by stage? The former should be avoided at all costs.

8. Is he knowledgeable when applying MBO to staff jobs, or is his experience confined to applications to line jobs, where the application is much easier?

9. Can he cite some of his work where MBO hasn't been 100 percent effective? If he's had the requisite experience, he's had a few of these.

10. Is he trying to peddle a large number of forms and paperwork? Does he insist that all forms must be used exactly as recommended? Excessive paperwork is a major weakness of MBO and too many forms usually indicate a person who is more skilled in method than analysis. MBO requires an analytical mind.

CONCLUSION

The wealth of experience of the countless, diverse organizations dictates several conclusions that should be of benefit to those who may be considering installing an MBO system, to those who have just begun, and equally, if belatedly, to those who profess to practice MBO but wonder why they aren't. These conclusions may be summarized as follows.

In the hands of a competent management, MBO can be a potent vehicle for improving individual managerial productivity and total organization performance.

Far too many installations have been made without sufficient preparatory work.

Many of the later weaknesses can be traced back to the lack of proper implementation earlier.

The later success of MBO is directly proportional to the thoroughness of implementation.

The analysis preceding the decision whether or not to adopt MBO is of paramount importance, especially in determining the degree of commitment on the part of management.

Implementation is time-consuming, laborious, and often frustrating, but well worthwhile.

While the actual implementation stage is highly important, the actions that precede and follow this stage are equally important.

Only the more successful organizations practicing MBO have appreciated that implementation is the real guts of the system.

28

Using
an MBO Adviser

THE USE OF an internal MBO adviser (or MBO coordinator, as the job is frequently titled) is growing in popularity in the United States. Originally used primarily in Europe, the concept spread to Canada and then to the United States.

THE JOB IN GENERAL

An MBO adviser is the "in house" expert on the practice, operation, and applications of the MBO system. He/she functions as a top-level staff manager assisting the organization's management team in the identification and selection of key results areas, the analysis of capability to achieve results, and the formulation of objectives and plans to achieve the objectives and advising generally in the implementation and practice of MBO. The adviser spends considerable time training others in MBO and acting as a catalyst to management thinking. In many ways, he is a teaching "professor of MBO." His major contribution is made during the implementation period.

SPECIFIC DUTIES

The MBO adviser is a staff member of management and as such has no line authority over anyone except himself. His influence and contribution develop from his ability to impart his knowledge to others in a manner that will help them manage better through the use of MBO. He assists higher-level managers in gaining a working knowledge of MBO practice, operation, and applications in the following ways:

1. Assisting in the identification and selection of key results areas—those high-payback areas of the job in which they must achieve a high level of performance to be successful.
2. Helping them complete their operating plans—their objectives, plans, and budgets.
3. Acting as a catalyst between two levels of management to help them reach agreement.
4. Counseling managers in problem-solving techniques.
5. Performing management-styles analyses.
6. Conducting organizational analysis.
7. Assisting in the preparation of MBO implementation schedules and plans.
8. Establishing feedback and monitoring techniques; for example, progress and performance measures.
9. Assisting in the preparation of policies and procedures relative to assembling and submission of operating plans.
10. Assisting in the determination of the context of interim reviews during the target period; counseling them in conducting such reviews.
11. Counseling and training in team development.
12. Providing on-the-spot coaching.

QUALIFICATIONS

Ideally, the MBO adviser has a sound educational background, usually including graduate study. He should be a broad-gauged manager, preferably with a good track record in both line and staff positions. Peer respect of his management ability is important, and he should be selected from fairly high up on the management ladder. Skills in training and interpersonal relations are essential. He must be a clear, analytical thinker who can communicate with enthusiasm and credibility. In-depth knowledge and understanding of the MBO system is a must.

To be avoided at any cost when selecting an MBO adviser is the brilliant, brittle person with an inferiority complex. He'll spend roughly one-third of his time trying to impress others with his intelligence, one-third espousing complicated concepts, and the other third trying to do the work of others just to demonstrate that results are being achieved from his efforts.

REPORTING RELATIONSHIP

For maximum impact, especially during the critical implementation period, the adviser should normally report to the chief executive officer or to the chief operating officer where all line and staff functions report to the latter. Having him report to some top staff officer such as the vice-president of finance or personnel exposes the company to the risk of having MBO viewed too narrowly; that is, as primarily a financial or personnel approach. The "filter" problem is also avoided when the adviser reports directly to the top officer. The most successful total company approaches are line-directed.

POTENTIAL PITFALLS FOR THE ADVISER

Much like other staff managers, the adviser must avoid several major pitfalls. These traps are especially damaging when they befall an adviser because of his role in furthering the total management system of the organization. The following are some of the more serious pitfalls.

Overselling MBO. While the adviser must be enthusiastic, his main emphasis should be placed on helping managers practice MBO. Constantly chanting MBO's virtues, instead of providing them, will turn off many managers.

Telling them rather than showing them. A certain amount of lecture is necessary, but this should never take priority over practical, workshop-type learning experiences.

Doing it for them rather than making them think and do it themselves. The adviser is responsible for showing managers how to do it and letting them gain experience by doing it themselves.

Trying to do too much too quickly. Patience is necessary in any type of training activity and certainly when managers are mastering a broad system like MBO. The adviser must aim for progressive accomplishment, not rapid, spectacular results.

Creating unnecessary forms, procedures, and paperwork. The adviser should be analysis-oriented, not process- or method-oriented. The latter can lead to generating complicated, painstaking detail.

Becoming and end in himself; not using other available disciplines and expertise. In many respects, the title "MBO Coordinator" is an apt description. One of his tasks is to coordinate all the various disciplines to ensure that MBO is practiced in the most effective manner. He should never let his actions replace or neglect these other disciplines: the external consultant for his overall expertise; the specialist in planning for his services; the financial experts for the feedback and financial analysis they provide; personnel people for their skills in performance evaluation and in giving rewards and recognition; and organizational development people for their abilities in staff development and training.

Replacing the president. Because of his vast knowledge of MBO, the adviser must be constantly on guard against the possibility that his words or action will be interpreted as speaking or acting in the president's place. The MBO system belongs to the president and the managers, not to the adviser. An effective MBO adviser maintains low visibility while keeping the focus on the top officer and the other managers.

SOURCE OF MBO ADVISERS

Obviously, a company has two choices when selecting an adviser—internal and external. It can hire the adviser from another organization where MBO has been successfully practiced for the requisite period of time or it can select a competent manager internally and provide him with the necessary training in MBO. Both alternatives have advantages and disadvantages.

The person hired from another company will have both MBO knowledge and experience as an adviser. He won't, however, be familiar with the operations of his new company (some consider this to be an advantage as he won't be steeped in past practices and customs). He may face the added problem of being regarded as a "whiz kid."

Selecting the adviser internally has the major advantage that he is knowledgeable in company operations and, assuming that the right person has been selected, the additional advantage of already enjoying acceptance by his peers. However, he must be trained to serve as an adviser. By necessity, his MBO training must be undertaken outside the company because it probably isn't already practicing MBO. Following is a topical outline of the major subjects in which the adviser must be trained.

The MBO System
    Its evolution.
    Definitions and terminology.
    How it operates.
    The components of the system.
Prerequisites to a Successful System
The Applications of MBO to the Total Management Function

The Use of the Behavioral Sciences
  Their importance.
  Their application.
  How they work.
The Sequence in the Objective-Setting Process
  Preparatory work required prior to writing objectives.
  Establishing objectives from the top to lower levels of
  management.
  Differences in objectives by management levels.
  Coordinating and balancing of all objectives.
How to Write Objectives
  Criteria for effective objectives.
  Types of objectives.
  Testing objectives for effectiveness.
Staff Managers and MBO
  Objectives for staff managers.
  How they differ from line objectives.
Planning or Programming Objectives for Achievement
  How to program objectives.
  Evaluating the effectiveness of the programming.
Evaluting, Measuring, and Controlling
  Tailoring the measuring tools.
  Establishing the basis for revisions and corrective action.
Implementing MBO
  Guides and practices.
  Implementing for the whole organization.
  Implementing in only one department or division.
Executive Direction of the MBO System
Administration and Monitoring of the System
How to Avoid the Common Pitfalls in MBO
Preparing an MBO Adviser Action Plan
  What are the next steps?
  Where do you go from here?
  Action back on the job.

THE ADVISER'S NEXT JOB

The major responsibility of an MBO adviser ends when the MBO system
has been implemented and is functioning smoothly, probably somewhere
around three years after initial implementation. Once this point has been
reached, the adviser is usually overqualified to continue serving in this ca-

pacity. He's probably overqualified for two reasons. First, he was a highly qualified person in an important job before he began his advisory role. Second, he has gained additional topflight, broad company experience.

For these reasons, he should be given a responsible job somewhere else in the company. Assuming he's been successful as an adviser, he should be qualified to fill a wide range of top management responsibilities, after having trained a more junior manager to carry on the more routine, but important, task of assisting in the administration of the ongoing MBO system.

29

CASE STUDY

The Western Company of North America

AUTHOR'S COMMENT: *This case study of The Western Company of North America is provided so that the reader can benefit from the actual experience of one of the organizations that have successfully practiced the MBO principles and approaches discussed in this book. The Western Company has been benefiting from its MBO system for more than eight years.*

THE WESTERN COMPANY of North America, with headquarters in Fort Worth, Texas, derived its sales of approximately $100 million in 1975 by providing technically oriented, on-shore services to the oil- and gas-drilling companies operating in the producing regions of Texas, Louisiana, Oklahoma, New Mexico, Colorado, Wyoming, and to a limited extent in Arizona and Utah. It also provides off-shore drilling operations under contracts to major oil companies in the North Sea, Persian Gulf, South China Sea, South America, and Gulf of Mexico. Western now includes The Western Petroleum Services Group, consisting of:

—The headquarters group, with analysis, marketing research, and personnel departments as well as engineering, manufacturing, and research divisions.

—The Stimulation Division, which increases the productivity of wells through the use of various chemicals and fracturing fluids designed to solve the flow-retarding problems of oil wells.

—The Wire Line Division, which identifies and evaluates petroleum-producing zones by means of intricate electronic equipment and provides access to those zones by perforating the pipe with holes through the use of a perforating gun firing shaped charges.

—The Cementing Division, whose purpose is to provide complete primary and remedial services during the drilling of new wells or the workover operations on established wells.

The Western Oceanic Group consists of:

—The headquarters group, with an operations division and marketing–sales and personnel departments.

—Several operating areas where Western provides drilling platforms, rigs, and crews for drilling, workover, and completion services to off-shore oil and gas producers. While the location of its areas of operation will change, the present operational areas are the Gulf Coast/South America, North Sea, and Far East.

As a technically oriented company requiring large investments in off-shore drilling rigs, rolling stock, equipment, and instrumentation, the company necessarily is typified by a high fixed cost of operation. The off-shore operation is capital-intensive. The on-shore operation is people-intensive. To maintain and improve its profitability with this diverse organization, the company must press for high volume and the maintenance of strict quality standards for its on-shore operation and a definite superiority in the maintenance of quality performance by the crews and drilling equipment for its off-shore operation. Numerous worldwide competitors and a rather static on-shore market impose an additional premium on all managers of the company to continually improve their performance. In this area Western has developed a unique Key Managers Training Program in the skills and functions of management that apply to all Western Company managers.

In the early 1960s, the company organized a research division with the mission of maintaining Western in the forefront of oil service companies by ensuring that the services provided by the company are the most advanced in terms of the latest methods and techniques. Today research is done by each service organization. Similarly, engineering for the specialized equipment, which must be designed and manufactured by the company, is performed by each of the two major operating units. This specialized engineering and manufacturing function reports to the president,

Western Petroleum Services, and the specialized research divisions report to the managers of the stimulation, wire line, and cementing divisions. With entrance into off-shore drilling in the latter 1960s, it was necessary to provide a highly technical specialized engineering and construction capability to oversee the building of the off-shore drilling rigs. This specialized function reports to the operations division manager in the Oceanic Group Headquarters.

Purchasing, except for the more routine supplies and services required at the corporate headquarters, is handled on a centralized basis by each of the two groups for their particular type of operations: on-shore or off-shore.

Legal matters are performed by Western Company Counselors with the assistance of specialized technical counsel.

The financial operations of the company, consisting of payroll, accounting, disbursement, computer (software and hardware operations) are centralized in the corporate offices, where they perform all financial functions for both operations groups.

Chart A illustrates the organization of The Western Company today and represents the second reorganization since MBO was instituted. This organization has resulted from organizational analysis of tasks that must be performed to satisfy the growth objectives of the operating groups, reflected in their current and long-range plans. The company considers its management group as comprising all line and staff managers from its chief executive office through the first level of supervision in both on-shore and off-shore operations and includes all this group in the MBO system. Unlike other companies that start with the top group and then bring in succeedingly lower levels at various stages, Western covered all three top levels at one time. Much of 1967 was devoted to extensively educating and indoctrinating managers in the rationale, operations, and techniques of MBO. The bulk of upper- and middle-level managers were operating under MBO beginning with 1968. While additional training activities continued for managers at lower levels, staff managers were included as an integral part of MBO from its inception. In late 1973, when the company had its first organizational change under MBO, an extensive Key Managers Training Program for the first two levels of management in the functions and skills of management was developed for all key managers. This training was completed in 1975. The continued emphasis on training all managers in the concept of MBO and the management knowledge they must have is the direct result of the chief executive officer's interest in providing necessary in-house management talent for the company's growth.

Chart A. Organization of The Western Company.

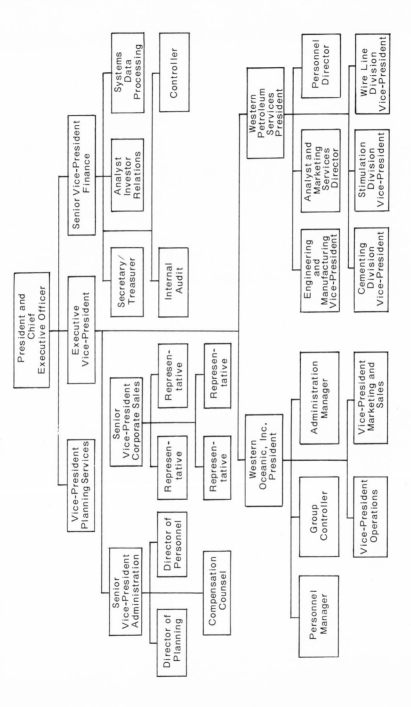

HISTORY OF MBO

The Western Company of today had its beginnings in the mid-1960s. Following the general industry recession, which began in 1958, the company went into a gradual decline. By 1964, Western's situation had become critical—rundown equipment, unsuccessful diversification efforts, declining market penetration, and insufficient profits. Western had fallen into a hole and there was no easy way out. The company considers that much of this hole was of the company's own making.

During its first 25 years, Western's management style could be described as personalized management with near-term perspective. The company decided that a complete change was necessitated in its basic management system. During the mid-1960s, the company began adopting management by objectives; however, only one operating division was successfully using the system by 1967. Beginning with 1967, major emphasis was placed on modern day MBO and in 1968 the full impact of the evolving management system became evident. The trends of the early 1960s had been broken and reversed. By the end of 1973, a balanced team of proven veterans and a new group of competent, aggressive managers had spelled out the long-term objectives of the company and the short-term objectives and plans by which the future goals would be achieved.

Western's adoption and implementation of MBO has been marked by two major successes: the dispatch with which all levels of management became involved and the apparent results the company has achieved to date.

WESTERN'S MBO SYSTEM

Western summarizes its MBO program as consisting of six major facets. The following is a brief description of the system as it is practiced in the company.

Management by objectives is The Western Company's system of management, which binds individual goals to corporate goals through the process of:

1. Fixing the current position of the company and each organizational unit within the company. (This involves an objective delineation and analysis of strengths and weaknesses and an evaluation of threats and opportunities that are present in the company's environment.)

2. Determining where the company wants to go and how it will achieve its desired position. (This involves an active, continual recognition of the environment in which the company operates and its impact on the company.)

3. Organizing the company so that plans to achieve the desired position can be implemented. (This involves defining organizational functions and accountabilities and authorities of each position in the organization.)

4. Passing responsibility for setting and achieving objectives down in the organization. In this fashion, actions of each organizational level support the achievement of the objectives of the next higher level. (This involves the commitment of each manager to the achievement of objectives through the process of individual participation in goal selection and in laying out plans to achieve these goals.)

5. Reviewing on a periodic basis the performance of each organizational unit and each individual toward the "committed for" objectives.

6. Taking corrective action if a deviation exists between the actual condition and planned-for condition to ensure the achievement of the agreed-upon objectives so that overall corporate objectives are met.

Through the process of goal setting, commitment to objectives, and appraisal of results, the individual is motivated and developed to the fullest in achieving his own goals by directing his efforts toward organizational objectives.

COMPONENTS OF THE SYSTEM

Chart B shows the five major components, or subsystems, of the total MBO system as practiced in The Western Company. These subsystems constitute the implementing, or action, vehicles of MBO. The financial

Chart B. Components of The Western Company's MBO system.

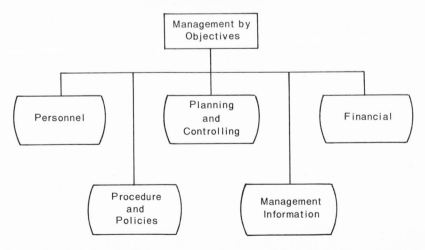

system has been previously discussed. The planning and controlling system is accomplished by an annual planning cycle generated at the corporate level by providing the operating groups with planning guidance that includes environmental analysis, projections as to labor markets, and operating markets. The circle is completed when the groups, using this planning guidance, develop their plans and submit them to the corporate planning office for consolidation into the overall corporate objectives and corporate plan. This system emphasizes planning from the bottom up so that individual managers are committed to the objectives they developed. If objectives do not meet the criteria for a Western Company objective, discussions between the organizational elements and top management resolve these differences.

MANAGEMENT INFORMATION SYSTEMS

In The Western Company all interoffice memoranda forms have preprinted at the bottom of each page the following: "A man's judgment is no better than his information." Because of the rapid growth of The Western Company the information systems of the 1960s and early 1970s have become outmoded. Western has instituted a comprehensive management information system to provide information from its widely separated operating locations to assist top management in the decision-making processes.

POLICIES AND PROCEDURES

Corporate policies and procedures are the communication vehicles to provide direction to MBO and its subsystems. Each group is required to develop policies and procedures on the technical and operational aspects of its particular type of business.

PERSONNEL

The total personnel system in The Western Company clearly outlines the responsibilities and accountabilities for this resource through each phase; that is, establishment of requirements, employment, utilization, evaluation, and compensation (evaluation will be discussed later). See Chart C for the elements of this system.

Chart C. The Western Company's personnel system.

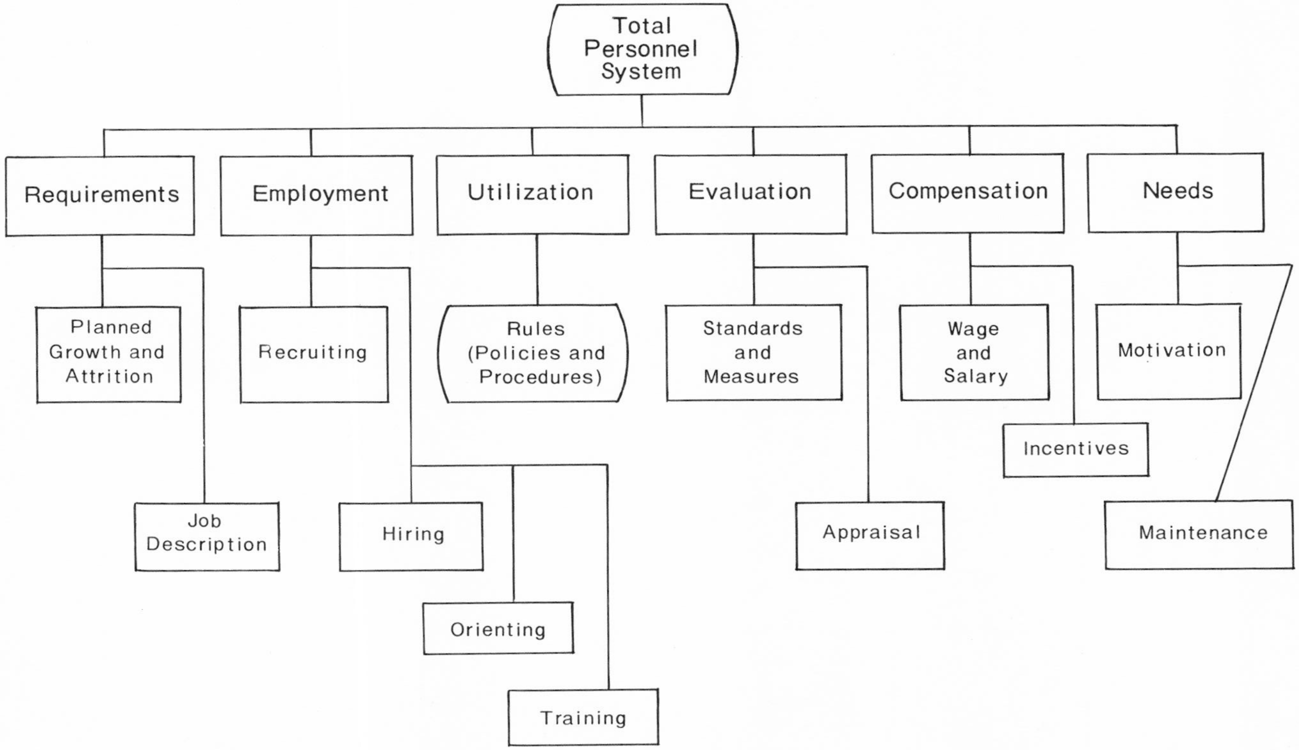

DEMANDS ON MANAGERS

Western has issued a specific policy statement that provides that the management system best serving the needs of the company, and the individual within the company, is management of objectives. In this regard (1) all managers must be proficient in goal setting—in planning to achieve their goals under time and cost constraints, in building an organization, and training subordinates who can plan and execute according to plan. (2) All personnel will be evaluated and rewarded on the basis of their performance according to plan and execution of their job accountabilities on the basis of function guides and standards of measurement. (3) The Western Company will maintain an internal environment that favors the creative individual and encourages him/her to perform at the level of his/her full potential.

ORGANIZATION CHANGES

The 18 months following the adoption of MBO were marked by extensive changes in the organization, particularly among personnel of all Western's staff departments except engineering. The heads of three functions were replaced. Two functions, marketing services and purchasing, were eliminated as general staff departments at the corporate headquarters level. A new planning function was initiated to assist the president and officers in the administration of the MBO system. These major changes resulted from a thorough analysis of the contributions and costs of all departments in light of the results that were required by the staff departments in terms of the company's short- and long-range objectives. A more detailed explanation of the changes in each of the staff departments follows.

Purchasing. Prior to the adoption of MBO in January 1968, purchasing was responsible for procurement of materials and supplies for the company's offices and certain, but not all, materials, supplies, and equipment for the three operating divisions and the Research Division. Purchasing also was responsible for a limited amount of inventory control. A study of the company's total purchasing requirement indicated that most of the purchasing needs of the operating divisions involved special-purpose materials and equipment; each division used different materials and equipment peculiar to its division. In certain instances, headquarters purchasing was duplicating purchasing and inventory control activities of the divisions.

The headquarters purchasing function was eliminated and through the reorganizations is now the responsibility of each of the operating groups for its specialized types of equipment. The office services manager at corporate headquarters became responsible for the procurement of office supplies and materials.

Marketing services. The job of the marketing services manager in Western's headquarters initially was eliminated. This manager had carried out general duties in the areas of contacts with the advertising agency, trade relations, and customer relations as well as certain loosely defined responsibilities for assisting divisional sales personnel in making sales. Because of the company's growth, this function and the coordination necessitated by on-shore, off-shore operations have been brought back to the corporate office under the direction of the vice-president of sales.

Through the evolution of the two reorganizations, the function of market analysis has been located in each operating group, as the requirements for analysis of the on-shore markets and the analysis of the worldwide off-shore markets can better be performed at the group headquarters than at a centralized corporate office.

Management replacements. The managers of three staff departments were replaced. These managers had considerable experience carrying out activities and administering programs of a general nature, which were difficult to evalute except in equally general terms. They were unaccustomed to operating in a manner that required establishing specific objectives and plans and making certain that the objectives were required by the company's needs and priorities. They were unable to make the transition from Western's traditional method of management to the new system provided for by MBO.

Planning. A planning function headed by a manager reporting to the president was added in 1968. At the same time it was clearly enunciated to all personnel of the company that the president continued to be responsible for the executive direction and effectiveness of the MBO program. The planning manager became responsible for assisting the president in the formulation of top objectives for the company and administering the MBO system.

The clear pinpointing of the planning manager's responsibility helped eliminate the confusion that frequently occurs when an administrative manager assists the chief executive in carrying out the MBO system. From its inception, Western's MBO system has borne the unmistakable mark of its chief executive officer. The expertise of the planning manager is invaluable, but in no way does it impinge upon the president's accountability. The planning function, through the two reorganizations, has continued to receive top priority and remains assigned to the corporate office and now, as an indication of its importance, the vice-president of planning services reports directly to the president.

ORGANIZING

We have alluded above to two reorganizations of The Western Company since it began operating under MBO. After approximately five years under the MBO system and the start of a rapid growth in both the on-shore and off-shore operations, the company reorganized into two operating groups—(1) The Western Petroleum Services, which would include the stimulation, wire line, and cementing divisions, with a centralization of the common staff functions in the group headquarters in Fort Worth, and (2) The Western Oceanic Group, headquartered in Houston, which at this time had three off-shore drilling rigs, two of the jack-up type operating in the Gulf of Mexico and a semisubmersible that began operation in the North Sea during the latter part of 1973. The Western Oceanic Group also had under contract the building of two more semisubmersible rigs in the United States, which became operational in 1974 and 1975, and three jack-up-type rigs in Singapore, one of which became operational in 1975; the other two became operational in early 1976.

With this dramatically expanded scope of operation, The Western Company recognized that a reorganization was necessary, but continued all phases of MBO under the new organization, with particular emphasis on providing its managers with extensive training in the skills and functions of management to carry out their increased responsibilities more effectively. A recent organizational change was required to better coordinate the continued growth of two widely diversified types of operations through the establishment of the executive vice-president indicated in Chart A.

PERFORMANCE EVALUATION

Evaluating personnel against performance standards is one of the most important aspects of the development and retention of good people in The Western Company. Feedback from the employee opinion questionnaires indicated that not all managers were properly establishing performance standards or discussing these performance standards and performance evaluations with employees. This was also determined to be one of the penalties of such rapid growth, and in its constant effort to recognize the importance of employee feedback to top management, the company has taken action in the past year to ensure that this manager/employee understanding of performance standards and how well the employee measures up to these standards is being accomplished.

Standards of performance and evaluations of performance should be on a consistent, objective basis; that is, related to desired results and well understood by the individual and his supervisor. Described below is a system for establishing standards of performance and conducting better evaluations that resulted from the organizational analysis that had led to the organizational restructuring.

Establishing standards and measures of performance begins with a review of organizational and individual objectives. The relative importance of each objective and each job must be determined, inasmuch as it is very seldom that those assigned to a given individual are all of equal importance.

Under this type of approach, the rater first conceives of the sum total of all individual objectives as being equal to 100 percent. Next, this 100 percent figure is divided by the number of objectives that have been assigned for the year. If the rater decides that not all the objectives of his subordinates are of equal importance, he must vary the weighting to correspond with his assessment of the relative importance of each objective. Since the total of all weights must always equal the 100 percent he started with, the rater must decrease the weight for one or more objectives whenever he increases the weight for one. This is called the Standard Percentage Weight.

In the example below, the Standard Percentage Weight was determined by concluding that the five objectives were not of equal importance (as might be expected) but that the sales and profit objectives are significantly more important than the other three. Thus the weight on one or more of the other objectives was increased.

Objective	Standard Percentage Weight
Achieve sales	20
Achieve profit	50
Reduce turnover	15
Reduce motor vehicle and loss-time accidents	10
Reduce heavy-vehicle accident cost	5
Total	100

There is now an order-of-magnitude representation of the relative importance of each objective. Of course, it must be remembered that although the finished weights look quite precise, the thought processes underlying them are basically subjective but require a more detailed thought process than the conventional systems of evaluating an employee as satisfactory, outstanding, and so on.

The performance Standard Percentage Weight as determined by the rates should be agreed upon by the subordinate at the beginning of the rating period. The assigned percentages will provide the subordinate with a good idea as to how he should apportion his time and channel his efforts. Prerating has two distinct advantages: (1) It helps the rater in determining whether the objectives are sufficiently challenging for the individual and gives guidance on priorities, and (2) it helps the individual to see how his supervisor will ultimately view his performance.

In assessing overall performance at year-end, the rating for each objective should be quantified, using the simple rating scale shown in Chart D. To do this, each objective's weight times its performance rating is calculated and the results are divided by 100, as indicated:

Objective	Weighting	Rating	Weighting × Rating
Achieve sales	20	104	2,080
Achieve profit	50	115	5,750
Reduce turnover	15	104	1,560
Reduce MVA and LTA	10	112	1,120
Reduce HVA cost	5	95	475
Total			10,985

$$\text{Rating:} \quad \frac{10,985}{100} = 109.85 \text{ or } 110$$

Chart D. Rated evaluation scale.

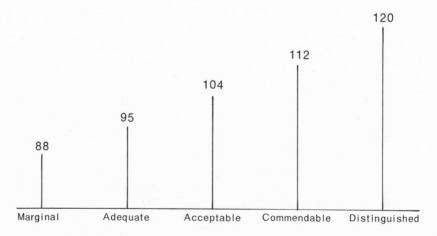

The individual's overall rating of 110 is evaluated against the rating scale. Thus, in this example, the performance of the individual has been judged to be within the commendable range and should be the basis for all compensation, bonuses and promotion or demotion.

RECOGNITION AND REWARDS

Under MBO employee compensation is based on individual performance toward the achievement of group/corporate objectives. As discussed, the individual's evaluation is conducted as a part of the manpower planning and development system at The Western Company. The company has implemented a wage and salary administration program. Ranges in pay for each job within The Western Company are determined by company evaluation committees on the relative worth of each job to the company. The individual's compensation is based on his performance on the job within the salary ranges that have been specified for that particular job. Evaluation committees annually review the worth of each job to ensure fairness and equitability. The evaluations are based on what is required of that job, not the individual in the job, to meet company objectives. The individual's performance in the job is the determinant of his salary level within his pay range, as explained in the preceding section on performance evaluation. Thus Western utilizes the results-oriented approach to both personnel evaluation and compensation.

CURRENT STATUS OF MBO

This case study covers the experience of The Western Company from 1968 through 1975. Seven years is not a long period of time in the life of an MBO installation, especially when one remembers that it usually takes a company at least three years to reach the point at which it can sit back with some degree of satisfaction knowing that it has climbed about 85 percent of the mountain. (The remaining 15 percent consists of reviewing experience to date, debugging, and refining.)

SUMMARY OF WESTERN'S EXPERIENCE

The vast bulk of Western's experience in applying MBO has been quite favorable even though efforts are continuing to improve the application and make it more beneficial. The following paragraphs contain the highlights of Western's experience to date.

Costs. The total general and administrative costs of providing staff services has decreased from the 1967 level, and there has been an increase in the quality of staff contributions. In certain instances (planning, for example), additional services are now available. The company is no longer paying for staff jobs it doesn't require.

Level of performance. There has been an overall increase in the performance levels of managers because their efforts have been closely aligned with the needs and priorities of the company. Needless activities have been eliminated and those incompatible with company objectives have been revised.

Organization structure. Western regards its organization structure, which is based on the company's short- and long-term goals, as closely meeting the mission it is intended to serve. It is lean and simple, and it has only six levels from the bottom level of supervision through the chief executive office. Minimal spans of control permit ready access to managers at all levels. Both line and staff managers now have definite accountabilities, which has resulted in a definite lessening of misunderstandings and confusion.

Results orientation. Managers have become more results-oriented. In lieu of emphasizing activities and programs, they have gradually become more and more conscious of the necessity for accomplishing profit-oriented results. They tend to approach problems with a businesslike attitude rather than viewing their roles in terms of getting involved to maintain or further the stature of their functions.

Staff acceptance. Western management makes no firm statements about the degree of improvement in the acceptance of staff managers. A combination of several new managers and a new management system makes precise evaluation premature. However, indications are that the acceptance of staff functions has increased. Staff managers have become more involved in many features of the company's operations. There has been a lessening of misunderstandings about the role of staff and less internal criticism of the costs of staff. Staff has begun playing a key role in planning the future of the company and ensuring its health. Three top staff managers now sit on the company's board of directors. Staff managers presently participate in the company's management incentive plan on the same basis as their line associates.

Last, the company believes its MBO system could have been improved if the company had had on its internal staff a person well grounded in the rationale and techniques of MBO. He could have provided the day-to-day expertise and counseling to managers to whom MBO represented a completely new ball game.

Like all other companies that have embraced MBO, Western could benefit from the hindsight knowledge it now possesses. While Western's management is objective enough to readily admit that its implementation activities weren't perfect, it is equally quick to enumerate the many advantages the company now enjoys from its MBO application.

OVERALL ORGANIZATIONAL PERFORMANCE

Western has made rather impressive strides in both sales volume and earnings since it implemented MBO in 1968, as indicated by Table A.

Table A. Sales volume and earnings, The Western Company.

Year	Sales	Net Income	Earnings per Share *
1968	$ 19,390,000	$ 1,093,000	$ .40
1969	23,566,000	1,260,000	.40
1970	24,003,000	287,000	.07
1971	29,709,000	1,507,000	.48
1972	31,772,000	1,744,000	.53
1973	40,439,000	2,372,000	.64
1974	61,753,000	2,961,000	.78
1975	100,000,000	15,200,000	3.02

* All years adjusted for 2-to-1 stock split in 1974 and 10% stock dividend in 1975.

While these increases cannot be directly attributed only to the impact of MBO, Western's senior management believes that MBO made material contributions to the achievement of this record.

In marked contrast to the short-term perspective mentioned earlier, Western has progressively moved to a longer-term analysis of the external environment and the company's ways of operating within that environment. Currently, the company looks into the future for a continuous period of eight years. The first five years of each eight-year period are then embodied in the formalized long-term plan of the company.

Another significant advantage that MBO brought to Western resulted from the timing of its implementation. MBO was implemented when, by usual standards, Western was a small company. Thus Western had a management system operational during its rather spectacular growth years. This management system aided it to grow in a planned, orderly manner. It was able to avoid the unplanned, haphazard, and costly growth attempts that have plagued many other small companies trying to operate without an effective system.

30

MBO in
Nonprofit Organizations

THE PROFIT MOTIVE is present in both profit and nonprofit organizations. A business makes profits depending upon the way it manages the resources (assets) entrusted to it. Business profits are enhanced in one or both of two ways: (1) by realizing a *higher* return on the *same* amount of assets and (2) by realizing the *same* or a *better* return on a *lesser* amount of assets.

Nonprofit organizations have the same mission, as illustrated by the following ways they use to realize a higher return on resources.

Increased productivity from present employees.

Improved patient care from present staff (in hospitals).

Increased quality and/or quantity of teaching from present staff.

Lower overhead costs of fund raising.

More effective crime prevention through improved law enforcement techniques.

Improved state of defense readiness by replacing troops with electronic or space hardware.

Better distribution of relief and disaster funds.

Greater results from volunteer workers.

Lower administrative costs of operating the organization.

Note: This chapter has been adapted from the author's article "Applying Management by Objectives to Nonprofit Organizations," *SAM Advanced Management Journal*, January 1973.

Reduction of wasted effort and/or wastes in the utilization of any assets.

Blending together of the efforts of all personnel to achieve an overall effectiveness that is greater than the sum of the individual efforts.

AN INCREASING PRIORITY

An increasingly higher priority is being placed on managing nonprofit organizations so as to achieve what Peter Drucker has called the prime duty of a manager; namely, to produce economically significant results. This upgrading of priorities results in large part from the dramatic changes taking place in the mix of organizations constituting our economy. Increasingly, the swing is proportionately away from manufacturing-type organizations to service types, including nonprofit groups. Most informed observers believe, with considerable justification, that we are rapidly approaching a service-oriented economy, which will overshadow the manufacturing sector in terms of numbers and their impact.[1] Thus nonprofit organizations now are and will continue to be challenged to adopt the more effective approaches for managing their resources.

The question that plagues most managers, administrators, and executive personnel of nonprofit organizations bent on effective performance is not whether they should increase their "profits" but how the improvement can be brought about and what means, methods, or tools are available to them.

One of the means used with increasing success for improving the effectiveness of both the organization and the individuals in these entities is management by objectives. Although MBO developed and has realized its major success in businesses operating for profits, the preponderance of the MBO system is equally applicable and beneficial to the nonprofit organization. This chapter will illustrate actual examples of successful MBO applications in various nonprofit organizations.

TESTING FOR APPLICABILITY

In light of the fact that MBO developed in an environment of profit-oriented business organizations, an examination should be made of the system's applicability and value to the nonprofit organizations before any decision is made to adopt it. Both writers and practicing managers in nonprofit entities have raised major questions concerning the system's value

[1] For in in-depth treatment of this shift, see "Selling the Services Society," *Sales Management*, March 6, 1972, pp. 23–38.

in the absence of the profit motive. The following questions will serve as an audit checklist for helping determine the applicability of MBO to non-profit organizations. The questions cover the major aspects of organizing and managing an operation. Also, they exert the major impact on MBO and, in turn, MBO exerts a major impact on them.

1. Does the organization have a mission to perform? Is there a valid reason for it to exist?
2. Does management have assets (money, people, plant, and equipment) entrusted to it?
3. Is management accountable to some person or authority for a return on the assets?
4. Can priorities be established for accomplishing the mission?
5. Can the operation be planned?
6. Does management believe it must manage effectively even though the organization is a nonprofit one?
7. Can accountabilities of key personnel be pinpointed?
8. Can the efforts of all key personnel be coordinated into a whole?
9. Can necessary controls and feedback be established?
10. Is it possible to evaluate the performance of key personnel?
11. Is a system of positive and negative rewards possible?
12. Are the main functions of a manager (planning, organizing, directing, and so forth) the same regardless of the type of organization?
13. Is management receptive to improved methods of operating?

The applicability and value of MBO to a nonprofit organization is directly correlated to the number of affirmative answers given to the above questions. Use of these questions as tests of the wisdom of applying MBO to profit-oriented entities has been well validated by about 20 years of successful practice in every type, size, and category of business entity both in the United States and abroad. Increasingly, the same tests are proving their validity when applied to nonprofit groups.

Naturally, the degree of conviction with which the questions can be answered with yes will vary with any limitations that may be imposed by the nature of the nonprofit organization, especially its locus of authority and its policies or regulations.

POSSIBLE LIMITATIONS

Limitations on the value of MBO to the nonprofit sector can be real and/or imagined. They are real when an organization's managers can do nothing to change them; for example, the compensation of federal civil service employees is established by Congress. The manager of a civil service organization cannot vary the compensation policy even though he/she could motivate better performance among his subordinates. The limitations, even if they do exist in fact, are imagined if they can be changed by the manager; for example, the false assumption that there is no way for a fund-raising organization to motivate volunteer workers to meet their targets.

Limitations probably do exist, again in varying degrees, in some nonprofit organizations. For example, a government or quasi-government organization may well have several constraints that would detract from realizing the full benefits of MBO that could be realized by a profit-oriented firm, such as:

Limitation	Impact on MBO
Many decision-making areas are preempted by law, rules, and regulations.	Less flexibility for making profit-oriented decisions. Tends to "level" all key personnel—less opportunity to prove individual metal.
Less opportunity to participate in setting objectives.	Lowered managerial motivation—lack of opportunity to determine own accountability and destiny.
Many forms of rewards and recognition are set by law.	Less flexibility to reward the outstanding performer over the mediocre one.
Emphasis on seniority rather than merit.	Tends to protect the inefficient and impede the efficient.
Performance measurement often lacking—emphasis on effort rather than output.	The achievement-oriented manager suffers. He demands results-oriented measurement.

A government organization was deliberately selected for this example because governmental units are more frequently cited as having so many limitations that MBO cannot be successfully applied.

Let's go back to these limitations and assume that they do in fact exist to a considerable degree. Does their existence destroy the value of MBO? Or does their existence merely limit the benefits and spotlight matters that, if changed, will increase the benefits? I submit that such limitations do not destroy the value of MBO but merely limit the realization of its full potential.

Management of most nonprofit organizations is starving for better management methods, and much of its hunger is being caused by increasing pressures from users of its services and those who finance its endeavors. Given this situation, even half a loaf of bread—possibly in the form of an MBO system whose full impact cannot be realized immediately because of the limitations—would appear eminently better than continuing to waste away as the hunger remains. At the same time, MBO will help to quickly spot the limitations so that all possible action can be taken to eliminate or minimize them. In the absence of MBO the limitations are destined to continue, often without recognition of their inpact on the progress of the organization. Concurrently, the organization's valuable resources continue to be dissipated. It often is said that much of the solving of a problem results from properly identifying and defining it; one of the chief virtue's of MBO is its ability to highlight sacred cows and other impediments to increased effectiveness.

MBO IN PRACTICE

Today MBO is making rapid strides in nonprofit organizations. While progress has not been as dramatic or as widespread as it has in business firms, finding a category of nonprofit organization in which MBO has not been successfully applied is becoming increasingly difficult.

The following examples of nonprofit organizations now practicing MBO were selected to show the wide range and diversity of the entities that have adopted MBO systems.

Schools

By virtue of their sheer weight of numbers and the importance of their end product—education—schools represent an area of prime concern to taxpayers with respect to first determining what the objectives should be and then coordinating all efforts to achieve those ends. Undoubtedly, this concern and the increasing burden on taxpayers have caused the rather sudden surge of interest in applying MBO to schools. Probably no other category of nonprofit organization is receiving more MBO attention than are schools.[2]

Dr. Donald W. Shebuski, superintendent of schools of Holt, Michigan, is very active in applying MBO to schools. He summarizes his experience as follows:

> School administrators have long endorsed the concept of a management team. Recently, however, a managerial strategy, known as

[2] For a general discussion of applying MBO to schools, see H. Merrell Arnold, "Management by Objectives and the School System," *The School Administrator*, April 1972, pp. 15–16.

management by objectives, has assisted scientific management-minded administrators to operationalize this team approach in education. Management by objectives is a method of participation and involvement of supervision and subordinates whereby decisions are reached and results explicated. Management at every level in schools has a continuing responsibility to improve the organization of the work under its supervision. It is accountable for the successful outcome of the team effort at any given level of responsibility.

The key word in the MBO approach is "improve." A primary responsibility of a school administrator is to improve the work of the people he supervises; to improve the product (students); and to improve the team effort that makes the organization successful. Through successful accomplishment of the above, he also improves himself.

Accomplishment of an accountability concept for schools means that we must explicate clearly defined goals, and have developed a management plan whereby goals can be reached in measurable ways.

MBO is not a panacea for all of education's many problems, nor is it an attempt to turn schools into a mechanized factory-like process. It is a procedure in which scarce resources (people and dollars) can be allocated to accomplish established goals, and then account for the degree to which goals and objectives have been reached.

Educational administrators have a great challenge before them as they face the durable concerns for accountability in education. At this point, educators are compelled to translate the educational process, which up until now has been considered an art, into a viable, scientific procedure. Management by objectives processes are proving to be a successful approach in this endeavor.[3]

The Management Institute of the University of Wisconsin-Extension, Madison, was one of the earliest university groups to adopt MBO. Its chairman, Professor Norman C. Allhiser, traces his experience with MBO:

"Before adopting MBO, our operations could be characterized as follows. The Institute had made good progress in a number of key areas:

Staff members were dedicated to the principles and concepts of adult education.

Subject matter was problem-oriented and practical.

Institute meetings were limited to 30 participants, and small group sessions within each group were utilized.

Resource leaders used directed discussion techniques for maximum involvement.

[3] Dale D. McConkey, "Applying Management by Objectives to Nonprofit Organizations," *SAM Advanced Management Journal*, January 1973.

The Institute was beginning to expand its activities and was developing an out-of-state following.

"However, weaknesses existed in our organizational structure. Valid description covering the accountabilities of faculty members had not been developed; quality of programs varied; the selection of speakers and resource leaders was erratic; programs were canceled; deadlines were missed; administration tended to be rather loose; and the evaluation of faculty and programming was extremely difficult.

"The need to improve the department's own management was apparent and in the early 1960s the Management Institute adopted the MBO concept. Emphasis was placed on improving and measuring the quality of the faculty and programming in a manner that encouraged the blending of individual efforts into a total team effort.

"The original MBO application was improved each year and now has culminated in a much more sophisticated approach. A long- and short-range planning meeting is held each year with active staff involvement. Overall objectives are established for that year, followed by the development of performance standards (objectives) for faculty members. These standards emphasize quality, quantity, and innovation and clarify individual accountability in the areas of programming, administration, self-development, teaching, services, innovation, and results achieved.

"Each member of the faculty prepares a 'planning guide' in which he spells out how he is going to achieve his objectives. Periodic conferences are held to discuss progress on objectives and plans.

"Our experience with MBO can be summarized in a number of ways. The number of our programs has increased more than sevenfold and enrollments by more than 30 times, although quality continues to be emphasized over quantity. MBO has helped us build this quality into our product. Greater decentralization for broader statewide service also has accompanied the growth. We believe MBO has helped us achieve and retain a leading reputation among the oldest and largest university-type programs. The Institute has weathered several 'recessions' and continues to grow even though some of its 'competitors' have suffered serious setbacks."

Another excellent example of a successful MBO application in schools is Harper College in Palatine, Illinois. A wide range of MBO applications has been made at this college.[4]

---

[4] See "Management by Objectives," by Robert E. Lahti, *College and University Business*, July 1971, pp. 31–33.

Government Laboratory

The U.S. Forest Products Laboratory located in Madison, Wisconsin, has recently completed a review of its first year of introducing management by objectives for its research management. The results are gratifying although there are many opportunities for continued expansion and improvement.[5]

Although project management in research requires goals and has been using them for many years, it was decided that management by objectives had some additional benefits that would be useful for all Forest Products research managers. The system was launched by first indoctrinating the top management group. Following this meeting, sessions were conducted for all project leaders and key scientists.

The mission of the laboratory was reviewed at the beginning of each session: "to conduct research leading to greater social and economic benefits for the people of the United States, and of the world, through the better utilization of their timber resources." The broad areas of concern of the laboratory were also reexamined during the sessions. Then each individual prepared objectives within the scope of his/her responsibilities consistent with the mission and within the following areas of concern:

The properties and behavior of wood and wood constituents.

Timber supply and utilization.

Efficiency in processing and use.

Better housing for the seventies.

The environment.

The rural economy.

Protection of wood in use.

Consumer interests.

Areas of improved management that the top management team has identified as a result of applying management by objectives include:

Clearer understanding of what is expected of research teams, project leaders, and individuals.

Specific connection between budget allocations and results accomplished on projects.

[5] This summary was prepared by Professor Fred C. Schwarz, University of Wisconsin, Madison, who served as a consultant during the installation. It is used here with his permission as well as that of the management of U.S. Forest Products Laboratory.

Increased involvement of entire staff in developing specific objectives to accomplish laboratory mission.

The management team is managing by objectives.

The management team now has a common language and there has been a demonstrated ability to attack a problem and approach it with a more positive attitude than before.

Canadian Post Office

MBO was applied to the Canadian Post Office in January 1970 beginning with a pilot project in the Ontario region, one of the four large regions into which the postal system is divided. Subsequently, it was decided to extend MBO to all four regions and the headquarters of the system.[6]

Several factors prompted the decision to adopt MBO. The Canadian Post Office employed up to 50,000 people annually and was known as the sleeping giant. Costs and deficits had mounted. Mail service, vital to both commerce and citizens, had been deteriorating. Increasing difficulty was being encountered in attracting competent personnel for key managerial positions.

A package of eight interrelated management programs was designed for the total planned change. The basis of these programs was the application of MBO, especially true delegation from the regional manager to the district manager to the area manager (the lowest level of management).

The experience gained in the pilot project leading up to the decision to adopt MBO for the total postal system included these benefits:

True delegation of accountabilities had taken place.

Management in the Ontario region was becoming stronger and more professional than the management at headquarters.

The potential for systemwide application was so encouraging that the decision was made to waive the two-year trial period planned originally for the pilot project and to accelerate the systemwide adoption.

Management of the Canadian Post Office doesn't kid itself into believing that MBO is a panacea. A turnaround the size of this giant will take time. There is no quick, magic cure. However, they feel that now the organization has an approach that is sufficiently flexible to meet the dynamics of work in the Post Office.

[6] This summary of experience is adopted largely from "Business Planning in the Canadian Post Office," by P. J. Chartrand, *Canadian Personnel and Industrial Relations Journal,* October 1971, pp. 17–22.

Hospitals

Plagued as they are with labor costs, which frequently average 70 to 80 percent of total operating costs, hospitals represent a fertile field for any management approach that promotes increased effectiveness. It seems only natural that hospitals have turned to MBO as a way of alleviating their plight.

Before assuming his present position as administrator of a large nonprofit hospital in Ottawa, Garry D. Cardiff played a significant role in applying MBO to another nonprofit hospital. In the following paragraphs, Cardiff summarizes the experience with MBO after three years:

1. Regardless of the effort put forth, enthusiasm and utilization of MBO are cyclic.

2. Only about 60 percent of those that started the program are still successfully using the approach. However, in light of factors such as background, personal limitations, and other organizational circumstances, this percentage seems acceptable to us.

3. The greatest enemy of an MBO program in a nonprofit organization is apathy. With the recent advent of "global budgeting," perhaps realistic incentive programs will be devised so that successful MBO performances can be rewarded in more tangible terms.

4. Many projects that "should be done" are done because of MBO. Procrastination generally is the result of lack of commitment.

5. The contribution to communications both horizontally and vertically has been immeasurable.

6. The contribution of MBO to our budgeting process has been equally rewarding.

7. Since MBO is an essential ingredient of writing and executing a long-range plan, the program will no doubt continue to prove invaluable, as we are currently in the primary stages of formulating such a plan.

8. On balance, the benefits we have gained far outweigh expenditures of time and money. Management by objectives is an interesting theory and a worthwhile practice.[7]

Volunteer Organizations

Volunteer organizations are considered among the more difficult for MBO applications. However, the fact that an MBO application is possible

[7] His experiences are described in "Management by Objectives—It Will Work in a Hospital Setting," *Hospital Administration in Canada*, November 1970, pp. 23–26.

is illustrated by the experience of a large volunteer organization that at this stage chooses to remain anonymous.

It operates nationally from a central headquarters, through regions, to local areas headed by a local manager, who is the lowest level of management. Managers of all these levels are paid professionals. Managers of the local areas are the real guts of the organization, as they are accountable for fund raising, motivating volunteers to carry out the bulk of the organization's work in the area, and directing the local programs.

Strict standards of accountability have been established for the area managers. Their primary accountabilities are program quality and quantity, financial stability, public relations, and internal relations.

Each accountability is assigned a weight, or value, which reflects its importance to the manager's overall effectiveness. Commendably, quality is weighted proportionate to quantity.

Next, each accountability is defined in terms of standards of performance required. For example, program quantity is spelled out in terms of the population size of the area, the percentage of the population represented by the age group the organization seeks to bring into its program, the number of eligibles who actually do participate in the program, and the percentage of total potential this number represents. Program quality is defined and measured by such factors as the number of participants who stay in the program and how this number compares with established medians.

The application now has endured several years of experience, and those to whom the organization is accountable are pleased with the results. The program emphasizes participation of all managers in goals setting, strict accountability, performance measurement and feedback to the managers, and maximization of benefits for all funds raised.

Municipal Organizations

Often, a nonprofit organization has functions and operations identical with those existing in a profit-oriented one. The more common of these include purchasing, personnel, finance, administration, operations, and public relations. Municipal governments often have suborganizations, which are almost exact duplicates of those of profit-making organizations. The port authority of cities like Boston and New York is an example. Madison, Wisconsin, has nine "enterprise funds," which include water and sewer utility, airport authority, bus utility, parking utility, golf courses, ice arena, concessions, and cemeteries. These funds are run on a consumer-reimbursement basis, whereby costs are paid by the users. Each of these constitutes a minibusiness within the municipal government.

Certainly, these organizations readily lend themselves to MBO, and applications are well under way in several instances.

Other Applications

The handful of examples described here should not mislead the reader into believing that they constitute the bulk of nonprofit organizations to which MBO has been applied. In the absence of space limitations, the number of case studies could be expanded considerably. For example, MBO has been applied in the U.S. Navy Supply Systems Command and in the major's office of the city of Sapporo, Japan, where in only one area—the tax division—major efficiencies have been realized through better methods of collecting taxes with substantial reductions in personnel. Nursing homes, churches, and child care centers all have embraced MBO, as have many other nonprofit organizations. On the basis of experience to date, it appears only logical that nonprofit applications will continue and accelerate.

CONCLUSION

In essence, MBO is a systematic approach to achieving desired ends. When viewed in this, its true perspective, it is obvious that MBO has considerable value when applied to nonprofit organizations. Those who would hold otherwise place themselves in the untenable position of advocating that the desired end—for example, quality education—should be approached by hit-or-miss methods. Nonprofit organizations have no landed right to assume this unique position.

Nonprofit organizations are not unique. Like all organizations, they have an objective to achieve; namely, to provide the highest quality product or service consistent with the funds available. They have assets entrusted to them: people, capital, and plant and equipment. They serve in a stewardship capacity to those upon whom they depend for their continued existence. Managers of these organizations have no inherent right to waste any of these assets or to violate their stewardship. They must be held accountable for results.

Highly successful MBO applications have been made in every conceivable type of organization—profit and nonprofit, the private and public sectors, large and small organizations, organizations in the United States, Canada, Europe, Japan, and elsewhere. These include hospitals, schools, police departments, nursing homes, defense departments, municipal government units, and agencies of the federal government.

Over 20 years of MBO experience have demonstrated the value and applicability of MBO to all types of organizations. The nonprofit sector is no exception. This same experience has demonstrated that MBO can be applied to these organizations only if they insist upon and meet the same demands that the system imposes upon other categories of organizations and endeavors. As a minimum these include:

1. The selection of highly competent managers, administrators, and professionals in all key positions.

2. In-depth training in the complete MBO system before any attempt is made to apply it.

3. A period of three to four years to make a successful installation.

4. Maximum participation from all personnel rather than the sometimes autocratic and despotic ideas of a few.

5. A complete tailoring or adapting of the MBO system to the individual problems or conditions existing in the individual entity to which it is applied.

6. The removal, or diminishing, by legislative or executive action of many of the impediments that act as limitations on the ability of MBO to achieve the full potential of which it is capable—limitations such as emphasizing effort rather than results, provisions that protect ineffective personnel, practices that stifle individual initiative and permit flexible decision making, and systems that fail to provide recognition and rewards.

7. Constant reexamination of the system after installation to improve it and render it responsive to the changing conditions in the environment in which it is being practiced.

MBO cannot be blamed for failure to meet these exhaustive and exhausting demands. Any failure must be placed squarely upon the shoulders of the real culprits—the persons who fail to meet the demands imposed by the system.

31

MBO:
Practical Reality
or Elusive Myth?

FOR SOME MANAGERS MBO has become a reality; for other managers it has become an elusive myth.

As I look back over the roughly 20 years that managers have been applying MBO, I'm concerned about several aspects of the applications. First, I'm concerned about the alarmingly high rate of failure on the part of managers as they have tried to practice MBO, possibly somewhere around 50 percent. Note that I said that the *managers* fail, not that the system fails. Second, I'm concerned about the undeserved black eye MBO is receiving because of the amateurish approach to MBO that many managers have adopted, either because of their own failings or because of their gullibility in letting themselves be sold by some of the overly zealous and undercompetent consultants. Last, I'm extremely concerned at the growing number of self-styled MBO consultants who continue to emerge each week. Many of the latter can best be described as individuals with a packaged solution in search of a problem. They constitute purveyors of the "chocolate-covered pill"!

Admittedly, there is a wide range between an elusive myth and a practical reality. This chapter addresses itself to some of the overwhelming reasons why some MBO attempts can fall into either of the two extremes. Also, I'd like to suggest at the outset that a competent management group can largely determine into which category it wants its efforts to fall.

ENERGETIC STUPIDITY

Probably the number one problem in MBO today is what I like to refer to as energetic stupidity on the part of some managers. This description is not intended to imply that most managers are lacking in normal intelligence. Certainly they are not. It is meant to describe a common situation in which managers devote an inordinate amount of precious time, energy, and resources to a subject (MBO) without first determining the end result they are seeking and the better way to get there! In other words, they get extremely busy without first determining at *what* they should get busy.

Three major areas seem to predominate when characterizing this state of extreme busyness. All lead to major failures in MBO.

Adopting in ignorance—adopting MBO without first determining what it is all about, what impact it will have on the organization, and whether it can benefit the organization.

Implementing in haste—endeavoring to implement MBO throughout the organization practically overnight and thus overlooking the high degree of patient tailoring, training, and understanding that is necessary.

Administering in myopia—attempting to administer MBO as just another simple program rather than considering it as a total management system. Many of us have continually advocated that MBO should be kept as *simple* as possible, but we never said it could be *simplistic*.

The following paragraphs enumerate several of the more meaningful reasons why some MBO attempts become a practical reality while others turn into frustrating myths.

WHAT IS MBO?

Reality begins with an organization reaching agreement as to what it means by MBO. There is no such thing as *the* MBO system. While MBO does have proven principles, these do not lead to any one, ideal MBO approach. The better approach for any organization is the one that has been closely tailored to that organization and one that meets the needs and expectations of that organization.

Only if an organization first determines what it means by MBO and defines when MBO will be operational can the organization evaluate whether or not MBO has succeeded. Undoubtedly, much of the frustration existing today results from not formulating these definitions. To state that MBO has succeeded or failed implies that some predetermined conditions existed against which progress was measured.

It should not be difficult for any organization to specify what it means by MBO. However, what is required is to reject the mystique with which many have attempted to surround MBO. There is really nothing too new or mystical about MBO. Basically, the unique quality of MBO should be its simplicity and common-sense approach to improving results.

As suggested earlier, MBO is really nothing more than the pulling together of all the better-known and proven management practices into one, organized and integrated way of managing—the integrated MBO system. Viewed in this light, an organization should have little difficulty in enunciating what MBO means to it.

MBO AND CHANGE

A major responsibility of any manager is to stay in control of the destiny of his operation or organization even in the face of rapid change. MBO can and should provide substantial help to the manager in carrying out this responsibility. But this help will be available only if *change* is built into an organization's MBO system.

Effective MBO begins by assuming that nothing in management is static. Management is dynamic; change must be anticipated and, in fact, encouraged if progress is to be achieved. The objectives written by a manager are little more than his best estimates *of the moment*. He must build in methods of revising his estimates as conditions change, as he gains additional data on which to base revised estimates. Building in the capability to cope with change and stay in control requires each practicing MBO manager to (1) identify those major future factors that can exert a significant impact on his operations, (2) establish an early-warning system for spotting these important changes as they do occur (and they will occur), and (3) take immediate corrective action to adjust to or cope with the change.

MBO is in itself a major change agent. Thus it is contradictory to fail to build change into it as this failure will have much to do with whether MBO is a myth or a reality.

A SYSTEM OR PROGRAM?

I recently spent two days explaining and discussing MBO with a corporate president and his senior officers. At the conclusion of the two days, the president said: "I'm convinced that MBO has a lot of merit and much to offer our company. However, right now we're busy installing a new cost accounting program. When this has been installed, we plan to put in a revised managerial evaluation program. After both of these, we'll un-doubtedly install an MBO program."

These comments are highly significant. They indicate that this presi-dent is treating MBO as just another program—that he'll be adding on just another program. He's well on his way to chasing an elusive myth.

Reality and success occur when MBO is viewed as a management system rather than another program. A program is part of a system, not the system itself. The system should be installed and then all programs folded into it.

Probably one of the better ways to disenchant managers is to con-tinually add on new programs that bear little discernible relationship to other programs. Management should be stating, "MBO is *the* way we manage our organization. Programs are specific approaches that help us carry out this way of managing."

MANAGEMENT IS THE KEY WORD

Frequently, I hear managers make statements to the effect that "I'll soon have to sit down and write my MBOs for next year." When asked what they mean by "writing my MBOs," they invariably respond that they must write their "objectives." Their answer points up one of the most common reasons for failure. MBO is considered as synonymous with writ-ing objectives.

The importance of formulating well-written, meaningful objectives cannot be minimized. However, objectives are just one part of the sys-tem, not the system itself. Management is what makes MBO and objec-tives successful.

The inevitable result of emphasizing objectives over management is the requiring of all managers to come up with a list of objectives. When written in this manner, objectives are seldom worth the paper they're written on. They're written in isolation or a vacuum; they're not suppor-tive of other objectives either vertically or horizontally. The preparatory steps necessary to lead to meaningful objectives have been omitted. Also, the steps necessary to translate the objectives into action during the target period have been similarly ignored. Thus the manager has written only a sterile list of words that will not cause anything to happen.

Reality requires "management" to come first. Management gives life and action to objectives and permits them to become more than just words on paper.

THE PARADOX OF MBO

Potentially, MBO has built into it a major paradox, which can be stated very simply:

> The more effective the MBO system, the more trouble it can get an organization into—*if* the organization neglects the long-term in favor of the short-term.

MBO is designed to line up all the resources (time, money, people, plant and equipment) of an organization to achieve the predetermined results.

I know of one individual who has been president of three major corporations in the short period of eight years. He has been a spectacular success, as of the moment, in each of his three positions. Sales, profitability, and capital returns all have been outstanding. However, the first two corporations have fallen apart in the years following his departure, even though he allegedly managed them along the lines of what he describes as "good MBO." Current indications abound that he mortgaged the future growth of these two organizations to make himself look good today.

The primary emphasis of any MBO system must be placed on the *long-term* health and growth of the organization. In fact, the real measure of any manager must be whether or not his organization grows over the long pull. The easiest way to look good today is to eliminate those actions designed for future growth but which have a low present return—for example, research, management development, and capital expenditures.

Reality requires that MBO first address itself to long-term, strategic matters. Once these have been agreed to, MBO can help managers accomplish the desired actions for tomorrow by being more efficient and effective today.

MANAGEMENT STYLE

Achieving realism in MBO requires that a particular management style be practiced by a preponderance of an organization's managers. Experience demonstrates that MBO has often failed because of attempts to impose it on an organization regardless of the management style of that organization.

MBO myths have frequently been the result of trying to draw a line through an organization's present management style and writing in the

MBO style to substitute for that which was lined out. This is tantamount to trying to change the contents of a can by merely changing the label.

Successful MBO requires a generous helping of what is commonly referred to as a participative management style. When one cuts through all the verbiage popularly associated with "participative," he finds that it is essentially a way of managing in which each manager is given the greatest practical latitude in managing his/her own operation but always within the requirements of what the total organization must achieve during a particular target period; that is, the overall objectives and priorities of the organization as a whole.

REWARDS AND RECOGNITION

Another great way to change potential reality into actual myth is to over-emphasize the first part of the equation that states Performance = rewards.

Over the short range it is entirely possible to increase performance by continually emphasizing it. But not for long. Too many MBO efforts have failed because emphasis was placed on getting managers to achieve higher and higher levels of results without the corresponding practice of equitably rewarding the results when they were achieved.*

The crux of the problem is the compensation time lag that exists when MBO is installed and an organization doesn't update what is usually a traditional approach to managerial compensation. Traditional compensation approaches usually are incompatible with the aims and rationale of MBO. Usually, especially in the absence of a full-strength and variable incentive compensation plan, traditional compensation doesn't permit the recognizing of the truly outstanding performer over the average performer. Traditional compensation has tended to level all the unit's managers into narrow, restrictive groups. Also, the methods by which compensation rates and ranges are determined are largely outdated for an MBO system.

Nor should rewards and recognition be limited to compensation dollars even though an equitable, motivating plan should be operational. In at least three instances in which the usual flexibility for utilizing compensation dollars wasn't available—one a large church, the second a government health department, and the third a unit of the U.S. Air Force—each of the organizations formulated about 100 different ways of recognizing performance without using compensation dollars.

* For a detailed treatment of this subject, see Dale D. McConkey, "The 'Jackass Effect' in Management Compensation," *Business Horizons*, June 1974, pp. 81–91.

Regardless of the form of the rewards and recognition, it must be sufficiently significant to let the achievement-oriented manager know that his/her efforts have been measured and appreciated.

CONCLUSION

I'm completely sold on the virtues and benefits of MBO when it is practiced in a manner that generates positive results. I've seen it do so under many varied and diverse circumstances in many organizations having varied and diverse product and service lines. The positive benefits to the organizations have been appreciable. MBO does work!

And as the benefits to the organization represent the sum total of the benefits that have accrued to the managers in these organizations, it follows that the individual manager benefited. So far, we've identified 25 major benefits that managers may realize.

Today I'm convinced that we stand on the threshold of substantial opportunity for improving, refining, and furthering meaningful MBO efforts in the future. However, we must benefit from the mistakes we have made in the past. To continue to perpetuate these mistakes and the elusive myth they foster would defeat the very purpose of MBO—namely, increased managerial effectiveness at all levels of management.

Whether the organization and its managers do enjoy these benefits from MBO depends upon whether MBO has become a practical reality or an elusive myth.

INDEX

DATE DUE